Editors
Anna Nylund
Faculty of Law
University of Tromsø
Tromsø, Norway

Kaijus Ervasti
Faculty of Law
University of Helsinki
Helsinki, Finland

Lin Adrian
Faculty of Law
University of Copenhagen
Copenhagen, Denmark

https://doi.org/10.1007/978-3-319-73019-6

Preface

With this book, we present interesting Nordic mediation research to an English-speaking audience. Much mediation research in our region is published in national languages (Danish, Finnish, Norwegian and Swedish) and, consequently, not accessible to those outside the Nordic countries.

With a generous grant from The Joint Committee for Nordic Research Councils in the Humanities and Social Sciences (NOS-HS), we set out to remedy this.

During three explorative workshops, a group of mediation researchers from four Nordic countries came together to discuss mediation research across borders, academic backgrounds and methodological approaches and to work on the collection of articles in this volume. All articles are peer-reviewed.

In addition to presenting mediation research here, we have established a website where you can find all the articles in this volume, information about Nordic research and researchers, legislation and a selection of literature on this subject; see www. mediationresearch.org.

We wish to thank Satu Svahn for her contribution in checking the English language in the articles.

We hope that you will find our research inspiring.

Tromsø, Norway   Anna Nylund
Helsinki, Finland   Kaijus Ervasti
Copenhagen, Denmark   Lin Adrian
November 2017

Contents

List of Contributors

Lin Adrian Faculty of Law, University of Copenhagen, Copenhagen, Denmark

Ida Helene Asmussen Faculty of Law, University of Copenhagen, Copenhagen, Denmark

Camilla Bernt Faculty of Law, University of Bergen, Bergen, Norway

Kaijus Ervasti Faculty of Social Sciences, University of Helsinki, Helsinki, Finland

Eva Fromholz Department of Social Work, Stockholm University, Stockholm, Sweden

Christian B. N. Gade Department of Anthropology, Aarhus University, Aarhus, Denmark

Maija Gellin Finnish Forum for Mediation, Helsinki, Finland

Vaula Haavisto Faculty of Educational Sciences, University of Helsinki, Helsinki, Finland

Maritha Jacobsson Department of Social Work, Umeå University, Umeå, Sweden

Solfrid Mykland The Norwegian Land Consolidation Court, Bergen, Norway

Anna Nylund Faculty of Law, University of Tromsø – The Arctic University of Norway, Tromsø, Norway

Katrine Barnekow Rasmussen Faculty of Law, University of Copenhagen, Copenhagen, Denmark

Kirsikka Salminen Faculty of Law, University of Helsinki, Helsinki, Finland

Astrid Strandbu Department of Education, University of Tromsø – The Arctic University of Norway, Tromsø, Norway

Renee Thørnblad RKBU North, Faculty of Health, University of Tromsø – The Arctic University of Norway, Tromsø, Norway

Lottie Wahlin Institute for Mediation Training in Sweden, Stockholm, Sweden

Introduction to Nordic Mediation Research

Anna Nylund, Kaijus Ervasti, and Lin Adrian

Contents

Abstract This is an introduction to a collection of articles in the book Nordic mediation research. The background and history of mediation in the Nordic, or Scandinavian, countries is presented. The areas of mediation practice in the Nordic countries and Nordic mediation research are also introduced.

1 Background and History of Mediation in the Nordic Countries

The Nordic—or Scandinavian countries[1]—Denmark, Finland, Iceland, Norway and Sweden have close geographic, historical, social, economic, cultural, linguistic and legal ties. The economies are organised in a similar manner in what is sometimes

---

[1]The term Nordic is preferred in this volume, as it is more precise. Geographically, only Norway and Sweden are situated on the Scandinavian Peninsula. Often Denmark is included in Scandinavia, since Danish is a Scandinavian language. So is the Icelandic language, although Iceland is

A. Nylund
Faculty of Law, University of Tromsø – The Arctic University of Norway, Tromsø, Norway
e-mail: anna.nylund@uit.no

K. Ervasti
Faculty of Social Sciences, University of Helsinki, Helsinki, Finland
e-mail: kaijus.ervasti@helsinki.fi

L. Adrian (✉)
Faculty of Law, University of Copenhagen, Copenhagen, Denmark
e-mail: lin.adrian@jur.ku.dk

© The Author(s) 2018
A. Nylund et al. (eds.), *Nordic Mediation Research*,
https://doi.org/10.1007/978-3-319-73019-6_1

1

called the 'Nordic model'. In this model, societies seek to blend a market economy with 'economic efficiency'—presented in the form of generous welfare benefits. Welfare benefits are awarded to the individual rather than the family and much of the benefits are tax-funded (Andersen et al. 2007). Decision making in politics, and in many other organisations, is based on consensus and corporatism. Culturally, people in the Nordic countries value egalitarianism, low hierarchy, directness, collectivism and gender egalitarianism (Warner-Søderholm 2012). In the legal area, the countries share legal traditions and have historically inspired each other's legislation and legal systems (Letto-Vanamo and Tamm 2016). This is also the case when it comes to alternative dispute resolution (ADR) and mediation. Because of these similarities, it makes sense to present mediation research from this particular region in the same book.

Mediation in some form has a long history in the Nordic countries (Adrian 2014; Ervasti 2014; Nylund 2014; Vindeløv 2012). For example, in 1795, the Danish King instituted national conciliation boards in Denmark and, 2 years later, in rural Norway by royal resolution (Adrian 2014). In the preamble of the resolution,[2] the King states that the purpose of the resolution is to prevent unnecessary and costly litigation between subjects. Accordingly, cases could be filed in court only after failed attempts to settle by a board. We also find traces of mediation in legislation in the medieval and early modern times (Adrian 2014; Nylund 2017; Sunde 2014). See more on the history of mediation in the Nordic countries in Ervasti (2018).

Modern-day mediation dates to the early 1980s in Finland, Norway and Sweden and to the 1990s in Denmark. The ideology of modern mediation in the Nordic countries is often attributed to Nils Christie and his ideas of conflict and conflict resolution presented in *Conflict as Property* from 1977. His main idea is that conflict should be resolved by those involved or affected by it rather than by the judicial system. Additionally, mediation in the Nordic countries is inspired by the development in other countries, in general, and influenced by U.S. mediation efforts, scholars and practitioners, in particular.

2   Mediation Practice and Training in the Nordic Countries

Mediation exists in all of the Nordic countries. However, the level of activity varies. There is only minimal activity in Iceland and consequently no contribution from there in this volume. In Sweden, there is some activity but mediation has not quite caught on as a common conflict resolution practice. Both Norway and Finland seem

---

geographically situated between North America and Europe. The Finnish language is not Scandinavian. Indeed, unlike most European languages, it is not even Indo-European. However, the historical, societal, cultural and legal structures in Finland are similar to the other Nordic countries.

[2] 10. juli 1795 Fr. om Forligelses-Commissioners Stiftelse overalt i Danmark, samt i Købstæderne i Norge.

to be moving towards a conflict resolution culture with mediation as a natural component. Denmark is somewhere in-between.

Mediation is offered by private providers as well as by public institutions but is most prevalent in public, highly institutionalised settings. For example, the judiciary in Denmark, Finland and Norway uses mediation as an alternative to adjudication in civil cases. Similarly, many family disputes are resolved in mediation or mediation-like settings. In Norway, for example, parties must go to mediation prior to filing a lawsuit (see Nylund 2018). Victim offender mediation is a widespread practice in all countries except Iceland. In Sweden, victim offender mediation is in place for young people under the age of 21 (Jacobsson et al. 2018) and, in Finland, regional mediation offices offer mediation all over the country. In the private sector, workplace mediation is on the rise and mediation is increasingly—albeit still only modestly—used to resolve commercial matters. In Denmark, for instance, attorney-mediators offer mediation services in commercial disputes along with two arbitration institutes.[3] Mediation of consumer disputes is an area of emerging mediation practices. Consumers have traditionally had access to cheap and relatively informal and fast dispute resolution mechanisms in all Nordic countries and now mediation, too.

There is limited regulation of mediator practice in the Nordic countries. None of the countries has general regulation in their legislation or by national professional bodies. Mediators in some areas of practice have, however, instituted their own professional requirements. For example, a court-connected mediator in Denmark must be trained in mediation and follow a set of ethical guidelines.[4] In many other settings, such as in Norwegian victim offender mediation, the only requirement is mediator training. However, in neither this setting nor elsewhere is there a set standard for training requirements nor any kind of certification procedures in place. Mediation training in the Nordic countries varies from short courses with a couple of days training to longer programmes all the way to a two-year part-time master's degree programme.

3   Nordic Mediation Research

With the emergence of mediation practices, research has emerged as well—in particular, in the last 10 years. Today mediation research constitutes an established field of inquiry with contributions from several academic disciplines (law, psychology, history, anthropology etc.) based on multiple methodological qualitative as well as quantitative approaches. The development of mediation research has not been coordinated cross-border and across academic approaches, and much is published in the researchers' national languages only. This volume is the result of three explorative

---

[3]See http://mediatoradvokater.dk/, http://voldgiftsinstituttet.dk/ and https://voldgift.dk/ (last assessed 23.10.17).

[4]See https://www.domstol.dk/saadangoerdu/retsmaegling/Pages/Etiskeretningslinjerforretsmaegling. aspx.

workshops conducted in 2016–2017 where 16 mediation researchers from a variety of fields and four different countries came together for the first time to explore and develop their research, as well as taking steps to making it available in English.

As a very tangible result of this work, this volume presents a collection of Nordic mediation research spanning over several types of mediation and different theoretical and methodological approaches. The contributions are random rather than representative, as sought to find interesting contributions in an organic process. Thus, the contents do not reflect all Nordic mediation research, neither is it representative of all forms of mediation available or the research on them.

Although the contributions are not representative of all mediation practice and research, they still reflect some generic trends described above. First, the articles reflect the proliferation of public-sector mediation in highly institutionalised settings and the strong connection between the justice system and mediation. Consequently, most of the contributions discuss court-connected civil or family mediation, victim offender mediation, and pre-action voluntary or mandatory family/child custody mediation.

Second, although mediation is present in all Nordic countries, it seems to be more common in Denmark, Finland and Norway, than in Sweden and Iceland. Not surprisingly, research and researchers are distributed unevenly as well and the contributions in this book reflect this. Third, across areas of practice and countries, some topics and perspectives are more frequent than others. We see that in the research presented in this volume, too.

The articles in this volume are arranged thematically rather than by country, area of practice or research methodology, as we think that themes provide the most interesting categorisation for readers. The articles in *Part I* focus on the systemic aspects of mediation. They are, in particular, concerned with how mediation is understood, developed and organised in different contexts and how the understanding and organisation of mediation is reflected in the use and practices of mediation. The articles in *Part II* critically examine the role of the mediator and mediation processes and try to answer questions such as: To what extent does mediated agreements reflect party self-determination and creative problem-solving? What role(s) are assigned to the mediator? What unspoken expectations do the parties in mediation face and how do these influence the mediation process and outcomes? In *Part III*, the articles focus on children as an active subject in mediation. They look at how children can participate in decision-making in mandatory mediation processes and examine whether mediation is in the best interests of the child seen from a legal perspective. The over-arching themes of these first three parts are the vagueness or over-inclusiveness of mediation and related concepts, how mediation interacts with and sometimes is co-opted by other dispute resolution mechanisms and social services, and how these processes influence the role of the mediator, the mediation process and the outcomes of mediation. The articles in *Part IV* discuss the relationship between mediation theory and mediation practices, as well as describe school mediation in Finland as an example of a particular area of practice.

The entire volume is available through open access on mediationresearch.org, together with other resources on mediation in the Nordic countries.

References

Adrian L (2014) Court-connected mediation in Danish civil justice: a happy marriage or a strained relationship? In: Ervo L, Nylund A (eds) The future of civil litigation – access to courts and court-annexed mediation in the Nordic countries. Springer, Cham, pp 157–186

Andersen TM, Holmström B, Honkapohja S, Korkman S, Söderström HT, Vartiainen J (2007) The Nordic model – embracing globalization and sharing risks. The Research Institute of the Finnish Economy (ETLA), Helsinki

Christie N (1977) Conflicts as property. Br J Criminol 17:1–15

Ervasti K (2014) Court-connected mediation in Finland: experiences and visions. In: Ervo L, Nylund A (eds) The future of civil litigation. Access to courts and court-annexed mediation in the Nordic countries. Springer, Cham, pp 121–136

Ervasti K (2018) Past, present and future of mediation in Nordic countries. In: Nylund A, Ervasti K, Adrian L (eds) Nordic mediation research. Springer International Publishing, Cham, pp 225–245

Jacobsson M, Wahlin L, Fromholz E (2018) Victim offender mediation in Sweden: an activity falling apart? In: Nylund A, Ervasti K, Adrian L (eds) Nordic mediation research. Springer International Publishing, Cham, pp 67–79

Letto-Vanamo P, Tamm D (2016) Cooperation in the field of law. In: Strang J (ed) Nordic cooperation: A European region in transition. Routledge, London, pp 93–107

Nylund A (2014) The many ways of civil mediaiton in Norway. In: Ervo L, Nylund A (eds) The future of civil litigation. Access to courts and court-annexed mediation in the Nordic countries. Springer, Cham, pp 97–120

Nylund A (2017) An introduction to Finnish legal culture. In: Koch S, Skodvin KE, Sunde JØ (eds) Comparing legal cultures. Fagbokforlaget, Bergen, pp 285–316

Nylund A (2018) A dispute systems design perspective on norwegian child custody mediation. In: Nylund A, Ervasti K, Adrian L (eds) Nordic mediation research. Springer International Publishing, Cham, pp 9–26

Sunde JØ (2014) Daughters of god and counsellors of the judges of men: changes in the legal culture of the Norwegian realm in the high middle ages. In: Brink S, Collinson L (eds) New approaches to early law in Scandinavia. Brepols, Turnhout, pp 131–183

Vindeløv V (2012) Reflexive mediation – with a sustainable perspective. DJØF Publishing, Copenhagen

Warner-Søderholm G (2012) But we're not all Vikings! Intercultural Identity within a Nordic context. Immigrant-institutet (IMMI), Packhusplatsen

Part I
Systemic Aspects of Nordic Mediation

A Dispute Systems Design Perspective on Norwegian Child Custody Mediation

Anna Nylund

Contents

Abstract In this article, I analyse why and how the Norwegian child custody system fails to provide early resolution to many families. Resolution of these conflicts should be timely and adapted to the level and sources of conflict. Child custody mediation is mandatory in Norway for all separating couples with children, yet the number of child custody disputes in courts is similar to the other Nordic countries with voluntary mediation schemes only. Particularly, high conflict families seem to receive inadequate services and support to manage their conflict, although the aim of the system is to prevent conflicts from being prolonged and escalating. In addition to an analysis of the failure of the system, I explore the different tiers of mediation services (the Family Counselling Office mediation and court-connected mediation)

A. Nylund (✉)
Faculty of Law, University of Tromsø – The Arctic University of Norway, Tromsø, Norway
e-mail: anna.nylund@uit.no

© The Author(s) 2018
A. Nylund et al. (eds.), *Nordic Mediation Research*,
https://doi.org/10.1007/978-3-319-73019-6_2

and their relationships—or lack thereof. This interrelationship influences the mediation system and its outcomes. To understand the context, I offer a brief account of the development of child custody mediation and give a societal background for the Norwegian child custody mediation system.

1 Dispute Systems Design and Family Mediation

Conflicts related to child custody and the amount of contact each parent should have following a divorce are a major challenge in contemporary Western societies. Prolonged high levels of conflict after parental separation is recognised as a central risk factor for the well-being of the children. Applying inappropriate mechanisms of dispute resolution may offer the parents no help in resolving their disputes and developing constructive co-parenting habits. Ultimately, inappropriate dispute resolution may result in prolonging the dispute and providing a solution that is not in the best interests of the child. The best interests of the child is the paramount factor in the resolution of disputes in custody and contact, along with the lifetime relationship between the parents vis-à-vis the child long after the separation.

The aim of dispute systems design theory is to help organisations and society manage and resolve disputes[1] in an efficient and constructive manner (Rogers et al. 2013; Menkel-Meadow et al. 2010; Smith and Martinez 2009; Bingham 2008). By creating systems for early management, destructive conflicts are avoided. Organisations and society can then funnel resources into productive activities instead of unproductive methods of handling conflicts. Dispute systems design recognises conflict resolution is about finding appropriate dispute resolution mechanisms: not every mechanism fits every dispute. Although originally developed to manage disputes within specific organisations, dispute systems design has spread to many types of contexts. In a court context, the concept developed by Frank Sander (1976) of a multi-door courthouse matches the ideas of dispute systems design theory.

In conflicts related to child custody, the level of dispute between the parents vary greatly, as does the reasons for the conflict and the number, nature and difficulty of unresolved issues. Relationships among family members are often complex, and a divorce involving children is seldom, if ever, a clean slate. On the contrary, some form of co-parenting is required at least until the youngest child reaches the age of 18 and often the parents have at least occasional contact long after their children are grown. Consequently, new issues giving rise to new conflicts may occur long after separation. Because the situations of each family is different, families should be offered a range of dispute resolution and other services.

---

[1]In conflict theory, some authors make a distinction between disputes and conflicts. In this text, the terms are used interchangeably.

This text discusses the Norwegian system for resolving child custody and contact disputes in the light of current knowledge on child custody mediation and other forms of child custody alternative dispute resolution (ADR). Particular emphasis is on high conflict families, a diverse group of families with prolonged conflicts, as finding appropriate mechanisms for this group is particularly challenging.

First, this text discusses the development of child custody mediation from facilitative mediation to both diversification of services and dilution of the idea of mediation (Sect. 2). In Sect. 3, the Norwegian child custody mediation and its background are presented. Thereafter, the Norwegian system is subject to criticism both from the perspective of dispute systems design theory and child custody mediation theory. Finally, some proposals to improve the system are offered.

2 Child Custody Mediation from Facilitative Mediation to Diverse Mediation Models

2.1 Child Custody Mediation as Facilitative Mediation

Child custody mediation draws on the theory of facilitative mediation. The role of the mediator is to facilitate negotiation between the parents by helping them identify and name the disputed issues, their interest and needs. Based on these, the mediator helps create options the parents can select to fulfil their interests. Child custody mediation theory recognised early the particular character of the disputes related to children: the close relationship between the parents, the high level of emotions, the social, psychological, emotional and economic importance of the outcome, and the need for future cooperation. The parents are recognised as the persons who are best equipped to solve disputes in the family. The task of the mediator is to help the parents overcome emotional, social and cognitive barriers to conflict resolution and teach the parents conflict resolution skills (Firestone and Weinstein 2004; Schepard 2004; Kelly 1997).

The best interests of the child is recognised as the epitome of the process. Consequently, mediation needs to focus on the interests of the child, on emotions and social relationships, and on teaching dispute resolution skills. For mediation to be an appropriate method of dispute resolution, both parents must be capable to offer the child adequate care. Additionally, for the outcome to be in the best interests of the child, both parents must be able to perceive the needs and interests of the child and to act accordingly. The parents often need the mediator to help them in recognising the needs and interests of the child (Schepard 2004; AFCC Model Standards of Practice for Family and Divorce Mediation 2000).

Divorce is not a single event. Rather, it is as a long-term process of restructuring a family. Furthermore, new disputes may arise as circumstances change: children's needs change as they grow, the parents' employment changes, new partners and half- or step-siblings become part of the family. To ease adjustment and family restructuring, mediation should preferably consist of short hearings over a period of time rather than a one-off ("marathon") session.

From the late 1980s and onwards, in the wake of proliferation of child custody mediation, critical voices were raised at some of its shortcomings. One shortcoming is related to the diverse needs of families, in particular, families with high levels of conflict. Another problem is related to how mediation is implemented as a shortcut to swift resolution and cost-savings rather than recognising the qualities of mediation and the preconditions for achieving successful results.

2.2 Adapting Mediation to the Needs of Diverse Families

Domestic violence was the first problematic issue to receive attention in mediation theory. Violence, be it physical, sexual, economical, emotional or psychological, shifts the power balance between the parents and hampers the parents' ability to solve problems. It has adverse effects on the children, regardless of whether the children are the direct target of violence. Therefore, (facilitative) mediation may lead to undesirable outcomes. However, violence is not always easy to spot and not all violence is the same. In some families, it is a single episode triggered by frustration. In other families, one or both parents regularly resort to violence to resolve conflicts. In still others, one parent uses violence to exert power and dominate the entire family. Consequently, in order to determine the appropriate type of dispute resolution process, one must assess whether violence is present in the family and what type of violence is present (Holt et al. 2008; Jaffe et al. 2008).

A persistent high level of conflict is typical for families experiencing domestic violence. Research shows many other factors may also result in high conflict. An estimate of 15–25% of families are believed to be high conflict in many Western countries (Ottosen 2016; Helland and Borren 2015; Brown 2011; Johnston et al. 2009). High conflict families are not a coherent group: The conflict may arise *inter alia* from health problems, substance abuse, socio-economic problems, and psychological factors. In some families, the children run a risk of abuse or neglect. They may also be a witness to violence. The risk factors for high conflict are also factors that increase the level of care the child needs, the capability of a parent to provide care for the child, the parent's ability to make decisions, or any combination of theses.

Facilitative mediation, as a short-term intervention, focusing on removing some obstacles of rational decision-making, is often not appropriate or sufficient to solve the disputes in these families. However, litigious court proceedings with an expert evaluation often leads to further escalation (Sauer 2007). Therefore, new forms of mediation have emerged particularly in the English-speaking world to better serve high conflict families. Mediation may be conducted in exclusively in separate meetings (caucuses) where the parents sit in different rooms and the mediator moves between the rooms. The parents may be offered services such as parental education, individual discussions or therapy in addition to mediation. Mediation may be combined with other types of dispute resolution processes, such as regular court proceedings, evaluation or arbitration. In helping families with particular challenges, the mediator must have sufficient knowledge and skills to help the family. For example, disputes arising from cultural and religious issues may require a different set of skills than disputes arising from substance abuse, parenting a disabled child, or handling a parent who has developed pathological hatred towards the other parent.

Examples of more intensive forms of mediation is therapeutic family mediation developed by Irving and Benjamin (2002), where mediators use methods and theories from family therapy. Johnston et al. (2009) have developed a method where parents and children are required to participate in short-term therapy on a group or individual level as a parallel process to mediation. Other types of dispute resolution combine mediation with evaluation or arbitration. The most widespread is perhaps parenting coordination, also known as parenting consulting or special master. The parenting coordinator helps the parents to implement the mediated agreement and to solve problems by giving advice, mediating and evaluating. The coordinator may have the right to arbitrate limited issues (Barsky 2011; AFCC Guidelines for Parenting Coordination 2005).

To offer appropriate services, parents participate in a triage—a screening process—to assess the level of conflict, presence of violence and other risk factors at the intake to the mediation programme. The extent and methods used in the screening process vary, but the main goal is to direct the family to an appropriate mediation or other dispute resolution process. In some programmes, other services, such as parent education, therapy and anger management courses are also available.

The result of recognising the diverse situations of dissolving families has been a diversification of mediation and other dispute resolution processes offered. The system must distinguish between different types of services offered to the families. Families should be offered a range of services: advice, therapy, dispute resolution and other services. Each of the services should be labelled appropriately.

2.3 Mediation Is Diluted to Settlement

The other development in child custody mediation is less encouraging. Mediation is often introduced both to provide more appropriate dispute resolution than an adversarial trial, which is often detrimental for co-parenting, and to provide cheaper services. However, in many systems the idea of settlement becomes dominating. Mediation is just about settlement, as settlement is seen as something inherently good and in the best interests of the child. Mediation dilutes to a process of settlement: settlement is more important than the quality of the process (and outcome). This view obscures the assets of mediation: the possibility to find interest-based, individualised solutions, teaching the family dispute resolution skills, and—at least to some extent—managing the underlying conflicts. Settlement-oriented mediation may be contrary to the best interests of the child, as the parents may be pressured to accept a solution that is not in the best interests of the child.

Additionally, they may gain little or no help to solve current and future conflicts. The best interests of the child may become subordinate to settlement.[2]

In this context, the definition of mediation is overly broad. Mediation is the same as any process for reaching settlement. A highly evaluative process where the mediator suggests solutions, or at least indicates a solution, may be, in fact, an adjudicative process, but labelled "mediation". Similarly, a process consisting mainly of therapeutic methods may be labelled "mediation". Mediation may be then almost any type of dispute resolution process or any type of service—or combinations thereof—offered to post-divorce families (c.f. Bernt 2018; Salminen 2018).

The overly broad definition of mediation leads to several problems. It is difficult to direct a family to an appropriate dispute resolution process if everything is labelled mediation. Norway serves as an example. Parents are offered a mixture of services, including some or all of the following: advice, light evaluation, small-scale family therapy, and mediation. Parents may, in practice, not select appropriate services, as all services are offered under the umbrella of mediation. As Bernt (2018) explains, offering mediation as an indistinct group of services also leads to role conflicts. The system is opaque particularly to the families involved—it is difficult to make meaningful selections when the choices are unclear. The family may find itself in a different process than it thought it would enter. In a policy perspective, it may be difficult to develop and assess the services for divorcing and post-divorce families when one does not distinguish between different processes.

3 Norwegian Child Custody Mediation Systems

3.1 Norwegian Welfare State as the Backdrop

All dispute systems are contingent on the social, cultural and economic context of the surrounding society.

In the Nordic countries, the Nordic welfare state is a paramount societal (and cultural) factor setting the stage of solving issues related to child custody. The Nordic welfare model is highly individualised and based on universal services. Each member of society is expected to provide for himself or herself by working, and pension rights are individual. Spousal maintenance is a rare exception. The government offers a vast range of high quality services free of charge or at a low cost: day care, school, after-school care, higher education, health services, etc. Up until recently, private school and the use of private health care has been limited. Today, private schools are more common, but most of them are state subsidised and

---

[2]Studies indicate that some families in court-connected divorce mediation in Norway feel pressured to settle and some parents settle even if they believe the settlement agreement is contrary to the child's best interests. See Koch (2008), Nordhelle (2011), Breivik and Mevik (2012).

tuition costs are modest. Consequently, in the aftermath of a separation, finance issues are less weighty than in many other Western countries. However, particularly low-income families are often in need of social benefits and may need help to orient themselves to their rights.

Nordic countries encourage parents to solve their issues out-of-court. The preferred way of solving disputes is informal negotiation between the parents or third-party facilitated dispute resolution out-of-court. In Norway, only an estimated 10–15% of parents instigate court proceedings in child custody cases (Koch 2008; Skjørten 2005).[3]

Today, co-habitation is very common in Norway. Approximately one-half of all first-born babies have parents who are not married. The socio-economic differences between co-habiting couples and married couples are small.[4] Co-habiting couples with children have much of the same rights and obligations as married couples—both during and after co-habitation.

3.2   Current Structure of Child Custody Mediation in Norway

The Norwegian child custody dispute resolution system is three-tiered. All three tiers are regulated by the Children Act.[5] The first two tiers consist of out-of-court mediation, one of which is mandatory for all separating or divorcing parents with children under the age of 16. The second step is mandatory pre-action mediation and the third step is court-connected custody mediation.

Children Act section 51 mandates all separating couples with children under the age of 16 to attend mediation at the local Family Counselling Office or a similar service provider. Parents must attend mediation for 1 h. After the first hour, the parents receive a mediation certificate and are entitled to apply for separation and receive benefits for single parents. The mediator may offer the family three additional hours once the first hour has passed. After the four first hours, the mediator may offer an additional 3 h for a total of 7 h (Children Act section 54). After 7 h have passed, mandatory mediation ends, but the Family Counselling Office may continue to work with the family under voluntary services. According to Children Act section 52, the goal of mediation is to achieve a written agreement on custody, residence and contact and to inform the parents on the financial consequences of the agreement. The Family Counselling Office is mandated to provide parents with information,

---

[3]The percentage is similar in Finland, see Valkama and Lasola (2009).

[4]Co-habiting parents are, on average, slightly younger than married parents, have a shorter history as a couple and have younger children, but the differences are rather small in total, see Ådnanes et al. (2011b), pp. 17–19. The level of conflict is approximately the same in both groups.

[5]Lov om barn og foreldre 8 April 1981 no 7. An unofficial English translation is available at https://www.regjeringen.no/en/dokumenter/the-children-act/id448389/.

advice and dispute resolution services. In most parts of Norway, children seldom participate in mediation.[6]

The second tier is pre-action mediation where a parent intending to instigate child custody proceedings at court must attend mediation for at least 1 h and up to 7 h. At the end of the hour, the parents obtain a mediation certificate that is valid for 6 months. During those 6 months, the parents may instigate court proceedings. The license from the initial "mediation" during separation (first-tier mediation) is valid for 6 months: within that period, the parents are not required to participate in additional mediation before instigating litigation. Thus, pre-action mediation takes place several months, or even years, after the initial separation. Mandatory pre-action mediation is subject to the same regulation as mandatory mediation during separation. Yet the target group is different, as only parents who have not found agreement in the initial mediation and parents who face new or recurrent conflicts are included. Although many families face conflicts long after separation, most of them are able to solve the conflicts on their own. Thus, in the pre-action mediation group the level of conflict is, on average, higher than in families participating in mandatory post-separation mediation.

The third tier is court-connected alternative dispute resolution processes, in practice, almost exclusively court-connected mediation. Mediation is the preferred method of dispute resolution in court, and it is used unless there is reason to believe the child could risk abuse or neglect (Children Act section 61). In addition to court-connected custody mediation, the court may order evaluation, out-of-court mediation and other types of help. However, these are seldom used. In practice, the court appoints an expert to (co-)mediate the case with the judge hearing the case. The expert mediates, provides advice to the parents and the court. The expert-mediator may also make an expert evaluation.

The first two tiers of dispute resolution have a long history. The purpose of mediation was originally to help parents to mend their relationship to avoid divorce. Today, the purpose is to help parents find an agreement that is in the best interests of the child. The minimum number of hours of mandatory mediation was reduced from three to one in 2007. Since mediation should be voluntary, the reduction of mandatory hours could be characterised as a positive development. However, because "mediation" refers to a broader set of services, particularly families with prolonged conflicts could benefit from a longer session with an opportunity to discuss the conflict, its implications for the children and to teach co-parenting skills.

Court-connected custody mediation was introduced in 2004 to offer a form of dispute resolution that would not escalate conflicts in the manner litigation and other adjudicative processes does. Although the legislator recognised that mediation does not fit situations where the child risk neglect or abuse, the model does not take into account the varying needs of families, and, in particular, high conflict families. The

---

[6]Ådnanes et al. (2011b) found children participated in mediation in only 4% of the cases. Some Family Counselling Offices have adopted a mediation model where the children, as a rule, are included in mediation. See Thørnblad and Strandbu (2018).

model is based on a vague concept of mediation as a conflict reducing dispute resolution mechanism. The legislator recognised many of the promises of mediation, but disregarded research and experience from other countries indicating short-comings and pitfalls of short-term facilitative mediation, including the limited help it offers to many high-conflict families and some of the perils of mixing different types of services under the label of "mediation" (Nylund 2008, 2011).

4 Critical Perspectives on Norwegian Child Custody Mediation

In this part, three key points of criticism will be raised. Firstly, the current system has an unclear target group, is an incongruent mixture of elements and a connection between the forms of mediation is lacking. Furthermore, Norwegian mediation can be criticised for allowing the mediator to mix roles, for not securing the children's right to participation in decision-making and for having mandatory mediation. However, the three latter issues will not be discussed in this text.

4.1 Unclear Target Group

Norwegian child custody mediation has an unclear target group. Two decades ago, Ekeland and Myklebust (1997) noted that mediation in Family Counselling Offices did not recognise the various need of families. Mandatory mediation at separation is targeted at all separating families. Thus, the level of conflict and the number of and severity of risk factors for the well-being of the child and for high conflict vary. Many parents would find, and actually have found, a solution on their own. Low conflict families do not need dispute resolution services. However, they may wish to have information on shared parenting, supporting the children, factors they should take into account when selecting care arrangements and social benefits.

Families with moderate conflicts may benefit from mediation. However, settlement, as such, may not be the key issue in the family. Rather, the parents may need help to improve communication, discuss specific issues and recognise the best interests of their child(ren). Discussing some of the issues or providing facilitative mediation requires more than 1 h and may require, in many cases, more than 7 h.

Finally, high conflict families often need more intensive and more specialised services than low to moderate conflict families. In some cases, mediation may not be an appropriate dispute resolution method and may even put the child at risk of abuse or neglect. In other high conflict families, dispute resolution services should be tailored to give the families proper help. In absence of a screening mechanism and in light of the limited first session, one may ask if the particular needs of each family are identified and if, and how, the services can be tailored to each family

(Gulbrandsen 2013; Gulbrandsen and Tjersland 2013; Ådnanes et al. 2011a). More than one-half of the high conflict families leave mediation after 1 or 2 h without agreement and without reduction in the level of conflict (Tjersland et al. 2015). Currently, some Family Counselling Offices are piloting a model for high conflict families where a set of individual, family and group sessions are combined. In the model, two employees "co-mediate" to offer the best help to reduce the level of conflict. The initial results are encouraging, with more families engaging in mediation beyond the first mandatory hour.

In Norway, neither mandatory pre-action mediation nor court-connected custody mediation has been designed with high conflict families in mind. Considering that only 10–12% of families instigate child custody proceedings in court, there is reason to believe a notable part of the families have a persistent high level of conflict. Yet the bill that introduced court-connected custody mediation hardly touches upon the topic of high conflict families. It seems to presuppose families belong to two categories: one where the child risks abuse or serious neglect and one where the parents are stuck in a conflict but are able to resolve it if the mediator focuses on constructive communication and the positive experiences of co-parenting. In fact, many families fall between these categories: the child does not risk serious neglect, but focusing on improving communication and positive experiences will not suffice to reduce the level of conflict (Tjersland et al. 2015; Nylund 2012; Nylund 2011; Ådnanes et al. 2011a; Nylund 2008). There is also a widespread notion that a conflict is never the fault of one party. Rather, the reason for persistent conflict lies with both parties. However, often the behaviour of one parent is an important source of conflict (Gulbrandsen 2013; Dutton et al. 2011; Demby 2009). Nonetheless, a skilled mediator cannot regard one parent as the "good one" and the other as the "bad one". Nor can a mediator necessarily assume that both parents have equal fault and equal parenting skills. Given the complexity of familial relationships, the mediator needs sufficient tools to deal with a range of reasons for persistently high levels of conflict.

Norway is the only Nordic country with mandatory mediation for all separating couples and the only Nordic country with mandatory pre-action mediation. Denmark has a system with a mandatory pre-trial counselling or mediation session. The service is similar to the Norwegian model of services, but it distinguishes between family counselling and mediation. Both services are in addition separate from adjudicative processes (www.statsforvaltningen.dk). In Finland and Sweden, mediation is offered on a voluntary basis outside courts. Yet the percentage of divorcing families instigating child custody litigation is roughly the same.

Although the research community has recognised that the current system does not serve the needs of high conflict families, the system has been subject to limited discussion. Currently, no triage mechanisms are in place to assess the conflict level in the family and the sources of conflict, nor to determine appropriate services. Mediators are not offered systematic training on issues related to high conflict families. Therefore, families are offered inappropriate or inadequate services to help them manage their conflict and teach them effective post-divorce parenting skills.

4.2 Overly Broad Definition of Mediation

Mediation is defined very broadly. At the Family Counselling Office "mediation" consists of information, advice, brief therapy and dispute resolution. Mediation may be facilitative, evaluative, therapeutic, narrative, transformative or simply trying to induce the parents to settle. The consequence of an unclear concept of mediation and bundling of services is that families often leave mediation after the first hour (Kjøs et al. 2015; Tjersland et al. 2015; Gulbrandsen 2013; Ådnanes et al. 2011a, b; Gulbrandsen and Tjersland 2010; Haugen and Rantalaiho 2010). Thus, the positive potential that mediation and other services could offer remains untapped.

According to the mediators, mediation is often ritualised, as the regulations do not give them the power or tools to deal with the underlying conflicts. Most parents leave after the mandatory first hour without getting much help to manage the conflict. Furthermore, both parents and mediators find that many of the settlement arrangements arrived at during mediation are sub-optimal. Parents agree to a mediated settlement because they fear court proceedings could lead to a worse option, not because they find the mediated agreement good.

When mediation is a mélange of services, the family may not pick the most relevant services. Families with low or moderate levels of conflict may reject the services because they do not need help to resolve a conflict, as they have already agreed on most issues. This may be true, however, they may like to discuss the needs of the children or challenges related to co-parenting. Families with underlying risk factors, regardless of the level of conflict, could find it helpful to discuss the underlying problem. However, they may not be aware of the services available to them or the mediator may lack (sufficient) training on the issue. In some families, key issues may remain unnoticed due to a lack of proper screening and awareness of the mediator.

As the source of the persistent conflicts is not recognised or the mediator lacks the knowledge and skills to provide a successful intervention, many families run a risk of not receiving the help they need. If the families perceive that the Family Counselling Office has limited help to offer, they may not be induced to participate in mediation apart from the mandatory first hour.

The limited timeframe for mediation may also hamper mediation. Successful interventions may be time-consuming—both in terms of the number of mediation sessions and the time-span of mediation. Hence, mediation is often not an avenue to swift resolution. The more limited the timeframe and the more the focus lies on settlement, the more parents may feel pressured to adopt a dissatisfactory settlement. This is probably particularly true in a country such as Norway where going to court is the exception. In Norway, it is generally understood that a "successful" divorce is a "happy" divorce where the parents agree on all issues.

In third-tier court-connected custody mediation, the understanding of mediation is broad. The tasks and roles of the mediator are manifold and may lead to conflicting roles and use of contradictory strategies. The methods of "mediation" are not standardised, nor is there committed work towards developing guidelines for best practices. While uniformity should certainly not be a goal in itself, continuous and persistent work towards developing practices would be beneficial to improve the quality of services and assure appropriate interventions.

Section 61 of the Children Act regulates court proceedings in child custody cases. In addition to court-connected custody mediation (expert-led or assisted) and a regular trial, the judge can request the parties to mediate at the Family Counselling Office or another out-of-court mediation programme. Although the provision is silent on the use of other types of dispute resolution processes, the legislator has clearly understood mediation in a broad manner. The role of the court-appointed expert-mediator is to give advice to the parents. Moreover, the expert-mediator may use evaluative techniques. Thus, mediation could be a highly, or almost purely, evaluative process. Evaluation could be appropriate in some situations, but, in other situations, it could be counterproductive. Therefore, using evaluation requires knowledge and skills on the when and how evaluation is appropriate (Bernt 2018).

Court-appointed experts and staff at Family Counselling Offices are licensed psychologists, social workers or psychiatrists, often with a specialisation in families and some additional training. However, no mediation training is required, nor are there any guidelines as to the content of such training. Training on issues related to specific issues is haphazard. The lack of comprehensive mediation training reduces the awareness of the concept of mediation, its uses and abuses, techniques used in mediation and the relationship between mediation and other forms of dispute resolution.

A particular problem related to offering mediation as a mélange of different services relates to consent. If almost any service or method for resolving disputes fits within the definition of mediation, then the families will not know which type of process they consent to. The right to informed decision-making and self-determination is reduced. Monitoring quality becomes difficult or almost impossible. In court-connected custody mediation, leaving the process may be difficult, particularly when the option is litigation where the expert mediator shifts to the role of expert evaluator, and the judge-mediator becomes the judge (Bernt 2018).

4.3   Relationship Between the Three Tiers of Mediation

Ideally, a dispute system should be designed to prevent conflicts from arising and escalating. Disputes should be resolved at the lowest possible level using the least intrusive mechanisms. Each level in the system should build on the earlier levels and bring loops back to the lower levels of the system.

The Norwegian child custody dispute system is incoherent. The same rules regulate the first two tiers, mandatory post-separation mediation and mandatory pre-action mediation, but fail to recognise the difference between the needs of the target group. In mandatory pre-action mediation, the family has already faced separation and lived with separation for at least 6 months. The conflict level is on average higher, and risk factors are more prevalent. Still, the rules and regulation are identical.

Court-connected custody mediation is, in practice, fully separated from mediation in Family Counselling Offices. Family Counselling Offices do not provide information to the court on mediation or risk factors present in the families. Thus, mediation in courts starts as if there had not been earlier attempts to mediate the case. Even though a family has only participated in the first mandatory hour of pre-action mediation, only a few courts regularly loop cases back to the Family Counselling Office. Although exchange of information may compromise the confidentiality of mediation, and sending a case back for mediation may pressure parents to settle, out-of-court mediation and court-connected custody mediation should be coordinated. The system should be more coherent with each level building on previous levels and better coordination between the levels.

In a comparative context, mandatory mediation for separating families and mandatory pre-action mediation does not seem to have reduced the percentage of families resorting to court proceedings. The system's design does not seem better than in countries with voluntary mediation.

4.4 Particular Problems Related to Court-Connected Custody Mediation

Court-connected custody mediation is the rule in cases on child custody, residence and contact. Mediation is seen quite uncritically as a superior method of dispute resolution, suitable to most cases. The only exception is cases where the child risks abuse or neglect.

The regulation is based loosely on theories of general child custody mediation and blatantly disregards the discussions on high conflict families. Considering only approximately 10 % of all separating parents instigate court proceedings, many if not most of these families could probably be characterised as "high conflict". Consequently, the dispute resolution system should be set up accordingly.

Currently, no triage is in place. Judges trust that legal counsel will mention any relevant information indicating child abuse or neglect to enable the judge to direct the case to traditional court proceedings rather than court-connected custody mediation. There is no uniform standard of what constitutes abuse or neglect disqualifying the case from mediation. If physical violence is present in the family, does only violence against the child disqualify mediation? Does severe violence against a parent also disqualify a case and, if so, on what grounds? Although the families have attended mediation at the Family Counselling Office, there is usually no exchange of information between courts on the level of conflict or sources of conflict. Neither does the court use triage.

The content of mediation and the role of the mediators are discussed in more detail by Camilla Bernt (2018). Here, it is sufficient to make a few remarks on mediation vis-à-vis providing diversified services. First, the court invites an expert to assist the court in mediating the case by providing information and advising the parents, and, if necessary, to decide the case. In spite of the widespread use of experts, the training does not have sufficient focus on mediation and issues in high conflict families. Experts without the specific training are frequently used. The content of the training is geared particularly towards the traditional role of a court appointed expert rather than that of a mediator, parenting coach and counsellor (Agenda Kaupang 2017).

Awareness of different causes of high conflict levels is relatively low particularly among judges, as is the knowledge of their consequences on parenting and the children.[7] When combined with an understanding of mediation as an inherently good form of dispute resolution and settlements as inherently good outcomes, the result may be less than optimal. Some parents report that when they voice a concern for substance abuse problems, or even (sexual) abuse of the child, the allegation might turn against them. The parent voicing the concern is accused of using a tactic of escalation or an attempt at disrupting the process towards settlement. The focus on settlement results in some parents feeling pressured into a settlement they do not agree with (Stang 2013; Koch 2008).

5   Improving Child Custody Mediation

The Norwegian child custody dispute system should be improved in several ways to address the issues of a lack of coherence and differentiation between families. First, differences in the family situations should be recognised, as the level and sources of conflict vary significantly. Consequently, families should be offered different types of help. Second, conflicts should be solved early to avoid escalation and the family taught dispute resolution skills to reduce future conflicts. Third, the system should offer transparent, coherent services where the different types of services are distinguished and where each step builds on the former steps.

5.1   Recognising the Needs of High Conflict Families

An essential step to improving the system is to recognise the diverse situations and needs of families. Since solving—or at least managing—disputes in high conflict families is a challenge, identifying families with a high conflict level is essential. In order to do so, services should be based on an initial assessment, triage of the situation, and needs and wishes of each family. Assessment of the conflict level

---

[7]The Norwegian Institute of Public Health issued a report on high conflict families (Helland and Borren 2015). The report provides research on how a high level of conflict is manifested, the reasons for high conflict and risk factors behind it. However, the report does not discuss how the high conflict level can be managed or reduced or how mediators should identify or deal with it.

and sources of conflict does not presuppose an extensive triage. Rather, simple tools and increased awareness, vigilance and knowledge may suffice. Based on the assessment, families should be directed to appropriate services. The Family Counselling Offices have the infrastructure and much of the tools necessary to do so. Ideally, an assessment tool would be developed to ensure consistent quality and limit the resources spent on assessment.

Currently mediators report having too little knowledge of particular problems and sources of conflict such as violence, child abuse, substance abuse and questions related to ethnicity and religion (Agenda Kaupang 2017; Ådnanes et al. 2011b). By increasing the competency of mediators, family counsellors, psychologists and other professionals working with child custody and contact issues, the needs of families facing particular challenges and high conflict families will be recognised and addressed earlier and in appropriate ways.

5.2   *Preventing Conflicts and Conflict Escalation*

A key concept in dispute systems design is to create an organisation that reduces the number of disputes and prevents disputes from escalating. Teaching conflict management skills and implementing mechanisms for early intervention is essential.

To improve the Norwegian child custody mediation system, services should be unbundled and distinguished from each other. I do not advocate total separation of processes, where a mediator is banned from using any type of therapeutic or therapy-inspired intervention, or where a mediator should never give parents any general information. Rather, different services should be offered, and each family should be able to assemble a set of services.

Families with low- to medium-levels of conflict may find information on post-divorce parenting, conflict management and supporting the children emotionally helpful. Online resources on parenting skills, discussion groups or meetings where a member of the staff facilitates a discussion on adjustment to a new family situation could be some of the services fit for families. Helping the parents recognise the views and perspectives of the children would probably be beneficial for many families. Labelling the help "mediation", as is currently done, makes the system opaque, as the families do not know what services are available. Further, many families may not find the services attractive, since the level of conflict is low, and they have settled all issues.

Appropriate labelling is not sufficient to unbundle services. Families, including children, should be informed of the services offered. Role conflicts and confusion of services should be avoided by letting different people perform different roles. This should be the case particularly when a family receives services that are more extensive. Thus, one counsellor could offer information and a discussion on post-divorce parenting and the impact of conflict on the well-being of children, a second could offer therapeutic services and a third could function as a mediator. Different services requires different skills from the person offering the service. Although a family therapist may also be a good facilitative or therapeutic mediator, not all family therapists are qualified mediators; nor does a mediator have to be a therapist.

If families believe the services offered are appropriate for their needs, they are more likely to be motivated to use them and return for more help and assistance when needed. Focus should not be on settlement, but on offering families help to adjust to post-divorce life and specialist services for post-divorce families. Conflict may arise long after the divorce, as new partners and children become part of the family, as the children grow and as the life-situations, such as employment and health, of the family members change. Parents who have learned co-parenting skills and dispute resolution skills, or who are at least aware of the services offered, are probably more likely to return for early dispute resolution services, if necessary.

5.3 Transparent, Coherent and Unbundled Services

Today, the system lacks coherence. A family is directed through a set of sessions labelled "mediation". In the Family Services Office, the session far too often ends after the first hour, and in courts, the sessions are longer but their content is mixed and often evaluation-driven. The entire system is also settlement-oriented rather than focusing on finding interest-based, child-friendly solutions.

A mandatory intake discussion, where the family discusses its current situation and, when appropriate, receives advice could be combined with an intake assessment, triage, where the family counsellor informs and advices about services and assesses the needs of the family.

After the intake assessment, families where the children risk child abuse or neglect would be directed directly to the court. Other families receive appropriate services based on the assessment. Although mediation and counselling should not be mandatory, parents should receive information about the content and benefits of the services. Keeping families within the Family Counselling Office system would provide them with an opportunity to solve their conflicts early.

Second-tier mediation, mandatory pre-action mediation, should to a greater degree be connected with court proceedings. Requiring the families to take part in an intake discussion and assessment at the Family Counselling Office would serve two aims. First, to encourage the family to use dispute resolution process on a lower level to reduce the level of conflict, to keep the decision-making power within the family, to reduce costs and obtain better outcomes. Second, the Family Counselling Office would assist the court in assessing the level and sources of conflict.

Courts should still offer court-connected custody mediation, but building on the work done at the Family Counselling Office. Courts should also loop back families to the Family Counselling Office when appropriate.

By making the system more coherent, overlapping services could be avoided and families could be encouraged to use less invasive, less conflict-driving dispute resolution mechanisms and other services that enhance the ability of the family to solve conflicts and provide children with good parenting.

References

Ådnanes M, Haugen GMD, Jensberg H, Husum TL, Rantalaiho M (2011a) Hva karakteriserer vanskelige saker i foreldremekling, og er meklingsordningen godt nok tilpasset? Fokus på Familien 39:86–115

Ådnanes M, Haugen GMD, Jensberg H, Rantalaiho M, Husum TL (2011b) Rapport. Evaluering av mekling etter ekteskapslov og barnelov. SINTEF Teknologi og samfunn. NTNU Trondheim

AFCC Model Standards of Practice for Family and Divorce Mediation (2000) Association of Family and Conciliation Courts

AFCC Guidelines for Parenting Coordination (2005) Association of Family and Conciliation Courts

Agenda Kaupang (2017) Evaluering av utdanningsprogramme for barnefaglige sakkyndige. Barne- og likestillingsdepartementet, Oslo

Barsky AE (2011) Parenting coordination: the risks of a hybrid conflict resolution process. Negot J 27:7–27

Bernt C (2018) Custody mediation in Norwegian courts: a conglomeration of roles and processes. In: Nylund A, Ervasti K, Adrian L (eds) Nordic mediation research. Springer, Cham, pp 105–132

Bingham LB (2008) Designing justice: legal institutions and other systems for managing conflict. Ohio State J Dispute Resolut 24:1–51

Breivik FL, Mevik K (2012) Barnefordeling i domstolen. Når barnets beste blir barnets verste. Universitetsforlaget, Oslo

Brown H (2011) Mediating high conflict couples. In: Deleuran P, Jarner S (eds) Conflict management in the family field and in other close relationships. DJØF Publishing, Copenhagen

Demby S (2009) Interparent hatred and its impact on parenting: assessment in forensic custody evaluations. Psychoanal Inq 29:477–490

Dutton DG, Denny-Keys MK, Sells JR (2011) Parental personality disorder and its effects on children: a review of current literature. J Child Custody 8:268–283

Ekeland T-J, Myklebust V (1997) Foreldremekling: brukarperspektiv. Møreforskning, Volda

Firestone G, Weinstein J (2004) In the best interests of children family. Court Rev 42:203–215

Helland MS, Borren I (2015) Foreldrekonflit; identifisering av konfliktnivåer, sentrale kjennetegn og risikofaktorer hos høykonfliktpar. Folkehelseinstituttet rapport 2015:3

Gulbrandsen W (2013) Foreldrekonflikter etter samlivsbrudd: En analyse av samspill og kilder til det fast-låsende. Tidsskrift for norsk psykologforening 50:538–551

Gulbrandsen W, Tjersland OA (2010) Mekling ved samlivsbrudd: en oversikt over effektstudier. Tidsskrift for norsk psykologforening 47:705–714

Gulbrandsen W, Tjersland OA (2013) Hvordan virker obligatorisk foreldremekling ved store konflikter? Tidsskrift for velferdsforskning 16

Haugen GMD, Rantalaiho M (2010) Barns rettigheter i mekling ved separasjon og samlivsbrudd. In: Kjørholt AT (ed) Barn som samfunnsborgere. til barnets beste? Universitetsforlaget, Oslo, pp 111–131

Holt S, Buckley H, Whelan S (2008) The impact of exposure to domestic violence on children and young people: a review of the literature. Child Abuse Negl 32:797–810

Irving HH, Benjamin M (2002) Therapeutic family mediation. Sage Publications, Thousand Oaks

Jaffe PG, Johnston JR, Crooks CV, Bala N (2008) Custody disputes involving allegations of domestic violence: toward a differentiated approach to parenting plans. Fam Court Rev 46:500–522

Johnston JR, Roseby V, Kuehnle K (2009) In the name of the child. A developmental approach to understanding and helping children, 2nd edn. Springer, New York

Kelly JB (1997) The best interests of the child. Fam Court Rev 35:377–387

Kjøs P, Madsen OJ, Tjersland OA (2015) 'Barnets beste' i mekling ved samlivsbrudd. Tidsskrift for Norsk Psykologforening 52:570–579

Koch K (2008) Evaluering av saksbehandlingsreglene for domstolene i barneloven – saker om foreldreansvar, fast bosted og samvær. Barne- og likestillingsdepartementet (Department of Children and Equal Opportunity), Oslo

Menkel-Meadow CJ, Love LP, Schneider AK, Sternlight JR (2010) Dispute resolution: beyond the adversarial model, 2nd edn. Wolter Kluwer, New York

Nordhelle G (2011) Praktiseringen av sakkyndighetsarbeid i barnefordelingssaker. Tidskrift for familierett, arverett og barnevernrettslige spørsmål:176–197

Nylund A (2008) Til domstol – med barnet i fokus. Tidskrift for familierett, arverett og barnevernrettslige spørsmål 6:229–243

Nylund A (2011) Mekling i barnefordelingssaker på godt og ondt. Tidskrift for familierett, arverett og barnevernrettslige spørsmål 9:302–322

Nylund A (2012) Barnefordelingssaker og 'familier med høyt konfliktnivå'. Tidskrift for familierett, arverett og barnevernrettslige spørsmål 10:215–235

Ottosen MH (2016) Analyse om udviklingen i familieretlige konflikter. SFI Det Nationale Forkningcenter for velfærd, Copenhagen

Rogers NH, Bordone RC, Sander FEA, McEwen CA (2013) Designing systems and processes for managing disputes. Wolters Kluwer, New York

Salminen K (2018) Is mediation in the best interests of the child from the child law perspective? In: Nylund A, Ervasti K, Adrian L (eds) Nordic mediation research. Springer, Cham, pp 209–222

Sander FE (1976) The multi-door courthouse. Barrister 3:18

Sauer JJ (2007) Mediating child custody disputes for high conflict couples: structuring mediation to accommodate the needs & desires of litigious parents. Pepperdine Dispute Resolut Law J 7:501

Schepard AI (2004) Children, courts and custody. interdisciplinary models for divorcing families. Cambridge University Press, Cambridge

Skjørten K (2005) Samlivsbrudd og barnefordeling. Gyldendal, Oslo

Smith S, Martinez J (2009) An analytic framework for dispute systems design. Harv Negot Law Rev 14:123–170

Stang EG (2013) Når vi ikke får gehør i rettsapparatet har vi tapt på vegne av barnet. In: Søvig KH, Schütz SE, Rasmussen Ø (eds) Undring og erkjennelse. Festskrift til Jan Fridtjhof Bernt 70 år. Fagbokforlaget, Bergen, pp 665–678

Thørnblad R, Strandbu A (2018) The involvement of children in the process of mandatory family mediation. In: Nylund A, Ervasti K, Adrian L (eds) Nordic mediation research. Springer, Cham, pp 183–208

Tjersland O, Gulbrandsen W, Haavind H (2015) Mandatory mediation outside the court: a process and effect study. Confl Resolut Q 33:19–34

Valkama E, Lasola M (2009) Lasten huoltoriidat tuimioistuimissa. In: Litmala M (ed) Oikeusolot 2009. Katsaus oikeudellisten instituutioiden toimintaan ja saatavuuteen. Oikeuspoliittisen tutkimuslaitoksen julkaisuja, vol 244. Oikeuspoliittinen tutkimuslaitos, Helsinki, pp 233–256

"Restorative Justice": History of the Term's International and Danish Use

Christian B. N. Gade

Contents

Abstract In this article, I explore the historical origin and development of the use of the term "restorative justice" in published sources. The main argument is that the growing popularity of the term and its expanding use makes increasingly blurred what restorative justice is. I begin by investigating the term's international usage, tracing it back to written sources from the nineteenth century. Then, I cite personal communication with Howard Zehr to describe how his use of the term was inspired by Albert Eglash. Zehr initially popularised the term and, in the 1990s, use of the term expanded. In the 2000s, the term began to appear in United Nations and European Union documents, illustrating that restorative justice had become an internationally recognised approach to justice. After describing this international development, I analyse the Danish context, where the term "restorative justice" began to appear in writings around the year 2000. Around the same time, the existing Danish victim offender mediation programme became connected to restorative justice. Later, Danish practices outside the area of criminal justice became associated with the term. In conclusion, I argue that a potential problem of the expanded use of the term "restorative justice"—both in Denmark and internationally—is that usage may become so broad that the concept loses its meaning.

C. B. N. Gade (✉)
Department of Anthropology, Aarhus University, Aarhus, Denmark
e-mail: gade@cas.au.dk

27

A. Nylund et al. (eds.), *Nordic Mediation Research*,
https://doi.org/10.1007/978-3-319-73019-6_3

1   Introduction

The aim of this article is to explore the history of how the term "restorative justice" has been used in published written sources. I begin by exploring the international use of the term. I then explore its use in Denmark, which includes areas such as victim offender mediation. In the Danish context, I also explore the history of the Danish terms "genoprettende retfærdighed" and "genoprettende ret", which have both been applied as translations of "restorative justice". A thorough historicisation of the use of the terms will contextualize and thus form the basis of a deeper understanding of current texts about restorative justice. Such a historicisation will illustrate how the current texts, at least to some extent, are formed by history.

Historical research on the international use of the term "restorative justice" has been limited, and scholars have wrongly assumed that this term was coined during the second half of the twentieth century, though it already appeared in texts from the nineteenth century, as shown in this article. Furthermore, there does not exist any research that traces the historical development of how the term "restorative justice", and its Danish translations, have been applied in relation to practices in Denmark, and this article attempts to fill that research gap.

My data for this article has been collected through literature searches in Google Scholar, Google Books, JSTOR, Web of Science and Scopus. I have searched for texts that contain the terms "restorative justice", "genoprettende retfærdighed" or "genoprettende ret", and all the identified texts have been ordered chronologically to trace the historical development of the terms' usage.

2   International Use of the Term "Restorative Justice"[1]

Several scholars have suggested that the term "restorative justice" has a young history. For example, Christopher Marshall writes that "the term *restorative justice* was coined in the 1970s to describe a way to respond to crime that focuses primarily on repairing the damage caused by the criminal act and restoring, insofar as possible, the dignity and wellbeing of all those involved" (Marshall 2011). Daniel Van Ness has been even more specific in terms of genealogy, claiming that Albert Eglash coined the term in *Beyond Restitution: Creative Restitution* from 1977 (Van Ness 1993). Subsequent to this claim by Van Ness, many have credited Eglash as the father of the term (Llewellyn and Howse 1999; Ammar 2003; Chatterjee and Elliott 2003; Heath-Thornton 2009; Van Ness and Strong 2010; Daly 2013). Nevertheless, Ann Skelton managed to trace the history of the term back to the 1950s (Skelton

---

[1]In this section, I partly reuse and build on the historical text investigations that I made for my article *Restorative Justice and the South African Truth and Reconciliation Process*, published in the South African Journal of Philosophy, in 2013.

2005), and I have shown that the term is even older, as it appears in at least the following six texts from the pre-1950 period (Gade 2013):

- *The Christian Examiner and Church of Ireland Magazine* (1834): In this Christian magazine, it is explained that a certain Title Composition Act was "deservedly hailed by all well-thinking men, as beneficial to the clergy, and to the people, as a great act of restorative justice (Members of the Church of Ireland 1834).
- *The Signs of the Times* (1848): In one of this book's ten Christian lectures, Rev. Lebbeus Armstrong tells a story about two witnesses who had been imprisoned for perjury though they were innocent. He writes: "their release would be an act of restorative justice" (Armstrong 1848).
- *Thoughts on a Continuation of the Book of Common Prayer used in the Church of England* (1856): Here Rev. John Stow refers to Luke 19:8, where Zacchaeus says to Jesus that he will give half of his possessions to the poor and pay back fourfold if he has ever cheated anyone. He writes: "What a lesson of liberality and of restorative justice is here afforded to All, who profess faith in CHRIST and the adoption of the Tenets of His Gospel!" (Stow 1856).
- *A Woman's Story* (1863): In this book by Burton Abbots, it is explained that Cecil decided to give Salome a considerable amount of money that she had been entitled to since childhood. It is explained that "Cecil represented the case merely as an act of restorative justice" (Abbots 1863).
- *An Inquiry Concerning Justice* (1916): This article by Floyd R Mechem contains the oldest explicit definition of "restorative justice" that I have been able to find. The term is defined as "justice administrated by the judicial machinery which restores man to his proper rights" (Mechem 1916).
- *Address of Mr. Manuel Fourcade, Bâtonnier of The Order of Advocates, etc.* (1924): In this speech, Fourcade addresses the problems of peace after World War I and says that in Biblical times, the enthusiasm of the Psalmist exalted itself in a vision of justice embracing peace. It is specified that "[i]t is fitting to reaffirm our belief in these ideas of restorative justice" (Fourcade 1924).

My historical findings suggest that the term "restorative justice" first appeared in a Christian context, but—as already emphasised in my article from 2013—it is unclear to me what exactly "restorative justice" means in these texts. In the four texts from the nineteenth century quoted above, the term is used without any explanation of its meaning, either pointing to an unclarity in these texts or the possible scenario that the nineteenth century readers were familiar with the term and its meaning at this point in time, making further explanation unnecessary. Both could be the case. To me, it is also unclear exactly what is meant by "restorative justice" in two texts from the twentieth century, as Mechem does not explain what *rights* he is referring to, while Fourcade does not tell us anything about what *ideas* he has in mind.

Thus, there are many uncertainties regarding the meaning of "restorative justice" in the early texts, and I have not been able to establish any connection between these texts and the later restorative justice literature in the second half of the twentieth century. However, the texts demonstrate that Eglash did not have anything to do with the coining of the term "restorative justice". Despite this, his thoughts on creative restitution (Eglash 1957a, b, 1959, 1977) were indeed important for the later restorative justice literature, and I think Kathleen Daly was reasonable in suggesting that he was one of the founding fathers of the restorative justice movement, together with Randy Barnett, Howard Zehr and Nils Christie (Daly 2013).[2] In 1977, Eglash wrote that while retributive justice has "its technique of punishment for crime", restorative justice has "its technique of restitution" (Eglash 1977), thus pre-empting two ideas later unfolded by Howard Zehr in his article *Retributive Justice, Restorative Justice* from 1985. The first of these ideas is that restorative justice stands in sharp contrast to retributive justice and the second that restitution is an important element of restorative justice. Nevertheless, Eglash never went into further details about his understanding of "restorative justice".

No doubt, Zehr has been the single most influential author on restorative justice. The first text by Zehr that contains the term "restorative justice" is the abovementioned article from 1985. This article presents the first written formulation of most of the restorative justice ideas he later developed in his famous books *Changing Lenses: A New Focus for Crime and Justice* (1990) and *The Little Book of Restorative Justice* (2002). Most importantly, the 1985 article presents the idea that the current criminal justice paradigm—which Zehr refers to as "retributive justice"—is in crisis and that restorative justice should be adopted as a new paradigm. The article does not contain any definition of "restorative justice", but it includes an appendix where Zehr lists 17 differences between "retributive justice" and "restorative justice", including the five differences in the diagram below, which are directly reproduced from his article (Fig. 1).

In the article from 1985, Zehr does not explain who or what inspired him to use the term "restorative justice". However, in an e-mail of 6 June 2017—which I have received permission to quote—Zehr told me: "I found the term, among other terms, in an essay by Albert Eglash [the aforementioned text from 1977] (...) In one sentence, he listed a number of terms, and that was one. It seemed to fit what I was thinking, and contrasted nicely with the term 'retributive'; I was looking for terminology that would communicate and would be easy to remember". In the same e-mail, Zehr also explained: "In earlier writing I had laid out some of the basic concepts of what I came to call RJ ['restorative justice'], but we didn't have terminology. In the early '80s, I led a retreat for priests and nuns doing prison ministry and this was the first time, I think, that I put out the overall concept and used the term".

---

[2]The main reason to include Christie in this list is that his article *Conflict as Property* (1977) has inspired many restorative justice scholars, though he did not use the term "restorative justice" himself in his early writings. To my knowledge, Christie first began to use the term in the twenty-first century—see, for example, Christie (2005, 2010, 2013). The reason to include Barnett in the list is that his article *Restitution: A New Paradigm of Criminal Justice* (1977) was an important source of inspiration for Zehr as explained later. However, Barnett did not use the term "restorative justice" himself.

Retributive justice	**Restorative justice**
1. Crime defined as violation of the state	1. Crime defined as violation of one person by another
2. Focus on establishing blame, on guilt, on past (did he/she do it?)	2. Focus on problem-solving, on liabilities and obligations, on future (what should be done?)
3. Adversarial relationships & process normative	3. Dialogue and negotiation normative
4. Imposition of pain to punish and deter/prevent	4. Restitution as a means of restoring both parties; reconciliation/restoration as goal
5. Justice defined by intent and by process: right rules	5. Justice defined as right relationships; judged by the outcome

Fig. 1 Zehr's justice paradigms

As Zehr explains in his article, his thinking was also inspired by Randy Barnett's article *Restitution: A New Paradigm of Criminal Justice* from 1977. Here, Barnett used Thomas Kuhn's ideas about paradigm shifts as a background for arguing that the current criminal justice paradigm is in crisis and ought to be replaced by a new paradigm. Barnett chose the term "restitution"—the same term that had been promoted by Eglash—and not the term "restorative justice" to denote the new paradigm, meaning that Zehr was probably the first person to apply the term "restorative justice" to refer to a potentially new criminal justice paradigm.

The first time Zehr provided a definition of restorative justice seems to have been in *The Little Book of Restorative Justice* from 2002 (*Changing Lenses* from 1990 does not contain any definition). His definition is as follows: "Restorative justice is a process to involve, to the extent possible, those who have a stake in a specific offense and collectively identify and address harms, needs, and obligations, in order to heal and put things as right as possible" (Zehr 2002). This definition has become highly popular. However, the number of restorative justice definitions has increased with the increasing popularity of the term, resulting in the current situation where "restorative justice" is defined in various ways (for a list of definitions, see Gade 2013).

Kathleen Daly explains: "During the 1990s, restorative justice became immensely popular, eclipsing and overtaking other justice ideas circulating during the 1970s and 1980s – a range of restitution, reparation, reconciliation, and informal justice projects" (Daly 2013). This development went hand-in-hand with both an *upwards* and a *downwards* expansion of the terms use, as clarified by Gerry Johnstone. With the downwards expansion, the term began to be used in relation to non-criminal forms of misconduct, including misconduct in schools, inappropriate behaviour in the workplace and neighbourhood disputes (Johnstone 2011). Furthermore, "As well as shifting its focus 'downwards' from crime, the campaign for restorative justice has also looked 'upwards' from 'ordinary' crime to problems involving genocide, gruesome violence, gross violations of human rights, political oppression and historical injustice"

(Johnstone 2011). One of the most famous example of the upwards expansion occurred in post-apartheid South Africa, where Desmond Tutu and several others argued that the Truth and Reconciliation Commission attempted to promote restorative justice (Gade 2013). Other examples of the upwards expansion include the term's usage in relation to traditional African conflict management mechanisms such as *mato oput* in Uganda after the civil war and *gacaca* in Rwanda after the genocide (Mangena 2015).

Restorative justice, which Zehr had presented as a revolutionary alternative approach to criminal justice in 1985, became an internationally recognised approach to justice in the 2000s. For example, the United Nations Economic and Social Council adopted a resolution on *Basic Principles on the Use of Restorative Justice Programmes in Criminal Matters* in 2002, stating: "Member states should consider the formulation of national strategies and policies aimed at the development of restorative justice and the promotion of a culture favourable to the use of restorative justice among law enforcement, judicial and social authorities, as well as local communities" (United Nations Economic and Social Council 2002). The term also appears in the European Commission for the Efficiency of Justice's guidelines for a better implementation of the recommendation concerning mediation in penal matters (2007), and in Directive 2012/29/EU of the European Parliament on minimum standards on the rights, support and protection of victims of crime (2012). The former calls for increased awareness of—and focus on—restorative justice in various contexts (see ss. 36, 41, 42, 44, 47 & 50), while the latter points to issues that ought to be considered when using restorative justice to avoid negative effects (s. 46).

Thus, as described above, a lot has happened in restorative justice since Zehr wrote his foundational article *Retributive Justice, Restorative Justice* in 1985. Some of the most significant developments within academia include the emergence of critical research challenging common restorative justice assumptions and dogmas, as well as empirically informed research on the effects of restorative justice programmes. Kathleen Daly's writings represent an influential example of the first kind of research, for example, challenging the idea that restorative justice is radically different from retributive justice (Daly 2002, 2008, 2013), while Lawrence Sherman and Heather Strang's experimental research with randomised trials is an influential example of the second kind of research (Sherman et al. 2015a, b; Strang et al. 2013).

3   Danish Context

As already mentioned in the introduction, "restorative justice" is translated into Danish as both "genoprettende retfærdighed" and "genoprettende ret". Annika Snare's article *Restorative Justice – om genoprettende retfærdighed* (English: *Restorative Justice – On Restorative Justice*) from 1999 may have been the first text to use the term "genoprettende retfærdighed". The oldest text, in which I have found the term "genoprettende ret", is Beth Grothe Nielsen's article *Paradigmeskift – fra straffende ret til genoprettende ret: en canadisk højesteret viser vej* (English: *Paradigm Shift – From Punitive Justice to Restorative Justice: A Canadian Supreme Court Shows the*

Way) from 2001. These texts by Danish scholars were inspired by the emerging international literature on restorative justice, and they both referred to Howard Zehr.

The question of whether restorative justice is something that is found in Denmark first began to be addressed around the year 2000, and it only received little attention at this time. As a matter of fact, I have merely managed to identify a few texts from the first half of the 2000s that use the term "restorative justice"—or its Danish translations—in connection with practices in Denmark, and all these texts use the term in relation to the Danish trials with victim offender mediation (Snare 1999; Lemonne and Snare 2000; Aertsen and Willemsens 2001; Miers 2001; Lemonne 2003; Kyvsgaard 2004).[3] These early texts suggest that the victim offender mediation, organised by the Danish police, is an example of—or at least something closely related to—restorative justice. Thus, restorative justice became a new "wrapping" of victim offender mediation in Denmark, even though the Danish pilots with victim offender mediation had never previously been associated with the term "restorative justice". Some scholars also posed the question of whether this association was reasonable. For example, Anne Lemonne and Annika Snare argued that the Danish model is not a clear-cut example of restorative justice as the mediation programme is combined with prosecution in the penal system (Lemonne and Snare 2000). In contrast to a country such as Norway, victim offender mediation has always been a supplement, and never an alternative, to punishment in Denmark.

Prior to 2005, no other practices in Denmark than the abovementioned pilots appear to have been connected with restorative justice. Nevertheless, in 2004, Britta Kyvsgaard wrote: "It can be argued that the principles underlying restorative justice have long been part of the Danish penal system. The Danish Criminal Code of 1930 in section 84 mentions among mitigating circumstances freely and voluntarily averting the damage caused by the crime, fully restoring the damage of the crime, and otherwise freely and voluntarily making efforts to prevent the completion of the crime or to restore the damage caused by it" (Kyvsgaard 2004). This attempt to "project" restorative justice into the past has been a common, and sometimes criticised (Daly 2002), exercise in the restorative justice literature. In fact, Zehr already made the attempt in his article from 1985, arguing that restorative justice was the dominant form of justice in the past, thus presenting the turn to restorative justice as a *return* to a previous "golden age" that pre-empted the postulated decline period of state-centred retributive justice (for a discussion of similar *narratives of return* in other contexts, see Gade 2017).

Slowly, other Danish practices than the police trials began to be associated with restorative justice. In 2005, Karin Sten Madsen wrote that restorative justice is the concept of justice that lays behind the use of victim offender mediation (Madsen 2005a, b), and she described how the Centre for Victims of Sexual Assault at Rigshospitalet, which is Denmark's largest hospital, had conducted a 12-month project

---

[3]The first Danish victim offender mediation pilot ran from 1994–1996, and the second from 1998–2003 (the second pilot was prolonged to 2010—the year when the permanent, national programme started). For information about the pilots, see Henriksen (2003), Rambøll Management (2006), The Ministry of Justice's Committee on Victim Offender Mediation (2008).

with mediation between sexually assaulted women and their offenders from 2003 to 2004. In a feature article in the Danish newspaper Politiken on 22 July 2005, Madsen elaborated on the project and wrote that: "Without knowing *restorative justice . . .* the women [who took part in the project] followed their own feeling and invited to restoration [my translation]". Later, Mary Koss and Mary Achilles also referred to the mediations at the just mentioned Danish centre in their article *Restorative Justice Responses to Sexual Assault*, thus suggesting that restorative justice in Denmark occurs outside the police programme on victim offender mediation (Koss and Achilles 2008, see also Liebmann 2007; McGlynn et al. 2012; The Danish Health Authority 2012).

The term "restorative justice" began to receive increased attention in Denmark around 2008. The background was that the Danish Ministry of Justice had established a committee, which should propose the future organization of a permanent Danish victim offender mediation programme. The committee's report *Betænkning om konfliktråd* (English: *Report on Victim Offender Mediation*) was published in October 2008, and it presented restorative justice as a theoretical foundation of victim offender mediation, thus echoing the understanding of the relationship between restorative justice and victim offender mediation already presented by Madsen in 2005. In fact, this is not very surprising, as Madsen was one of the committee members. The report uses Zehr's aforementioned definition of "restorative justice", and its fifth chapter on international recommendations about victim offender mediation mentions two documents that have been presented earlier in this article: the United Nations' resolution on basic principles on the use of restorative justice programmes in criminal matters from 2002 and the European Commission for the Efficiency of Justice's guideline for a better implementation of the existing recommendation concerning mediation in penal matters from 2007, both dealing with restorative justice.

In connection with the establishment of the permanent victim offender mediation programme, *Foreningen for mediation/konfliktmægling* (English: *The Union of Mediation/Conflict Mediation*) held a hearing at Christiansborg, where the Danish Parliament is located, on 12 November 2008. At this event, the future permanent programme was linked to restorative justice, and Zehr—by then known as "the grandfather of restorative justice"—was invited to make a presentation entitled "Restorative Justice, Principles and Values". His book *The Little Book of Restorative Justice* was also published in Danish in 2008, which no doubt contributed to an increased Danish interest in restorative justice, not least among conflict management practitioners. Based on the aforementioned report *Betænkning om konfliktråd*, the Danish Parliament passed its *Lov om konfliktråd* (English: *Victim Offender Mediation Act*) in 2009, which resulted in the establishment of the national victim offender mediation programme on 1 January 2010.[4]

At this point in time, I was working with restorative justice in South Africa and was getting increasingly interested in the Danish context. Thus, I took initiative to the first Danish conference on restorative justice, which I organised together with Aase Rieck Sørensen, who was the director of the Danish Centre for Conflict Resolution, and

---

[4]For details about the Danish programme, see Storgaard (2013), Asmussen (2014).

Professor Vibeke Vindeløv from the University of Copenhagen. The conference was held at Aarhus University in May 2011, and it was attended by more than 60 people, including both conflict management practitioners and academics such as Karin Sten Madsen.[5] One of the people who made a presentation at the conference was Jacob v. H. Holterman who had written the first Danish doctorate thesis on restorative justice with the title *Everything you Always Wanted to Know About Restorative Justice* (*But were Afraid to Ask)* (2009). Ida Helene Asmussen, who was in the process of writing the first doctorate thesis on the Danish victim offender mediation programme, also attended. Her thesis was defended in 2013 and published as a book entitled *Fra retsstat til omsorgsstat: om syndsforladelse i konfliktråd* (English: *From a Nation of Laws to a Nation of Care: On Absolution in Victim Offender Mediation*) in 2014. Asmussen shows that some victims and offenders who have participated in the permanent Danish victim offender programme have been put under pressure to perform specific roles, which—needless to say—is problematic (see also Asmussen 2018). After the conference in 2011, a Danish network on restorative justice was established, which I have been facilitating together with Aase Rieck Sørensen.[6]

The last 5 years have included several attempts at describing the Danish restorative justice "landscape". The first attempt was made by Annette Storgaard in her report *Restorative Justice in Denmark* from 2013. This report was part of the project "The 3E Model for a Restorative Strategy in Europe", funded by the European Commission. Thus, it was linked to a broader effort to describe the European restorative justice landscape. Storgaard explains that almost nothing is happening in Denmark with regard to restorative justice, and she specifies: "The only program that comes relatively close to the ideas behind Restorative Justice is VOM [victim offender mediation]" (Storgaard 2013), and also: "The only element in Danish criminal justice practice that has a tiny 'taste' of Restorative Justice is the Victim-Offender Mediation" (Storgaard 2013). In later texts, Storgaard also explained that "[i]n Denmark, 'Restorative Justice' is not a particularly dominant issue in public political debates or among practitioners" (Storgaard 2015); and: "The only form of Restorative Justice in Denmark is Victim-offender mediation, which is organised by the police" (Storgaard 2017).

Until now, Storgaard has been the only person writing in English about the Danish restorative justice landscape, leaving the international community with the impression that next to nothing is happening in Denmark regarding restorative justice. Storgaard does not mention any texts on restorative justice written by Danes, nor does she take notice of restorative justice initiatives outside the police, such as the Danish restorative justice conference and the network. There are also other restorative justice initiatives that Storgaard leaves unnoticed in her writings. For example, on 9 December 2014, Karina Lorentzen Dehnhardt, Jonas Dahl and Trine Pertou Mach, all from the Socialist Party, made a parliamentary proposal about a pilot on "genoprettende ungemøder"

---

[5]All conference presentations were video recorded and can be streamed from the following website, which also includes a complete list of conference participants: http://cesau.au.dk/import/konferencer/afholdtekonferencer/genoprettenderetfaerdighed/.

[6]The network has an e-mail list with about 150 members, including academics and conflict management practitioners, and has a website with information about network meetings and other activities: https://genoprettenderet.wordpress.com.

(English: "restorative youth meetings"). This proposal, which was based on lobbyism from the SSP Committee on Restorative Justice,[7] was debated in Parliament on 18 December 2014, but did not generate sufficient political support to be implemented. Nevertheless, the mere proposal shows that restorative justice is something that has received political attention in Denmark.

Against the background of the conference on restorative justice, the Danish Centre for Conflict Resolution received funding from *Forskningsfonden af 1971* (English: *The Research Foundation of 1971*) to collect data on how restorative justice is practiced in Denmark. The data collection process resulted in the report *Genoprettende retfærdighed i Danmark* (English: *Restorative Justice in Denmark*), which was published in May 2015.[8] According to this report, restorative justice in Denmark is not confined to the police's victim offender mediation programme, but is practiced in various contexts. To illustrate this, the report presents seven stories with concrete examples of how restorative justice has been practiced in Denmark. One example is about a restorative circle process in *Ungdomsbyen* (English: *The youth town*) in Copenhagen, which was organised by a conflict management teacher in a fifth grade after a fight between two youngsters. Another example is about a restorative conference in a small town in Egedal Municipality, which was arranged by the SSP due to serious trouble in the community caused by a group of 16–17 boys. A weakness of the report is that it does not contain any quantitative data on the spread of such processes in Denmark. Such data does not exist.

In December 2015, the Danish Institute for Local and Regional Government Research (KORA) published yet another report on restorative justice entitled *Genoprettende retfærdighed overfor kriminalitetstruede unge* (English: *Restorative Justice for Youngsters in Danger of Crime*). This report was commissioned by the Danish Crime Preventive Council and TrygFonden. It contains a section about restorative justice in Denmark, which basically summarises the findings of the report from the Danish Centre for Conflict Resolution (Berger et al. 2015). Additionally, the KORA report presents an overview of international literature on restorative justice, including an overview of findings on the effects of different restorative justice programmes. Henrik Dam, the chairman of the Crime Preventive Council, wrote a feature article in the Danish newspaper Jyllands-Posten on 3 March 2016 based on the KORA report. In this article, entitled *Den genoprettende retfærdighed* (English: *The Restorative Justice*), he highlights the KORA report's conclusion that there are positive effects of restorative justice when applied for youngsters in danger of crime.

---

[7]SSP is a collaboration between schools, social service and police. The SSP Committee on Restorative Justice consists of conflict management practitioners who have actively attempted to promote the use of restorative justice in Denmark, for example, by organising a three-day course on restorative justice for Danish SSP workers in October 2015.

[8]I wrote this report with the support from several people, including the members of a consultation group that included Henning Maigaard, the head of the Secretariat of Victim Offender Mediation at the Danish National Police, Charlie Lywood and Jens Ansberg from the SSP Committee on Restorative Justice, and Bo Ørsnes from the Danish Centre for Conflict Resolution. For a complete list, see Gade (2015).

The positive effects of restorative justice, however, have been recently questioned in the Danish context by Britta Kyvsgaard. In her report *Evaluering af konfliktråd* (English: *Evaluation of Victim Offender Mediation*), published by the Danish Ministry of Justice in 2016, she concludes that the Danish victim offender mediation programme does not have *any* effect on recidivism. This finding has sparked a new collaborative research project between Aarhus University, the Danish National Police and scholars from the University of Cambridge.[9] The project will use randomised trials in seven police districts to test two different ways of carrying out victim offender meetings in Denmark: standard victim offender mediation (*konfliktråd*) versus restorative justice conferences. The aim is to compare the relative cost-effectiveness and impacts on victim harm and offender recidivism of these two restorative justice models. TrygFonden has provided funding for the project, which started in September 2017.

This research project is not the only new Danish initiative in the area of restorative justice. Belinda Hopkins, who has done a lot of work on restorative justice in schools in the United Kingdom (Hopkins 2004, 2009), has been in Denmark to train the teachers at Tovshøjsskolen, a primary school in Aarhus, and in Albertslund municipality, the staff at several schools and youth clubs are planned to be trained in restorative justice. These initiatives are organised by the SSP.

4   Expanding Use of "Restorative Justice"

This article has historicised the international and Danish usage of the term "restorative justice". First, it demonstrated that the international history represents a story about a term that became immensely popular and expanded into new areas. Existing practices were "re-labelled" as "restorative justice", and from the 1990s, the term began to be used in connection with practices outside the area of "normal" criminal justice: both in relation to forms of misconduct that do not constitute crimes (downwards expansion) and in relation to gross human rights violations committed during periods of political oppression, genocide and civil war (upwards expansion). The growing popularity of the term "restorative justice", and its expanding use, went hand-in-hand with an increasing number of restorative justice definitions, thus making it increasingly blurred what restorative justice is. This definitional vagueness meant that it was easy to "re-label" even more practices as "restorative justice".

About 15 years after Zehr wrote his foundational article *Retributive Justice, Restorative Justice* (1985), the term "restorative justice was translated into Danish and began to be used in connection with Danish practices. At first, the term did not receive much attention in Denmark and was only used in connection with the

---

[9]The research team includes Sarah van Mastrigt, Theresa Ammann and myself from Aarhus University, Lawrence Sherman and Heather Strang from the University of Cambridge and a not yet employed research assistant.

police's victim offender mediation (with was "re-labelled" as a form of restorative justice). Later, the term began to be used to denote other practices, such as conflict management practices in schools. This development constituted a downwards expansion of the term's use in the Danish context. Thus, the Danish story is a tale of how a term was adopted from the international context and gradually gained popularity and increased attention. The potential problem is, of course, that the use of the term "restorative justice"—both in Denmark and internationally—may become so broad that the term loses its meaning. If the term ends up denoting next to everything, it will end up meaning next to nothing.

References

Abbots B (1863) A Woman's Story, vol 2. T Cautley Newby, London

Aertsen I, Willemsens J (2001) The European forum for victim-offender mediation and restorative justice. Eur J Crim Policy Res 9:291–300

Ammar NH (2003) Exploring elements of restorative justice in the Islamic legal system. In: Safty A (ed) Value leadership and capacity building. Universal Publishers, Boca Raton

Armstrong L (1848) The signs of the times; comprised in ten lectures designated to show the origin, nature, tendency and alliances of the present popular efforts for the abolition of capital punishment. Robert Carter, New York

Asmussen IH (2014) Fra retsstat til omsorgsstat: om syndsforladelse i konfliktråd. Djøf, Copenhagen

Asmussen IH (2018) Mediation in light of modern identity. In: Nylund A, Ervasti K, Adrian L (eds) Nordic mediation research. Springer, Cham, p 133–143

Berger NP et al (2015) Genoprettende retfærdighed over for kriminalitetstruede unge: en kortlægning af viden. KORA, Copenhagen

Barnett R (1977) Restitution: a new paradigm of criminal justice. Ethics 87(4):279–301

Chatterjee J, Elliott L (2003) Restorative policing in Canada: the Royal Canadian Mounted Police, community justice forums and the youth criminal justice act. Police Pract Res Int J 4(4):347–359

Christie N (1977) Conflict as property. Br J Criminol 17(1):1–15

Christie N (2005) Restorative and retributive justice in the context of war and war crimes. Temida 8 (4):27–32

Christie N (2010) Victim movements at a crossroad. Punishment Soc 12(2):115–122

Christie N (2013) Words on words. Restorative justice. Int J 1(1):31–46

European Commission for the Efficiency of Justice (2007) Guidelines for a better implementation of the existing recommendation concerning mediation in penal matters. Council of Europe, Strasbourg

Daly K (2002) Restorative justice: the real story. Punishment Soc 4(1):55–79

Daly K (2008) The limits of restorative justice. In: Sullivan D, Tifft L (eds) Handbook of restorative justice. Routledge, Oxon

Daly K (2013) The punishment debate in restorative justice. In: Simon J, Sparks R (eds) The sage handbook of punishment and society. Sage Publications, London

Dam H (2016) Den genoprettende retfærdighed. Jyllands-Posten, 3 March 2016

Eglash A (1957a) Creative restitution: a broader meaning for an old term. J Crim Law Criminol Police Sci 48(6):619–622

Eglash A (1957b) Creative restitution: some suggestions for prison rehabilitation programs. Am J Correct 20:20–34

Eglash A (1959) Creative restitution: its roots in psychiatry, religion and law. Br J Delinq 10:114–119

Eglash A (1977) Beyond restitution: creative restitution. In: Hudson J, Galaway B (eds) Restitution in criminal justice: a critical assessment of sanctions. Lexington Books, Lexington

European Parliament (2012) Directive 2012/29/EU of the European Parliament and of the council of 25 October 2012 establishing minimum standards on the rights, support and protection of victims of crime. Official Journal of the European Union, Strasbourg

Fourcade M (1924) Address of Mr Fourcade, bâtonnier of the order of advocates, etc. Am Bar Assoc J 11:768–769

Gade CBN (2013) Restorative justice and the South African truth and reconciliation process. S Afr J Philos 32(1):10–35

Gade CBN (2015) Genoprettende retfærdighed i Danmark. Danish Centre for Conflict Resolution, Copenhagen

Gade CBN (2017) A discourse on African philosophy: a new perspective on Ubuntu and transitional justice in South Africa. Lexington Books, Lanham

Heath-Thornton D (2009) Restorative justice. In: Wilson JK (ed) The praeger handbook of victimology. ABC-CLIO, Santa Barbara

Henriksen CS (2003) Evaluering af konfliktråd. CASA, Copenhagen

Holterman JvH (2009) Everything you always wanted to know about restorative justice* (*but were afraid to ask). PhD Dissertation, University of Roskilde, Roskilde

Hopkins B (2004) Just schools. Jessica Kingsley Publishers, London

Hopkins B (2009) Just care. Jessica Kingsley Publishers, London

Johnstone G (2011) Restorative justice: ideas, values, debates, 2nd edn. Routledge, Oxon

Koss M, Achilles M (2008) Restorative justice responses to sexual assault. Applied research forum: National Online Resource Centre on Violence Against Women, 1–15

Kyvsgaard B (2004) Youth justice in Denmark. Crime Justice 31:349–390

Kyvsgaard B (2016) Evaluering af konfliktråd. The Ministry of Justice, Copenhagen

Lemonne A (2003) Alternative conflict resolution and restorative justice: a discussion. In: Walgrave L (ed) Repositioning restorative justice. Willian Publishing, Devon

Lemonne A, Snare A (2000) Genoprettelse af alternative konfliktløsning. Kriminalistisk årsbog 107–122

Liebmann M (2007) Restorative justice: how it works. Jessica Kingsley Publishers, London

Llewellyn JJ, Howse R (1999) Restorative justice – a conceptual framework. Law Commission of Canada, Ottawa

Madsen KS (2005a) Hvor ku' du gøre det? Konfliktmægling ved seksuelle overgreb. The Centre for Victims of Sexual Assault, Rigshospitalet, Copenhagen

Madsen KS (2005b) Ansigt til ansigt. Politiken, 22 July 2005

Mangena F (2015) Restorative justice's deep roots in Africa. S Afr J Philos 34(1):1–12

Marshall C (2011) Justice, restorative. In: Green JB (ed) Dictionary of scripture and ethics. Baker Academics, Grand Rapids

McGlynn C, Westmarlard N, Godden N (2012) "I just wanted him to hear me": sexual violence and the possibility of restorative justice. J Law Soc 39(2):213–240

Mechem FR (1916) An inquiry concerning justice. Mich Law Rev 14(5):361–382

Members of the Church of Ireland (1834) View of public affairs for the year 1834. Christ Exam Church Irel Mag 3(27):1–11

Miers D (2001) An international review of restorative justice. Home Office, Policing and Reducing Crime Unit, London

Nielsen BG (2001) Paradigmeskift – fra straffende ret til genoprettende ret: en canadisk højesteret viser vej. Juristen 6:205–216

Rambøll Management (2006) Evaluering af organiseringen af konfliktråd i Danmark. The Crime Preventive Council, Copenhagen

Sherman LW et al (2015a) Are restorative justice conferences effective in reducing repeat offending? Findings from a Campbell systematic review. J Quant Criminol 31:1–24

Sherman LW et al (2015b) Twelve experiments in restorative justice: the Jerry Lee program of randomized trials of restorative justice conferences. J Exp Criminol 11:501–540

Skelton A (2005) The influence of the theory and practice of restorative justice in South Africa with special reference to child justice. LLD thesis, University of Pretoria, Pretoria

Snare A (1999) Restorative justice – om genoprettende retfærdighed. Grønland – på vej mod et nyt straffesystem?: Rapport fra NSfKs 41. Forskningsseminar, Ilulissat, Grønland. Nordisk Samarbejdsråd for Kriminologi, Copenhagen

Storgaard A (2013) Denmark. In: The 3E model for a restorative justice strategy in Europe. European Commission, Strasbourg

Storgaard A (2015) Denmark. In: Dünkel F et al (eds) Restorative justice and mediation in penal matters: a stock-taking of legal issues, implementation strategies and outcomes in 36 European countries. Forum Verlag Godesberg, Mönchengladbach

Storgaard A (2017) Denmark. In: Decker SH, Marteache N (eds) International handbook of Juvenile justice, 2nd edn. Springer, Cham

Stow J (1856) Thoughts on a continuation of the book of common prayer used in the church of England. Printed at the School-Press, London

Strang H et al (2013) Restorative justice conferencing (RJC) using face-to-face meetings of offenders and victims: effects on offender recidivism and victim satisfaction. A systematic review. The Campbell Collaboration, Oslo

The Danish Health Authority (2012) Behandlingstilbud ved centre for modtagelse af voldtægtsofre. The Danish Health Authority, Copenhagen

The Ministry of Justice's Committee on Victim Offender Mediation (2008) Betænkning om konfliktråd. The Ministry of Justice, Copenhagen

United Nations Economic and Social Council (2002) Basic Principles on the Use of Restorative Justice Programmes in Criminal Matters. ECOSOC Resolution 2002/12

Van Ness DW (1993) New wine and old wineskins: four challenges of restorative justice. Crim Law Forum 4(2):251–276

Van Ness DW, Strong KH (2010) Restoring justice: an introduction to restorative justice, 4th edn. LexisNexis, New Jersey

Zehr H (1985) Retributive Justice, Restorative Justice. New Perspective on Crime and Justice 4

Zehr H (1990) Changing lenses: a new focus for crime and justice. Herald Press, Scottdale

Zehr H (2002) The little book of restorative justice. Good Books, Intercourse

Developing Family Mediation in Finland: The Change Process and Practical Outcomes

Vaula Haavisto

Contents

Abstract In this article, I discuss the process and outcomes of a successful developmental project on family mediation in Finland. Family mediation is a municipal service available for divorcing parents who cannot agree on child custody matters. In the Marriage Act of 1987, prerequisites were made for family mediation as an early intervention to help families in conflict. In practice, only few parents used the service. Moreover, the concept of mediation was fluid and diffuse and practitioners working

V. Haavisto (✉)
Faculty of Educational Sciences, University of Helsinki, Helsinki, Finland
e-mail: vaula.haavisto@sovittelu.com

© The Author(s) 2018
A. Nylund et al. (eds.), *Nordic Mediation Research*,
https://doi.org/10.1007/978-3-319-73019-6_4

with divorce families understood and applied mediation in different ways. Moreover, often family mediation was not undertaken as a distinct process. In the article, I describe the developmental work done in a project called "Fasper" whose aim was to change the present situation by exploring the concept of family mediation and producing new mediation models, practices and tools for family mediators. Following the methodological starting points of Developmental Work Research, the project did not offer a ready-made, top-down model for family mediation. Instead, practitioners studied divorce services and developed, tested and implemented new models and practices for family mediation. It is important to continue this work and bring it to the national level in order promote major changes in the system.

1 Introduction

In 2009, the Finnish Forum for Mediation—a non-governmental organisation promoting mediation in different fields of society—initiated a multi-disciplinary project to study and develop family mediation in Finland. The project was called Fasper, which was an abbreviation from Finnish words meaning facilitative family mediation.

Municipalities in Finland are required under the Marriage Act 1987 to provide family mediation as a voluntary service for families in dispute (Avioliittolaki 411/1987). The service is free-of-charge. The purpose of family mediation is to find a solution for the conflicts among family members through discussions and negotiations. Family mediators are usually employees of family counselling, child protection or other social welfare services who are assigned the task by the municipal social welfare boards. Family mediation is also available at other entities authorised to provide family mediation services, which mainly consists of the family counselling centres operated by the Evangelical Lutheran Church of Finland.

Focusing on the Marriage Act, one could assume that family mediation was an established service, available for all citizens. However, both the Parliamentary Ombudsman in her decision (Eduskunnan oikeusasiamiehen päätös 2004) and Sami Mahkonen in his investigation (2008) had reported just the opposite: in the municipalities, the organisation of family mediation varied a lot, there was a disruptive overlap between family mediation and different forms of family counselling, and the service was often poorly available. Project Fasper was launched to find solutions to these problems and study the potential of family mediation to serve as a central resolution method for family conflicts.

Project Fasper was conducted in 2009–2014 by a group of researcher-interventionists employed by the Finnish Forum for Mediation: a project manager, researcher and a senior researcher—the last one only for the first 3 years of the project. This group was supported by a scientific leader, a university professor in social work. While writing later in the article about "we", I refer to this group of researcher-interventionists who was responsible of the research and the interventions made in the project. As a project manager, I was part of the group.

Our study represents interventionist studies, where the focus is on *studying through experimenting*: changing human activities by experimenting and evaluating the new activities. The project followed the methodological starting points of Developmental Work Research (DWR),[1] an approach in which researcher-interventionists guide a community in its efforts to develop and transform practices (Engeström and Sannino 2010). Related with the tradition of Action Research (Lewin 1948), the potential new activities are in a similar vein pursued in collaboration with the researchers and practitioners. In project Fasper, this meant close collaboration between researcher-interventionists and front-line employees.

In this contribution, I will begin by describing the starting points of the project—the fluid concept of family mediation and the unorganised practices. After that, I will raise some theoretical concerns about the methodology needed in promoting change and learning in such complex systems as family mediation services. That will be followed by an overview of the developmental process in project Fasper. Some of the concrete outcomes—hence, the models created in the project—are presented. Finally, I will discuss the main conclusions concerning change and collaborative learning in developing mediation.

2 Family Mediation and Family Conflicts in the Service System

In Finland, a mutual settlement between the parents is considered the primary course of action after divorce or separation. According to the Child Custody and Right of Access Act 1983, the agreement parents make on the custody, living arrangements, visiting rights and maintenance of their child can be registered by the social board in a child's home municipality, allowing the agreement to be executed (Laki lapsen huollosta ja tapaamisoikeudesta 1983). In confirming the agreement, the best interests of a child must be considered. The child welfare officers—usually social workers or lawyers by training—who register the agreements can only register or refuse to register the parents' agreement, not alter it. If the parents cannot agree on children's matters, the municipal family mediation is one option available for them.[2]

---

[1]DWR is a methodology for simultaneous research and development in workplace settings created at the University of Helsinki, see Engeström (1995), Engeström (2005). Guided by Cultural-Historical Activity Theory with the origins in Russian social psychology, see Vygotsky (1978), Leontjev (1978), it is a theory-driven method for analysing developmental possibilities in complex, interacting systems. The approach is guided by Engeström's theory of Expansive Learning (1987), which emphasises learning as creation of new knowledge and practices.

[2]In addition to municipal family mediation, also court-connected mediation in custody and contact disputes is available for parents. This form of mediation is discussed in Kirsikka Salminen (2018).

The legal framework for family mediation comes from chapter 5 of the Marriage Act of 1987. Additionally, the Social Welfare Act sets the requirement for municipalities to organise family mediation (Sosiaalihuoltolaki 1301/2014). According to the Marriage Act, "disputes and legal matters arising in a family should primarily be settled in negotiations between the family members and decided by agreement". The family mediator's task is to "render assistance and support, upon request, when disputes arise in a family". An amendment was made in 1996, which says that family mediators may render assistance and support also "in the event that disputes arise as to compliance with a court order or an agreement on child custody and right of access" (Avioliittolaki 411/1987, chapter 5, section 20).

Section 21 of the chapter states the following: "A mediator shall aim for a confidential and open discussion between the family members. He or she shall aim for a consensus as to how to solve the disputes in the family in the best possible way for all the persons concerned." In addition, it is ruled that "[t]he mediator shall pay special attention to securing the position of the minor children in the family" (section 21, subsection 2) and that "[t]he mediator shall assist the persons concerned in concluding agreements and in other measures necessary for the settlement of disputes" (section 21, subsection 3). The rest of the sections deal with the monitoring, planning and controlling of family mediation; the authorization of service producers other than municipal authorities; as well as the duty of secrecy of the mediator, among other things.

As can be seen, the wording of the Marriage Act is broad and covers, in principle, all possible conflicts between different family members. In practice, family mediation has been interpreted to cover situations where a couple is divorcing or has divorced and they are in dispute over their children. Still, there is quandary whether mediation should be offered for spouses who are contemplating the possibility of a divorce or only for those who have already decided to get divorced. Similarly, there may be different interpretations about the content of family mediation: do there have to be a dispute over the children or can family mediation be a more therapeutically oriented assistance for dissolving the couple relationship.

For many years, the field of Finnish family mediation was blurred and discontinuous. The municipalities had no uniform guidelines on how to arrange the mediation services and very often the service was non-existing—almost a dead letter. No official statistics on how many municipalities offered family mediation were available. It is thus no wonder that Finnish parents only seldom had heard of family mediation services or knew what mediation could offer them (Mahkonen 2008; Eduskunnan oikeusasiamiehen päätös 2004; Karvinen-Niinikoski and Pelli 2010). If they entered the process, they were not necessarily aware of it (for the problems of the overly broad definitions of mediation, see Nylund (2018)).

Correspondingly, professionals working with divorced families were confused with the concept and practices of family mediation. In the interviews conducted in the early phase of project Fasper (see 4.1), professionals working with divorced families were asked how do they see family mediation, where does it take place, and do they mediate by themselves. Here are some quotes from the professionals:

Often it [family mediation] is kind of legal term, a work that has to be included in the statistics. Here at the family counselling centre, we don't compile statistics on family mediation. It is only a thin red line what is mediation and what is something else. Much of the work done here in family counselling is mediation, but it is included in the statistics as some other type of work, for example, guidance and consulting or family therapy. It becomes as part of the working process, mediation is inside the working process. I could imagine that family counselling workers of my generation see mediation as a bit superficial. *Psychologist at a family counselling unit, August 2010.*

Here at the family counselling unit I try to mediate a bit, find some connections between the parents, but it is not any real mediation. In our municipality it is very confusing, the clients roll around in this system. There is no clarity in this swirling system. *Social worker at a family counselling unit, May 2010.*

I think mediation is mostly giving information, not therapy in any way. Giving information and considering the child's situation. *Social worker at a family counselling unit, May 2010.*

I get acquainted with mediation weekly when I meet divorced parents who cannot agree with each other. I see that mediation is sprinkled into several job descriptions, into social work, the work of child welfare officers, family work in early child protection, family counselling units here in municipality and in the church. A systematic way of working is missing, but we can use the already existing tools. *Senior social worker at a family support unit, October 2010.*

The answers described ambivalence about what kind of work is considered as mediation and whether it differs from other services, such as counselling and guidance. They showed that family mediation was not recognised and organised as a discrete process. As a result, individual professionals used counselling, therapy and social work techniques under the generic label of mediation. With a lack of qualifying training for mediators, the concept of family mediation was under-developed and theoretically vague (Karvinen-Niinikoski and Pelli 2010; Mattila-Aalto et al. 2012).

At the same time, the service system for divorce families faced severe difficulties. There were several services available, but nobody knew or could predict how the clients moved in the system and used the services. Despite of several services, the parents in conflict over their children were not helped. The service system became overloaded and the frontline service providers exhausted and frustrated with not being able to help (Karvinen-Niinikoski and Pelli 2010; Mattila-Aalto et al. 2012; Julkunen and Karvinen-Niinikoski 2014).

The big number of unresolved parental conflicts had resulted in parents seeking help from all available services, leading to high public costs of custody disagreements (Hämäläinen 2011). Parents' disagreements produced a big number of submitted child welfare notifications to the authorities (Toimiva lastensuojelu -selvitysryhmän loppuraportti 2013). Several distinct service producers formed a disconnected field, which—at its worst—escalated parental conflicts instead of helping to solve them (Mattila-Aalto et al. 2012). If the parents could not settle their disagreements, there were guided from the social welfare services directly to the courts. It was clear that the zone of dispute resolution around the courts was missing. These observations suggested that re-considering the ideas and practices of family mediation could generate a new out-of-court way of handling and resolving parental conflicts.

In this situation, the Finnish Forum for Mediation initiated project Fasper to develop, test and implement new content and practices for family mediation—to give a fresh start for family mediation, so to say. The 5-year project started with six municipalities and their collaborators to create a unified approach to family mediation as a short-term, structured intervention for parents in conflict over their children.[3] The aim was also to develop a new service model that would help integrating family mediation into the service system so that it would be easily available for divorcing parents. In addition, one aim was to create a model for family mediators' elementary training. The project did not offer a ready-made, top-down model for family mediation to be locally implemented. Instead, it invited the practitioners to study the present divorce services and parents' needs and to develop, test and implement new models and mediation practices to better serve the parents' needs (Haavisto et al. 2014).

3 Methodological Questions in Developmental Mediation Research

3.1 Development: Top-Down or Bottom-Up?

"Implementation – how great expectations in Washington are dashed in Oakland" starts the title of the classic book by Jeffrey Pressman and Aaron Wildavsky (1984). They point to the problematic nature of and difficulties in promoting change and development: the reluctance of organisations to approve intended change and adopt new practices, as well as the failings of or alteration to planned changes. Is change something that can be adopted from above or does it have to be generated from within? Is it once-and-for-all or a series of small improvements, and finally, is it planned or emergent?

The early studies of policy implementation recognised the gap between legislative intent and bureaucratic action (Palumbo and Calista 1990; Bardach 1980; Pressman and Wildavsky 1984). Researchers tried to make sense of why the serious intents did not materialise when put into practice. The metaphor of gap between intent and outcome had its roots in *a top-down model* of implementation, which considered implementation to be the simple, purely technical execution of a policy maker's or legislator's intention, in which the rules are implemented as they were intended (Mazmanian and Sabatier 1983). A reverse perspective on implementation started to emerge when implementation was understood as a series of change efforts that emerge from within an agency or community, drawing on local knowledge and lived experiences. According to the *bottom-up model*, implementation is not

---

[3]For definitions of family mediation as a distinct process, see e.g. Parkinson (2014), Roberts (2008), and for mediation in general, Vindeløv (2007).

technical exercise, but rather a continuous, usually local project in which the reform is adjusted to local needs (Palumbo and Calista 1990; Eisenstein et al. 1988; Majone and Wildavsky 1984).

The acknowledged fruitlessness (Palumbo and Calista 1990) of these two opposing approaches has led to attempts to try to overcome the simplistic interpretations of the implementation problem. According to Yanow (1990), top-down policies are interpreted and given meaning—understood, explained and altered—from the bottom-up by the implementers. This potential for new and emergent urges to connect the issues of learning with the implementation of change.

3.2 Learning: Adopting Existing Knowledge or Creating New?

In studies of the top-down perspective on the implementation of change, learning could be best understood as *adopting* new rules, policies or practices (Haavisto 2002). Especially in the context of courts and law, adopting new rules has traditionally been the major form of learning. Learning is regarded as a non-problematic result of pouring the necessary information into those who are to implement it. The bottom-up perspective emphasising the discretion of local implementers, suggests that the implementation process is subject to constant modification and adjustments in goals, strategies and practical execution. According to this view, learning seems to be a continuous process of *adaptation*, where implementers learn to fit the policy to local needs (Haavisto 2002).

In addition to adopting and adapting as forms of learning, the implementation of change can be viewed as a process that also contains the questioning of current cultural models and production of novel local solutions. This potential for new and emergent is elementary in the theory of *expansive learning* (Engeström 1987). In expansive learning, people are not required to adopt change nor compelled to adapt to them. Instead, they initiate and seek new solutions and actively make sense of the situation they are in. Expansive learning is not about choosing between ready-made alternatives, nor merely re-defining something already known. It involves learning *new forms of activity that are not yet there* (ibid.).

The focus of this article can be described with the following four-square matrix (Fig. 1), where the horizontal dimension concerns whether learning is seen as the appropriation of culturally given knowledge or as the creation of culturally new knowledge. The vertical dimension determines whether we focus on development taking place as top-down or bottom-up. The interest of this article is on the bottom-up implementation of changes and on the learning of local solutions that go beyond existing traditions and models.

Focusing on the local implementation of changes and the creation of novel solutions raises a more finessed question about the learning taking place. If the practitioners are creating and learning something that is not yet there, how is the new

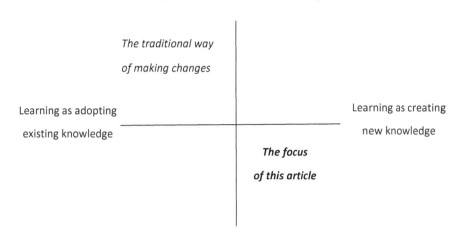

Fig. 1 The focus of this article

generated? Does it start as a creation of concepts and abstract models or does it start from creating and establishing new practices and concrete outcomes?

These questions are in the nucleus of the studies of concept formation and conceptual change, relevant to our understanding of change and learning. Concepts are traditionally understood as abstract, cognitive entities that are determined by an explicit definition (Greeno 2012). In addition to this kind of formal concepts, we can also distinguish functional concepts (Greeno 2012) or concepts of practice (Hutchins 2012). These are usually formed within and between complex activities, and they are typically collective (Engeström and Sannino 2012). They help people to organise their understanding of what they are doing (Greeno 2012).

Functional concepts develop within and from local practices. The changes pursued in project Fasper can be seen as collective learning and an effort of functional concept formation. The functional concepts are challenged, re-formulated and executed in practice. As Engeström (2014) states, collective concept formation is typically a long process in which the concept itself undergoes multiple transformations and partial stabilisations. This type of creation necessarily transcends the boundary between the mental and the material. It is both an endeavour of collective learning and a creative process of generating something culturally new (Engeström 2014).

4   The Developmental Process in Project Fasper

Following the principles of DWR, project Fasper aimed at local knowledge production and transformative learning through creation of new practices. In DWR, every participant's reflections and professional expertise are of genuine interest and brought forward to the advantage of both the learners and the activity they develop (Engeström 2009). Researcher-interventionists guide a community in its effort to develop and transform practices. The learners construct together their interpretations of events by searching for new meanings, reinterpreting phenomena and creating new knowledge, and, finally, putting the ideas into action (Engeström and Sannino 2010). In its active years 2009–2014, project Fasper followed the cycle model of expansive learning, consisting of the following phases: questioning and analysing the present activity, modelling the new activity, testing, implementing, and consolidation (Engeström 1987; Engeström and Sannino 2010).

In six municipalities around the Helsinki metropolitan area, practitioners from different organisations gathered together to study and develop family mediation. Social workers, child welfare supervisors, family workers, psychologists, family therapists, family counsellors, attorneys and judges participated in the project. They were organised in two similarly-composed local learning networks that met separately 12 times during years 2011–2012. Every session, with an average of 14 participants per session, lasted approximately 3 h. The two networks were given similar learning tasks by the researcher-interventionists.

4.1 The Mapping of Terrain

The objective of project Fasper was defined widely on purpose: the general aim was to study the possibilities of family mediation to resolve families' conflicts and promote family mediation practices that could facilitate parents to resolve their conflicts by themselves (Karvinen-Niinikoski and Pelli 2010). The project started with "mapping of the terrain". The researchers interviewed 90 professionals working with divorced families to uncover how the services were organised in the municipalities participating in the project and how the professionals understood family mediation. The picture given by the interviews as to the local conditions was in line with the previous national findings (Eduskunnan oikeusasiamiehen päätös 2004, Mahkonen 2008). Family mediation was not available as a distinct process (except in one of the participating municipalities) and there was no jointly shared understanding of mediation. Many of the interviewed said they were doing "kind of mediation"—in other words, they used different kind of working methods under the generic label of mediation. The conceptual unclarity resulted in different kind of practices and perceptions. Can one come to mediation alone or together with the ex-spouse? What does the mediator do in mediation? What can he or she not do? Is all counselling and guidance the same as mediation? (Haavisto et al. 2016).

4.2 Developing and Implementing Family Mediation Practices

After mapping the terrain, a landscape of family mediation in Finland opened. The service system was scattered, divorced parents occupied heavily the service system, family mediation was not easily available, and there was no joint understanding of its content and execution (Haavisto et al. 2016).

In our hands, there were a skein in which family mediation was a formal and authoritative activity regulated by law, but the practice appeared inconsistent and scattered. We faced a double bind: we could not train a ready-made mediation model for the practitioners, as it would have inevitable been a pre-given, top-down model, the establishing of which would have been highly uncertain. On the other hand, we could not simply start to develop new practices for family mediation, as the participants did not have any shared knowledge or concept of mediation on which to base the developmental work.

The tension could not be resolved by offering mediation training, neither by creating directly a new concept for family mediation. We could not choose between the clear-cut top-down and bottom-up models of implementing change, but had to find a third way of proceeding. We started to search for a way of developing, where the increasing of participants competence in mediation (the adoption of knowledge) and the local development of practices and service models (the creation of new knowledge) were intertwined as a process where the one feeds the other. The project progressed as an interplay between mediation trainings and the local developmental network sessions.

The local learning networks were organised on geographical basis so that neighbouring municipalities started to work together in spring 2011. In their first two network sessions, they examined the local divorce service system, both the present and historical situations. They found that divorced families move around the local services without anyone knowing their route and anyone having the big picture of their situation. They focused on the failure of the service system to meet the needs of divorcing parents in conflict and recognised this scattered service system as their shared problem space in need of change. This kind of questioning of the present system seems to be an elementary prerequisite for change and transformation (Bergman-Pyykkönen 2017).

After the sessions of examining and questioning, we organised the first mediation training. It was a one-day training to introduce mediation as a conflict resolution method in different areas of society and different kinds of conflicts. After that, we organised a more detailed three-day training in family mediation to deepen the understanding and practicing of family mediation as a distinct process. We invited family mediator and trainer Lisa Parkinson from the United Kingdom as the trainer. We considered important that the trainer was well-experienced not only in mediating family conflicts, but also in producing mediation models and practices.

After the training, we continued working in local networks, the goal being to test in practice the things learned in training. We had constructed interconnections between training and local development: the participants anticipated the training by addressing questions they needed to get answers. In the network sessions after the training, the given concepts and models were to fit the local conditions. Network sessions three through seven were to produce the new concept of family mediation and prepare for testing the paradigm and new tools. The participants tackled with questions such as how does mediation process in our area look like and how is the new family mediation service organised as part of the larger divorce service system.

The first trials of new methods were conducted in Spring 2012. One of the local networks made intensive experiments and, finally, they had 15 family mediation processes conducted, all documented by the researchers.[4] In the other network, the leap from adopting knowledge to the local creation of new mediation practices appeared more demanding and slow. In network sessions eight and nine, the new practices and emerging service system were evaluated through the experiences gained in the experiments.

The local trials were intermitted by a further training when Lisa Parkinson gave a workshop for those practitioners who participated in the mediation experiments. The workshop was based on pre-assignments in which the participants reported their observations in the experiments to the trainer and disclosed what kind of further knowledge they needed. The workshop discussions were documented for the participants as training material to be available when later needed. After the training, the experiments continued with new mediation cases.

The experimenting phase in project Fasper took approximately 1 year. During that period, the family mediation process and mediator's toolkit were gradually developed. As a result, from the discussions in the network sessions there started to emerge a more common understanding of what mediation could be about, what is the focus of family mediation, and what kind of practices and tools are needed in mediation. At the same time, the first envisions about how family mediation could be more accessible and available than before came to light, along with how the mediation service could be produced in a multi-organisational network and how the new mediation service could be integrated into the existing service system. The last network sessions 10 through 12 included enriching and evaluating the tested models. Examples of the created new models and practices are presented in the next chapter.

The new family mediation service was officially implemented in spring 2013 when a multi-municipal unit for family law matters was built and started to coordinate family mediation service on the area. The year 2013 was time for consolidating the new mediation practices. The interventions and network sessions organised by the researcher-interventionists finished, but the participants organised necessary guiding instruments of their own. The family mediators met regularly in team meetings, and they created also a form of competence development which they called "family mediators' sparring afternoons".

---

[4]After the mediation process was finished, the parents and mediators were interviewed; parents separately, the co-mediators together. A part of the mediation sessions was also audiotaped with the parents' permission.

4.3   Distributing the Created Models

The implementation and consolidation of the created models raised the question how the created models could be distributed to other municipalities as well. A training model for family mediators' elementary training was piloted in the fall 2013.

We organised a planning group of seven people—two researcher-interventionists and five practitioners from the project—who at first started to co-create the contents for the training and then finally executed it as eight-days training for workers who had not participated earlier in project Fasper, but who were interested to start as family mediators.

After the pilot training, we were granted an allowance to produce four corresponding elementary trainings for family mediators around the country. This meant that approximately 80 professionals completed the elementary training, supported by the financial aid from the government. Since then, family mediators' elementary training has been organised randomly, mainly in collaboration with summer universities.

4.4   Where to Go Next—Consolidating Family Mediation Nationwide

The first step to establish family mediation largely in municipalities is to organise it as *a distinct process*—as was done in project Fasper. If family mediation is palatalised as minor or marginal method or working approach, "mediation-kind-of work", family mediation cannot reach its full potential.

The second step in municipalities should be acquiring training for the employees working as mediators. When the demand for family mediation grows, it is important to have well-trained, competent mediators.

The third step is to integrate family mediation into the family service system and organise the service provision in a way that suits for local conditions. The experiences in project Fasper convinced researchers and practitioners that mediation is possible to organise and provide in collaboration of several municipalities and other service producers, such as the church counselling units and NGOs providing family and divorce services.

The municipalities can support the establishing of family mediation by defining the referral system to mediation, providing mediation actively and by making informative presentations and leaflets about family conflicts and mediation.

In addition to the municipal measures, national procedures of consolidation are needed. The role of the regional state administrative agencies should be strengthened in planning, steering and monitoring the execution of family mediation in municipalities. Similarly, the role of the ministry of social welfare and health in promoting mediation needs to be reconsidered. Also, the chapter ruling family mediation in the Marriage Act needs updating.

The municipal family mediation offers the cost-free mediation service for parents, guaranteed by the present legislation. In the future, there will be reforms in the provision of social services, which will transfer the services from municipalities to provinces. This will probably open the service production also for the private producers.

In the future, we need common rules concerning the qualification requirements of family mediators and the training required. We need to consider whether the provision of family mediation should be subject to license or authorisation. This question may actualise if also private family mediation markets will emerge. We need to consider should there be an acceptation system for family mediators, which would both accept competent mediators and monitor how do they maintain and develop their competence. In Finland, we are at our early steps of professionalisation and quality control.

4.5 Evaluating the Developmental Process

4.5.1 Developmental Work in a Multi-Organisational and Multi-Professional Network

In project Fasper, family mediation was developed as multi-organisational collaboration including several service units of the municipalities, family counselling units of the church, courts and private law firms—despite of the fact that mediation service was the statutory responsibility of municipalities. Our initial presupposition was that gathering together all the local service providers around parental conflicts would benefit the developmental work and result as higher quality of the dialogue. We also thought that the collaborative effort would increase the consciousness about family mediation in all participating organisations, which would later promote adequate referral system.

The participants of DWR informed projects construct new meanings, re-interpret and constitute new ideas (Engeström 2009). In the context of family mediation, the elementary question was how can the practitioners with different professional backgrounds create a unified, shared understanding of family mediation. How do they negotiate joint understanding of their new task as family mediators and how do they construct new professional identities as mediators?

The researcher of project Fasper, Marina Bergman-Pyykkönen, showed in her study (2017) on interprofessionality in the project how bringing together practitioners with different organisational and professional backgrounds to collaborate outside the shelters of their institutions was a demanding effort. It contributed, however, to the emergence of a discursive space allowing for diversity in knowledge. As there were representatives of different professions in the workshops, it compelled them to argue and explain their ideas more thoroughly than if the participants were own colleagues with similar backgrounds (Bergman-Pyykkönen 2017).

The intersection of diverse practices belongs to all the intersecting practices, but is not defined by any one of them. This was especially true with family mediation, which was not "a property" of any special profession, but instead, a no-man's land. The ambiguous nature of boundaries activated dialogue, but still required special methods and tools to facilitate communication between the participants. The inter-professional collaboration in Fasper increased talk at the boundaries and the trans-parency and thoroughness of discussions in the workshops, but in order to happen, demanded not avoiding confrontations, but using them to explore and promote dialogue (Bergman-Pyykkönen 2017). In the analysed two learning networks of project Fasper, the first one (called the client-centred network) avoided confronta-tions and the dialogue got closed, whereas the second one (called the service system-centred network) used confrontations to explore and promote dialogue (Bergman-Pyykkönen 2017). The latter one became the spearhead of development in the project.

Similarly, powerful discursive tools were needed to structure a shared problem space and to envision the future. In her study, Bergman-Pyykkönen found meta-phors, anecdotes and models as discursive tools used by Fasper participants and recognised them as elementary for understanding learning in multi-professional groups and collective developmental efforts.

4.5.2 Developmental Work as Collaborative Concept Formation

The developmental work done in project Fasper was a collaborative effort to create new concepts for family mediation. In his analysis of the dynamics of concept formation, Engeström (2014) found two main directions: concept formation with the name in the lead and concept formation with the practice in the lead. In the first case, there exists a name (a concept), but only a vague idea of what it represents. Collaborative concept formation is a search for contents for the name. In the latter case, concept formation moves the opposite order with the novel practice in the lead, but no name for it (Engeström 2014).

In our previous study on the concept formation (Haavisto et al. 2016), we found that, in general, project Fasper was an example of concept formation with a name in the lead. The concept of family mediation was recognised and defined by the law, and in the project, new mental and material content for it was created. The first question of the multi-professional and multi-organisational learning network was "what family mediation is about?" When the concept formation proceeded, the practical question was "how family mediation is organised?" Later, when the models for family mediation process and service organisation were defined, there emerged a need to ask more specifically "how and with what tools family mediation is conducted?"

Proceeding with the name in the lead does not, however, mean that concept formation was only mental, i.e., producing textual definitions of the phenomena and abstract content for the concept. In fact, family mediation could not be conceptualised as such—that is making universal definitions at a desk—but it occurred when the practical questions of organising and conducting family mediation were answered and resolved. Concept formation is predominantly a collaborative process, in which *the concept gets new practical and material manifestations while developing further*. The new tools implemented and models for family mediation process, service organisation and mediators' training were all manifestations of the emerging concept of family mediation.

5   The Outcomes of the Project

In this chapter, the practical outcomes—the models created—are presented. In project Fasper, the following models were created, implemented and established locally:

- The process model for family mediation
- The family mediator's toolkit
- The service model for organising family mediation in a multi-organisational network
- The model for eight-day elementary training for family mediators

In the following, I will at first present the process model for family mediation, in order to give reader a general picture on how the family mediation process is conducted. After that, I will give an overview of the content of mediator's toolkit and describe more closely one special tool used by the mediators, the ecogram. Then I will depict the service model for organising family mediation and, finally, present the training model for family mediators' elementary training.

5.1   The Process Model for Family Mediation

The process model implemented in project Fasper is described in Fig. 2. In this form, the process is established in some of the participating municipalities, and it is also the model disseminated in family mediators' elementary training. The model consists of preliminary meetings separately for both parents and usually three appointments with both parents present. The number of joint meetings may vary, keeping in mind, however, that mediation is to be short-term. In this model, there are two mediators in all meetings, also in preliminary individual meetings. If the parents reach an agreement, they are often offered a possibility to come to a follow-up meeting to discuss how the new arrangements are working.

The total duration of the process varies approximately from 3 weeks to 2 months, according to the pace favoured by the co-mediators who set the timetable. In this temporal dimension, the municipal family mediation differs from the Finnish court-connected mediation of child custody disputes, where the mediation is aimed to be handled in one day. A future research would be needed to see if there is any

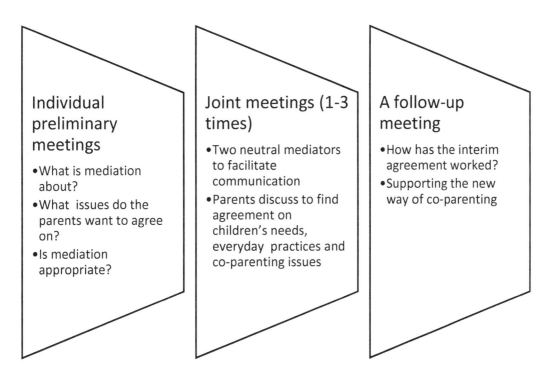

Fig. 2 The process model of family mediation in project Fasper

verification to our assumption that the prolonged process might better support and give room to the learning process of the parents and to the gradual growth of trust between them (see also Nylund 2018).

5.2   *The Family Mediators' Toolkit*

Family mediators' toolkit is a set of different kind of tools and models needed in conducting the mediation process in interacting with the parents and managing and resolving the conflict. We have distinguished two set of tools: "perceiving tools" and "technique tools". Perceiving tools are for increasing understanding and knowledge about the problem at hands; technique tools are for solving those problems.

   Perceiving tools can also be called "what is this about" tools, as they are different kind of models, figures, metaphors, etc., which help mediators to understand the complex phenomena around divorce and mediation. Examples of perceiving tools are the model of the phases of emotional and psychological separation and divorce presented by Lisa Parkinson (2014), the nine-step model of the escalation of conflict by Friedrich Glasl (1999), and the concept of the window of tolerance, introduced by Siegel (1999). These are all tools that help the mediators to understand why the parents find it difficult to communicate with each other or what might help the parents in making a settlement. Depending on mediators' discretion, some of these tools can be shared with parents in mediation sessions when they help also them to conceive their difficulties in communication or in parenting after divorce.

The technique tools are used in executing the mediation process. They can be tools for communicating about family mediation, for example, leaflets, brochures, referral instructions or process descriptions. An agreement to mediate form was used in the project to communicate to the parents the ground rules of mediation and increase their commitment. They can also be tools for managing the interaction and problem solving in mediation (e.g. different types of questions, techniques for focusing on the child, impasse strategies, re-framing techniques, managing power imbalances, methods for creating options and reality testing).

The most important perceiving tool used in the project was an ecogram, a model introduced by Lisa Parkinson in her training (Parkinson 2014). I will describe it more closely, as it incorporates the main theoretical ideas behind the mediation model created in the project.

During the project, the original figure was adjusted as the participants elaborated the model in the network sessions after Parkinson's training and when testing it in mediation sessions. In project Fasper, the ecogram was drawn as presented in Fig. 3.

The ecogram describes the children and their parents, and the two relationships between the parents: their relationship as a couple now terminated and their relationship as parents that usually needs to continue. The underlying assumption in the project was that it is useful to analytically distinguish these two and to focus family mediation on the parenting relationship and the children. Making this distinction is, however, emotionally difficult for the parents. It is difficult to end the marital or partner relationship yet continue to work together as co-parents (Parkinson 2014). It happens easily and is only human that the disappointments and rows flow into parental issues. That is why the parents benefit from mediators to facilitate their communication and help to overcome the emotional, social and cognitive barriers that are on their way in resolving their conflict (Nylund 2018).

According to the understanding adopted in project Fasper, family mediation is not about who did wrong in the couple relationship. Instead, family mediation is about children's matters and the organisation of their everyday life so that they could

Fig. 3 The ecogram (adapted from Lisa Parkinson 2014)

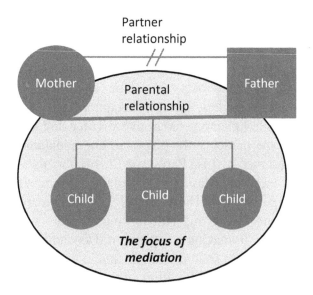

preserve close relationships with their both parents. This idea is encapsuled in the ecogram—as are the best interests of the child as a paramount foundation (see also Bernt 2018; Nylund 2018; Salminen 2018). When serving as a perceiving tool, the ecogram helps both the parents and mediators to keep this in mind. For this, mediators regularly draw the ecogram of the family on a flip-chart at the beginning the mediation process. To make the idea even more concrete, the mediators ask in the preliminary separate meetings of the parents to bring children's photographs when they come to the joint sessions. Then the mediators stick the photos on the ecogram on the flip-chart so that the children are made visible (Haavisto et al. 2014).

The experiences from the mediation experiments showed that when the ecogram was drawn on the flipchart, it started to serve also as a technique tool (Haavisto et al. 2016). Firstly, drawing the ecogram put the parents on the same map right at the beginning of the mediation. Secondly, it served as a memory to help the mediators keep in mind the names of the family members. Thirdly, the ecogram was a powerful tool in demonstrating for parents the entangling of the two relationships and that even though they are disconnecting themselves as partners, they still connect themselves as co-parents. Fourthly, the mediators could use the ecogram as a tool for facilitating the discussion. If the parents continued to talk about their unresolved marital conflicts, the mediators could point to the drawing on the flip-chart and redirect them back to children's issues (Haavisto et al. 2016, see also Parkinson 2014).

5.3 The Service Model for Organising Family Mediation in a Multi-Organisational Network

Previously in Finland, family mediation could be organised in municipalities so that workers in family counselling units or other workers of social welfare were appointed to the task. Especially in small municipalities this led to problems with disqualified mediators, as they might have been working with the same family or some of the family members earlier. Another problem was that the individual appointed mediators worked alone without support.

In project Fasper, we developed a multi-organisational model for providing family mediation services (Fig. 4). The stimulus for this was that on one of our piloting areas, three municipalities decided to set up a common unit for family law matters. This meant that family law services—child welfare supervisors confirming the child custody agreements—were provided in one unit for inhabitants of all these three municipalities. The new unit served as a natural base also for family mediation services which would be provided in collaboration by the three municipalities, the family counselling units of the church and authorised NGOs.

In the model, the client contacts the coordinator working at the unit for family law matters, who then appoints the mediators and fixes the timetables. The unit holds a "mediator reserve"—a certain number of trained mediators who have their main job

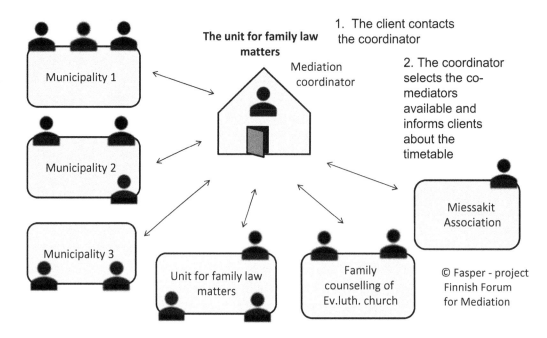

Fig. 4 The multi-organisational model for organising family mediation service

in the organisations belonging to the network. Instead of working as full-time mediators, they have an assignment from their employer to do mediation, for example, 60 h per year.

One advantage of the model is that it solves the disqualification problems effectively. If the clients come from Municipality 1, the coordinator can select for them mediators who work full-time in Municipality 2 or in some other organisation. Another advantage is that the unit for family law matters can also guide and support mediators' work and organise advanced training and competence development for the mediators.

5.4 The Model for Elementary Training of Family Mediators

The model for the elementary training for family mediators was created and piloted in 2013. Since then, the training model has kept the same structure, but there have been minor changes in the content. The overview of the content and structure is presented in Fig. 5.

The training model derives from the same theoretical ideas of expansive learning (Engeström 1987) as project Fasper, adjusted to the context of out-of-work training course. The training follows the idea that learning is not only adapting existing knowledge, but also creating new knowledge. When participants enter a training course they adopt new models, practices and tools, which they can use while practicing as a mediator. This is the acquisition of pre-given models, which, by

	Training days 1 & 2	Training days 3 & 4	Training days 5 & 6	Training days 7 & 8
P **r** **e** **-** **a** **s** **s** **i** **g** **n** **m** **e** **n** **t** **s**	Family mediation – past and present	Different stages in divorce	Observations and experiences in the practice period	Observations and experiences in the practice period
	Conflicts and dispute resolution Divorce as a conflict	How to keep children in focus	Parents' concerns and worries / trust Co-parenting after divorce	Mediator's identity; mediators' community and the competence development
	The mediation process and its phases – an overview	Acknowledging feelings Re-framing	Focusing on the details – focusing on the big picture	Family law issues in mediation
	Starting the mediation process and individual preliminary meetings	Preparations and starting the first joint meeting Clarifying issues	Negotiating Creating options / brainstorming	Reality testing The closure of mediation

Practice with a co-mediator

Reflections and feedback between the training sections

A travel story – how did I become a mediator

Fig. 5 An overview of the elementary training for family mediators

definition, is the focus in all training. In addition to that we saw it important that the students are encouraged to practice with a real case in between the training sections, either with a more experienced colleague, if they have one, or with another student from the same course. The experiences of the practicing are discussed and elaborated in the training. The personal experience of mediating opens up the possibility to not only adopt the pre-given models, but also to cultivate, enrich and transform them.

The same idea of transformative learning and students' own agency applies with the several role-plays during the course. The training follows the process of mediation: each day focus is on one phase in the mediation process. In the altogether six role-plays during the course, the students are practicing a determined phase of the mediation process and some theme or technique (e.g. re-framing or acknowledging feelings). They are not supposed to solve the conflict in one role-play, but only in the last one.

The theory of expansive learning sees that human activity is culturally mediated by tools and models (Engeström 1987). The idea of a mediator's toolkit was essential also in the training model. Our aim was that during the course we offer the students material from which they can collect themselves a toolkit of appropriate models and techniques to be used. The distinction between perceiving tools and technique tools, presented in an earlier chapter, was applied in the training.

5.5 Evaluating the Benefits of the Implemented Family Mediation Model

The interviews conducted in the 16 family mediation experiments in 2012 give some clues about the benefits of mediation for the families. The information is only tentative, as it is collected in a phase, when the mediators were only practicing the new way of working and many details were still in progress. No longitudinal statistics are thus far available about the possible effects on the service system level.

The first findings gave support to the idea that early family mediation can help parents to agree on their children's issues. The agreements can include solutions that can be confirmed by the child welfare supervisor to be enforceable. They can also include solutions that deal with the everyday details in children's life. The following excerpts describe the variation in the agreements:

> In the first meeting, we got an agreement on contact during the summer holiday. The result of the whole mediation process was an agreement on a flip-chart about the custody, living and contact. We went afterwards to see the child welfare officer who confirmed the agreement. The court case that was already pending was withdrawn. *A father*

> I was amazed how small things can help our everyday life. I mean, we defined how often we keep in contact, when the child is with the other parent, and how possible new partners are introduced to the child. And we agreed to have a small notebook for sharing information, and we agreed that we write every evening some sentences of what has been done with the kid, and then the other parent can read it. No need to start guessing what the five-year-old has meant, and no need to question who is right, the child or the adult. I think we succeeded to get our mutual trust on a new level. All in all, we talked quite much about trust. It was something we never couldn't discuss by ourselves. *A father*

Often mediation breaks the silence between the parents or cuts the circle of quarrelling, and helps to listen to each other's thoughts. This, in turn, helps to decrease the de-humanisation between the parents and encourages them to see each other as people who want best for their children. The most positive feedback for the mediators was given for preventing parents from fighting about their old marital conflicts and focus firmly on the child. It seems that parents approve mediators' active and even strict role in guiding the conversation when it supports the parents to communicate more constructively in children's matters and in getting things agreed.

> Maybe I went there to talk about our divorce. It was not so clear to me that in mediation, we think about the child. It appeared to be very good, cause many problems, even the practical ones, are resolved when we focus on the child. The child has been, anyway, our bone of contention. *A mother*

> I think they [the mediators] succeeded very well in calming us down. If the conversation got too heated, they said 'time out' and handled it very well. *A mother*

> The best thing was that the mediators always took the discussion back to the children. Every time we got out of it, they somehow put it back and brought in the viewpoint of the children. It really hit home for me a couple of times there. *A father*

I got gradually convinced that after all also the father wants best for the kids, and I could also say that to our children after the mediation. *A mother*

Early family mediation is, to a large extent, supporting the parents towards responsible parenting after their divorce. Managing conflicts is part of responsible parenting that can be supported in mediation. Many parents seemed to recognise their new, more responsible thinking as an important result of the mediation. Even though the parents could not make any agreement, they could still see some positive effects of the mediation process on the everyday life of the child (see last excerpt below). In this sense, mediation becoming more common may shape our contentious divorcing culture to a direction that better recognises children's needs.

The biggest effect was that it [mediation] made us think that if things go on like this, where does it lead. This really must end. The child is suffering from this. *A mother*

I think that from now on, I think more carefully what are the consequences of my own behaviour. *A father*

Our elder daughter is going to school in the neighbouring city, where also her father has his workplace. Now [after the mediation process] the father has spontaneously called in the mornings and offered her a lift, so that they can travel together. *A mother*

Family mediation is relatively inexpensive. In the project, it was estimated that a mediation process for one family takes approximately 10 h. This includes the individual preliminary meetings (45 min each), three joint sessions (90 min each), a possible follow-up session and time for planning and reflection between the co-mediators. Recently, the cost of a working hour in demanding professional work in social welfare has been estimated to be 75 euros (Hämäläinen 2011). Following this, the costs of mediation for one family would be 1500 euros with two mediators. The number is, however, an educated estimate, as mediation executed as a part of public office does not directly increase salary or other costs in the municipality.

What it requires, however, is new thinking in allocating the services. Family mediation could be offered to some parents instead of long-lasting counselling. In many cases, a short-term, structured procedure could be enough to help the parents get forward. We also believe that family mediation can be regarded as proactive child protection, which may prevent conflict escalation. In the future, it is important to investigate whether investing on early family mediation could decrease the number of child welfare notifications related to conflicted divorces, ease work pressure in family counselling and child protection or decrease the number of child custodies by the authorities.

6   Conclusions

Project Fasper showed that producing new understanding and conceptualisations of mediation is in a constant interplay with the more tangible changes in practices—in fact, they are two sides of the coin (Haavisto et al. 2016). While trying to understand what family mediation is about, the participants produced conceptualisation of family mediation, which received practical manifestations in the forms of models, artefacts, documents or structures of social organisation. Respectively, while tackling the mundane questions of practical details in the mediation service, the participants produced joint understanding of mediation.

The potential for novel practices and creating new knowledge—learning something that is not yet there—is in the core of the theory of expansive learning (Engeström 1987). The developmental work done in project Fasper suggests not to forget the importance of learning as adopting. For example, many of the mediators' new tools represented the acquisition of existing knowledge. Some of them were adopted from existing theories as such; some of them were adopted after alterations through re-defining and re-considering the context of use (Haavisto et al. 2016). What was fundamental was *the constant alternation and interplay in the project between adopting existing knowledge and creating new knowledge*. Because of this interplay, the adopting of existing knowledge resembled "making things one's own". The models and tools acquired in the mediation training, as well as the ways of using them, were collaboratively adjusted and cultivated to fit the local needs.

The alternation of the two forms of learning is visible also when all the phases of the project are considered. In the active years of the local development in the network sessions (approximately 2010–2013), the prevailing form of learning was the creation of new practices with the support of the family mediation training and adoption of existing models. After that, the focus has been in the organisation of an elementary training for family mediators and expanding the locally created models and practices nationwide (from 2014 onwards). Now the locally created models of project Fasper are pre-given knowledge to be adopted by family mediators in other municipalities. Still, the adoption of pre-given knowledge needs to be supported by local development and adjusting, wherever the models are implemented.

Regarding the implementation of change, project Fasper represented bottom-up implementation with its starting point in local development of new models and practices. Nevertheless, implementation of change is hardly ever a process of only one direction. In project Fasper, developmental process was not merely a local, grassroot contribution without any preconditions or limits. The ruling given in the Marriage Act set one prerequisite for the development, although diffuse. Correspondingly, family mediation was an existing part of Finnish service system for divorcing couples, even though it was diffused and unclear in its content. The elements of top-down implementation were intertwined with the bottom-up development. The existing concept—family mediation—was interpreted, enriched and concretised in ways that went beyond pre-given models. This supports a complementary view on *implementation as a learning process with a significant potential for expansion.*

The interplay of top-down and bottom-up implementation of change is also essential when viewing the larger picture of the consolidation of the implemented practices. The developmental project solved the local problems of organising family mediation, but, at the same time, disclosed the urgent need to unify the national prerequisites and top-down governing of family mediation. In addition to local guidelines and codes of conduct, also national, permanent infrastructure for supporting, guiding and supervising family mediation is needed—including the necessity to revise the legislation.

Top-down consideration is needed also in dispute systems design when the dispute resolution processes available for divorcing parents are viewed as a unity. As Nylund (2018) calls for, the different mediation services should be clearly distinguished from each other, and the differences between them appropriately explicated. Thus far, there has been no administrative or legal articulation concerning the prioritized sequence of municipal family mediation and the court-connected mediation in custody disputes. Although the dispute system should ideally consist of levels that build on the lower one and include a return mechanism (Nylund 2018), the reality is now that parents may enter family mediation after trying court-connected mediation or after having a court order in custody dispute. Similarly, there is no articulation about the differences in the aims, content, and the role of mediators between these two forms of mediation. A top-down dispute system design and articulation is needed to support the parents, as well as the professionals, in accessing the most appropriate dispute resolution alternative in each case.

Project Fasper was a collaborative effort to reform family mediation and create new conceptualisations, models and practices. It was an example of the possibilities and challenges of local learning and multi-view developmental work. From now on, it is important to continue the local developmental work, but also to take care of the prerequisites of family mediation on the national level and consider the totality of the dispute system. The efforts of those participating in the project were possibly an overture for a future sea-change in family mediation. The joint effort put the ball rolling, but no one can foresee where it will stop.

References

Bardach E (1980) The implementation game: what happens after a bill becomes a law, 3rd edn. MIT Press, Cambridge

Bergman-Pyykkönen M (2017) Towards interprofessionality in developing family mediation in Finland. Soc Work Educ 36(5):575–590

Bernt C (2018) Custody mediation in Norwegian courts: a conglomeration of roles and processes. In: Nylund A, Ervasti K, Adrian L (eds) Nordic mediation research. Springer, Cham, p 105–132

Eduskunnan oikeusasiamiehen päätös (2004) Havaintoja vanhempien välisiin ristiriitoihin tarjolla olevista sovittelu- ja neuvontapalveluista lapsiin liittyvissä kysymyksissä. Dnro 2059/2/03

Eisenstein J, Flemming RB, Nardulli PF (1988) The contours of justice: communities and their courts. Little, Brown and Company, Boston

Engeström Y (1987) Learning by expanding. An activity-theoretical approach to developmental research. Orienta-Konsultit, Helsinki

Engeström Y (1995) Kehittävä työntutkimus. Perusteita, tuloksia ja haasteita. Hallinnon kehittämiskeskus, Helsinki

Engeström Y (2005) Developmental work research. Expanding activity theory in practice. Lehmanns Media, Berlin

Engeström R (2009) Who is acting in an activity-system? In: Sannino A, Daniels H, Gutiérrez K (eds) Learning and expanding with activity theory. Cambridge University Press, New York, pp 257–273

Engeström Y (2014) Collective concept formation as creation at work. In: Sannino A, Ellis V (eds) Learning and collective creativity. Activity-theoretical and sociocultural studies. Routledge, New York, pp 234–257

Engeström Y, Sannino A (2010) Studies of expansive learning: foundations, findings and future challenges. Educ Res Rev 5(1):1–24

Engeström Y, Sannino A (2012) Concept formation in the wild. Mind Cult Act 19(3):201–206

Glasl F (1999) Confronting conflict. A first-aid kit for handling conflict. Hawthorn Press, Gloucestershire

Greeno JG (2012) Concepts in activities and discourses. Mind Cult Act 19(3):310–313

Haavisto V (2002) Court work in transition. An activity-theoretical study on changing work practices in a Finnish district court. University of Helsinki, Department of Education, Helsinki. https://helda.helsinki.fi/handle/10138/19754. Accessed 1 July 2017

Haavisto V, Bergman-Pyykkönen M, Karvinen-Niinikoski S (2014) Perheasioiden sovittelun uudet tuulet. Havaintoja, mallinnuksia ja arvioita FASPER -hankkeen pohjalta. Suomen sovittelufoorumi ry, Helsinki

Haavisto V, Bergman-Pyykkönen M, Karvinen-Niinikoski S (2016) Käsitteenmuodostus käytäntöjen kehittämisessä: tapausesimerkkinä perheasioiden sovittelu. In: Satka M et al (eds) Käytäntötutkimuksen taito. Heikki Waris -instituutti ja Mathilda Wrede –institutet, Hämeentie, pp 99–134

Hämäläinen J (2011) Kalliit erot. Selvitys huoltoriitojen kustannuksista. Lastensuojelun keskusliitto. Neuvokeskus, Helsinki

Hutchins E (2012) Concepts in practice as sources of order. Mind Cult Act 19(3):314–323

Julkunen I, Karvinen-Niinikoski S (2014) Socially robust knowledge processes of local and global interest in social work. In: Harrikari T, Rauhala P-L, Virokannas E (eds) Social change and social work. The changing societal conditions of social work in time and place. Ashgate, Farnham, pp 101–120

Karvinen-Niinikoski S, Pelli M (2010) Perheasioiden sovittelu – riitelykulttuurista vastuulliseen osallisuuteen. In: Poikela E (ed) Sovittelu. Ristiriitojen kohtaamisesta konfliktien hallintaan. PS-kustannus, Jyväskylä, pp 91–108

Leontjev AN (1978) Activity, consciousness and personality. Prentice Hall, Englewood-Cliffs

Lewin K (1948) Resolving social conflicts: selected papers on group dynamics. Harper & Brothers, New York

Mahkonen S (2008) Perhesovittelu. Selvitys avioliittolaissa 1987 säädetystä perheasioiden sovittelusta lähtökohtana lapsen aseman turvaaminen vanhempien erossa. Lastensuojelun Keskusliiton Neuvo-projekti

Majone G, Wildavsky A (1984) Implementation as evolution. In: Pressman J, Wildavsky A (eds) Implementation, 3rd edn. University of California Press, Berkeley

Mattila-Aalto M, Bergman-Pyykkönen M, Haavisto V et al. (2012) Konfliktiteoreettinen näkökulma eroihin ja palvelujen kehittämiseen. In: Kääriäinen A, Hämäläinen J, Pölkki P (eds) Challenges of divorce, interventions and children. Eron haasteet, väliintulot ja lapset. Ensi- ja turvakotienliiton julkaisu 39, pp 213–241

Mazmanian DA, Sabatier PA (1983) Implementation and public policy. Scott Foresman, Glenview

Nylund A (2018) A dispute system design perspective on Norwegian child custody mediation. In: Nylund A, Ervasti K, Adrian L (eds) Nordic mediation research. Springer, Cham, p 9–26

Palumbo DJ, Calista DJ (1990) Opening up the black box: implementation and the policy process. In: Palumbo DJ, Calista DJ (eds) Implementation and the policy process. Opening up the black box. Greenwood Press, Westport, pp 3–18

Parkinson L (2014) Family mediation, 3rd edn. Jordan Publishing Limited, Bristol

Pressman JL, Wildavsky A (1984) Implementation, 3rd edn. University of California Press, Berkeley

Roberts M (2008) Mediation in family disputes. Principles of practice, 3rd edn. Ashgate, Aldershot

Salminen K (2018) Is mediation in the best interest of a child from a child law perspective? In: Nylund A, Ervasti K, Adrian L (eds) Nordic mediation research. Springer, Cham, p 209–222

Siegel DJ (1999) The developing mind. How relationships and the brain interact to shape who we are. Gilford Press, New York

Toimiva lastensuojelu -selvitysryhmän loppuraportti (2013) Sosiaali- ja terveysministeriön raportteja ja muistioita 2013:19

Vindeløv V (2007) Mediation. A non-model. Jurist- og Økonomforbundets Forlag, Copenhagen

Vygotsky LS (1978) Mind in society. The development of higher psychological functions. Harvard University Press, Cambridge

Yanow D (1990) Tackling the implementation problem: epistemological issues in implementation research. In: Palumbo DJ, Calista DJ (eds) Implementation and the policy process. Opening up the black box. Greenwood Press, Westport, pp 213–228

Victim Offender Mediation in Sweden: An Activity Falling Apart?

Maritha Jacobsson, Lottie Wahlin, and Eva Fromholz

Contents

Abstract In Sweden, the government has invested considerable resources to implement victim offender mediation (VOM) for young people (under the age of 21). Despite this, the number of mediations is decreasing. What appears to be a gap between the legislator's intentions and practical applications raises questions about the reasons for this gap and the premises for mediation in penal matters in Sweden today. Our purpose in this article is to highlight and discuss some circumstances that can explain this decrease and the future of VOM in Sweden. We start by discussing the development of VOM in Sweden and continue by analysing possible reasons for why mediation is declining. The conclusion is that the decrease can be explained by problems related to legal and organisational structures as well as mediation practice. The conclusion is also that if the state and municipalities do not show more interest in VOM and restorative justice, then this activity will probably disappear.

M. Jacobsson (✉)
Department of Social Work, Umeå University, Umeå, Sweden
e-mail: maritha.jacobsson@umu.se

L. Wahlin
Institute for Mediation Training in Sweden, Stockholm, Sweden
e-mail: info@medlarutbildning.com

E. Fromholz
Department of Social Work, Stockholm University, Stockholm, Sweden
e-mail: eva.fromholz@socarb.su.se

© The Author(s) 2018
A. Nylund et al. (eds.), *Nordic Mediation Research*,
https://doi.org/10.1007/978-3-319-73019-6_5

1 Introduction

In Sweden, the government has altogether spent 66 million SEK (approximately EUR 6.4 million) between 2003 and 2007 to implement victim offender mediation (VOM) for young people (under the age of 21). In 2002, a new act concerning VOM, the Act on Mediation in Penal Matters (Lag 2002:445 om medling med anledning av brott) was introduced (hereafter, the Mediation Act). Furthermore, in 2007, there was a new provision introduced in Chapter 5, section 1c of the Swedish Social Services Act (Socialtjänstlag 2001:453) according to which it is mandatory for municipalities to offer mediation. Accordingly, the Swedish government has invested considerable resources to implement VOM in Sweden. Despite this, the number of mediations is decreasing (Wahlin and Jacobsson 2017). What appears to be a gap between the legislator's intentions and practical applications raises questions about the reasons for this gap and the premises for mediation in Sweden today. Our purpose in this article is to highlight and discuss some circumstances that can explain the decrease of mediation in penal matters and the future of VOM in Sweden.

After this introduction, we will give you a background and description of the development of VOM in Sweden. We will thereafter provide a brief description of the Swedish Mediation Act and the premises that it builds upon. In the following part, we will describe the mediation model that is mainly used in Sweden. Thereafter follows a discussion where we will highlight some problems that can have significance for the decreased use of mediation in penal matters in Sweden today. Finally, we will discuss the future of VOM in Sweden.

2 Background

Courts and social service authorities have common goals in preventing children and young people from committing crimes. In order to do that they use different means. In the Social Services Act (Socialtjänstlag 2001:453) Chapter 1, section 2 and Chapter 5, as well as in The Care of Young Persons Special Provisions Act (Lag 1990:52 med särskilda bestämmelser om vård av unga) in Chapter 1, section 2–3, emphasis is placed on the best interests of the child and the child's future development, in other words, prognostic assessments becomes central (Hollander 1985). Criminal law focuses instead on retributive values such as punishment, and discomfort, judgments made retrospectively based on a crime event (Edvall Malm 2012; Tärnfalk 2014). Hence, the social service authorities and courts share the same goals, but the means differ.

Also in VOM it is a goal to prevent children and young people from committing crimes. Furthermore, emphasis is placed on the best interests of the child and the child's future development, while in this case, the means are based on restorative values (Restorative justice, RJ), which means that emphasis is put on the involvement and welfare of both parties in the process following the offense (Zehr 2002). In Sweden, however, VOM is complementary to the trial (see description of the regulation below). It means that those involved have to deal with two different value systems.

In retributive justice, the focus is retrospective (Zehr 2002):

1. The crime: what laws has been broken?
2. The question of guilt.
3. The punishment.

The State is the main protagonist, and the emotional and moral aspects of those affected are left aside.

The restorative justice system is, in the same way, as the social service authorities, more concerned with prognostic values (Zehr 2002):

1. The parties: who has suffered damage and who has caused the damage?
2. The victim's needs.
3. The offender's responsibility to repair the damage.

Within the international movement for restorative justice, there has been a debate concerning contradictions existing between restorative and retributive values (Johnstone 2003). Some advocates of restorative justice believe this perspective should be the normal way to react to crime and that the legal processes only should be considered if the reparative processes have failed. Others claim that it is possible to combine both systems. Braithwaite and Zehr have, since the mid-1980s, argued for a strong dividing line between the retributive justice and the reparative systems (Braithwaite 1999; Zehr 1990). Later, Zehr (2002) changed his mind in some aspects, thinking that the two systems have a lot in common. For example, crime creates an imbalance between the victim and the offender; the victim can ask for compensation and the offender has obligations. He also claims that it is important to have a system that can deal with offenders who deny their responsibility. When the legal system is working at its best, it has essential qualities according to Zehr: respect for law and order, efficient processes and consideration of human rights. However, Zehr (1990, 2002) argues we should seek reparative processes as far as possible.

3   The Development of Victim Offender Mediation in Sweden

The interest in VOM was awakened in the late 1980s when some activities sporadically emerged in Hudiksvall by the police and in Solna/Sundbyberg by the social services authorities. In 1997, the National Council of Crime Prevention (*Brottsförbyggande rådet, BRÅ*) received a government mission to start pilot projects concerning mediation in penal matters with young offenders in the Swedish municipalities.[1] The evaluation from the pilot projects showed good results in terms of satisfaction (SOU 2000:105, Brottsförebyggande rådet 1999:14, 2000:8).

---

[1]Lottie Wahlin worked at BRÅ 1999–2007 with these issues.

According to BRÅ, mediation should be organised within the framework of municipal social services, but disconnected from the other social services activities. They were also of the opinion that there should be a clear regulatory framework for police and prosecutors on how mediation issues should be handled. BRÅ's opinion were not based on experiences from other countries, but they were aware of a need for knowledge development and education on how to organise VOM.

The issue of VOM was further investigated in a government commission (SOU 2000:105). A framework legislation was suggested, which means that the law allows extensive scope for assessing the circumstances in each case. The commission's proposal was based on the opinion that there was too little knowledge about mediation and that it, therefore, should not be taken into account in the legal process. Also, the commission would not introduce mediation as a penalty, given that it is based on voluntary involvement of the victims. Nor would it be possible with conditional allegations, since there was a risk that the perpetrators in such case would participate for "wrong" reasons, such as in order to get lighter punishment.

Instead, the commission shared BRÅ's assessment that VOM should be organised within the municipal social services. They did not, however, want to make any detailed regulations, as municipalities were assumed to have different conditions, depending on for example size and economy. Voluntary participation in mediation was emphasised and it was considered important that the parties really should be informed about that. To avoid that mediation would get the character of a minor trial the perpetrator should have acknowledged at least participation in crime.

The commission also considered that there was a need for a co-ordinating national unit that would be responsible for education, quality assurance and method development. However, The National Board of Health and Welfare (*Socialstyrelsen*—a national co-ordinating unit) considered in their reply that mediation is one of several methods social services can use to support both offenders and victims and that it, therefore, should be a part of the usual social services activities.

As described, in 2002, the new Act on Mediation in Penal Matters was introduced, based on the proposal by the government commission. At the same time, the government instructed BRÅ to allocate financial resources and provide training, methodology and quality assurance.

In 2003, BRÅ began their assignment. BRÅ's starting point was to develop methodologies and quality assurance by creating so-called model municipalities and regional co-ordinators who could assist and support other municipalities in the practical mediation work.

In December 31, 2007, BRÅ completed their mission of VOM. The government's idea now was that mediation should "stand on its own feet". During the assignment, four different reports had been written (Brottsförebyggande rådet 2005:14, 2007, 2008a,b). Experience is summarised in some important issues, such as the need for skilled and educated mediators, earmarked time for mediation, well-functioning routines and co-operation with various partners for effective mediation. The final report (Brottsförebyggande rådet 2008a) presented three different ways to organise mediation. The first proposal had an organisational structure, with an overall national co-ordinator, regional co-ordinator at the county level and finally municipal mediation organisations that should handle the practical activities. This organisation was inspired by the Norwegian model, National Mediation Services (*Konfliktråd*). The other proposal was based on municipal co-operation in regional networks, while the third was based on municipal co-operation in which one of the municipalities was responsible for co-ordination. The organisation that was used in practice was the second one, where each municipality is responsible for how mediation activities are organised.

In summary, the Swedish government has put great effort to build an effective and nationwide mediation activity, which could indicate that they want to strengthen prognostic values. Despite this, the number of mediations are decreasing and the interest in mediations seems to have reached a point of stagnation. There are no national statistics on VOM in Sweden, but there are other studies. There are a total of 290 municipalities in Sweden. When BRÅ conducted their review in 2008, they got answers from 287 of them, and 252 stated that they offered mediation to varying degrees. In studies made by Jacobsson et al. (2012, 2013) conducted in 2008–2010, they received questionnaires from 109 mediation co-ordinators responsible for mediation in a total of 212 municipalities. According to a more recent study (spring 2015–spring 2016) (Wahlin and Jacobsson 2017), 181 municipalities offered mediation. When interviews were conducted with the mediation officers in this study, they also told that they had fewer mediation cases compared to previous years. That indicates that the interest in mediation has substantially decreased.

4   The Act on Mediation in Penal Matters

The formulation of the act can have significance on how the relations between retributive and restorative values is perceived by, for example, the police, prosecutors, judges and mediators. As suggested by the government commission, the act is constructed as a framework legislation. It comprises ten sections.

According to the first section, the state or a municipality should organise mediation (section 1). The aim is that the plaintiff and offender, with help from a mediator, meet in mediation to talk about the crime event and its consequences (section 2). As it appears from the preparatory work, mediation is complementary to the criminal proceedings (see i.e. prop. 2001/02:126). Furthermore, mediation should benefit both parties in order to reduce harm from the crime event (section 3). According to the same section, mediation shall aim at the perpetrator gaining greater insight into the consequences of the crime and that the plaintiff is given the opportunity to process the experiences of the crime.

Furthermore, it is regulated in the act that the mediator should be a competent and upright person and impartial in regard to the parties (section 4). The mediator can either be a layman or a professional, but it is not clear from the law or the preparatory work what it means to be a competent and upright person, in this context. There is a discussion in the government bill about formalising the requirements, but the government was of the opinion that it would be sufficient that it appears from the law that it is the mediator's personal qualities, education and experience that should be decisive for the appointment as a mediator, and that the mediator thus "should be competent and otherwise suitable for the task" (our translation) (prop. 2001/02:126).

Mediation should be voluntary for both parties (section 5). According to the same section, the crime has to be reported to the police and the offender must have acknowledged the act or involvement in it. In the case of offenders below the age of 12, mediation shall only take place if there are special reasons. In the case of the plaintiff, no age is specified. According to the preparatory work, the victim should have achieved a sufficient age and maturity for mediation to take place (prop. 2001/02:126).

The mediation should be carried out promptly (section 6). It is also stated in this section that the mediator shall consult the investigator if a mediation is intended to take place before the preliminary investigation has been completed. If mediation is meant to take place thereafter, but before there is a statutory verdict, the mediator shall consult with the prosecutor.

Both the offender and the plaintiff should be informed about and prepared for the mediation process (section 7). Furthermore, the parents and legal guardians of both parties should have the opportunity to take part in the mediation meeting if there are no particular reasons against it (section 8). If this is not possible, it may be a circumstance that makes mediation inappropriate (cf. Sect. 5, above), especially if it is a child under the age of 15 (prop. 2001/02:126). Furthermore, according to the same section, there may be other people who can act as support persons to both parties if it is consistent with the purpose of the mediation and appropriate otherwise. It could be, for example, a close relative who is not a custodian, a family parent or other healthcare provider. According to the preparatory work, this must be decided on a case-by-case basis and should not be regulated in law in a binding manner (prop. 2001/02:126).

In the mediation meeting, the plaintiff should be able to tell about the crime experience and its consequences. Moreover, the plaintiff can also make demands for compensation (section 9). According to the same section, the offender should have the opportunity to give his view, tell why the crime was committed and apologize. The last section (section 10) in the act is about agreements concerning compensation. Stated in this section, the mediator shall only assist in the settlement of an agreement if it is clear that the agreement is not unreasonable. According to the preparatory work, the starting point is that the agreement should be reasonable in relation both to the crime committed and to the damage that has occurred. It is also pointed out that it is not always appropriate to deal with the issue of economic compensation in the mediation situation. If the parties disagree about the level of compensation, the question should instead be dealt with in the ordinary legal process, and this is also the case if the question becomes complicated due to the fact that there are several offenders (prop. 2001/02:126).

5   The Swedish Mediation Model

As described, it is the state or a municipality that should organise mediation. In practice, it is only the municipalities. It is most common with a meeting with one mediator, a victim and an offender before the trial (Wahlin and Jacobsson 2017). Most of the mediation offices had professional mediators (70%), some had only layman (17%) and the rest had both officials and laymen (ibid.).

The mediation model that is most common is the process-oriented (Strang and Braithwaite 2001), that was taught by BRÅ (Wahlin and Jacobsson 2017). There is one mediation office that stands out; they are using a transformative mediation model, inspired by Folger and Bush (1996). The characteristic of process-oriented mediation is that the mediation is regarded as a process that begins with the crime event and ends with a possible agreement between the parties. The process begins when a crime is committed and a police report is issued. Someone, generally the police, asks the perpetrator if they are interested in mediation and if a mediator can take contact. If the offender is willing, the case will be conveyed to mediation. The mediator then contacts the offender to try to meet him/her at a pre-meeting. At the pre-meeting the mediator assesses whether the offender has a true will to mediate. The offender is informed of what mediation means, telling the mediator about the crime event, the consequences, feelings, thoughts and other things that may be relevant in the context. In case the offender is interested to mediate the mediator will also take contact with the victim and have a pre-meeting with him/her. This meeting goes on the same way as that of the offender. If both parties are interested to mediate a joint mediation meeting is conducted.

If the meeting is intended to take place before the end of the preliminary investigation, the mediator must consult with the investigator. As described above, the mediator also contacts the prosecutor to inform the offenders willingness to mediate and to ensure that a mediation does not interfere with the legal process (section 6). Normally the mediation takes place before the trial. The mediation meeting most often follow a certain structure; introduction, the victim and thereafter the offender talks about the crime event, questions about the crime event, the victim and thereafter the offender talks about the consequences of the crime, questions about the consequences and, at last, agreements (Jacobsson et al. 2013; Brottsförebyggande rådet 2007).

It has been found that in practical applications mediators often say to the parties that confidentiality applies to all who attend the meeting (Jacobsson et al. 2013), but it is, according to the rules in the applicable law, Chapter 2, section 1, and Chapter 35, section 14, thirteenth section, of the Act on Publicity and Confidentiality (Offentlighets- och sekretesslagen 2009:400), only the mediators who are covered. It is also unclear how much information mediators can convey to the investigators and prosecutors. According to the rules, it should be sparingly.

As been described, parents and legal guardians should have the opportunity to take part in the mediation meeting if there are not reasons against it (section 8). In practice, it is the mediator who decides whether or not other persons will attend in the mediation meeting (Socialstyrelsen 2009). According to a study by Wahlin and Jacobsson (2017), mediators evaluate this differently. Some mediators believe that it is positive that parents or other actors are present, while others believe they may be interfering with the process, for example, by acting aggressively or trying to take control of the meeting.

6   Problematic Issues

What appears to be a gap between the legislator's intentions and practical applications raise questions about the reasons for this gap and the premises for mediation in Sweden today. In this part of the article, we will highlight and discuss some circumstances that can explain the decreased use of mediation in penal matters in Sweden.

The problems that we have identified is related to both law and practice. To begin with, it seems the formal technical construction of the legislation in which the act is constructed as a framework legislation, with many circumstances being unregulated or left to the practitioners to solve with little guidance in the preparatory work, is problematic (see also Marklund 2011).

One problem with the law is that there are no formal requirements concerning the mediator. This is not in line with the Council of Europe Recommendation No R (99) 19, which clearly emphasises that mediators are in need of education and support. As described, according to the Mediation Act, a mediator can either be a layman or a professional as long as the mediator is a competent and upright person, but it is not clear from the law or the preparatory work what it means to be a competent and upright person. In practice, this can be a problem since the mediators often work alone, without the opportunity to exchange experiences and knowledge with other mediators and educators (Wahlin and Jacobsson 2017).

Another problem is that parents and legal guardians should, according to the law, have the opportunity to take part in the mediation meeting if there are not reasons against it. Neither is this regulated in detail in law and preparatory work. As described above, in practice, it is the mediator who will decide whether or not other persons will attend in the mediation meeting, and mediators evaluate this differently. Some mediators believe that it is positive that parents or other actors are present, while others mean that they may be interfering with the process, for example, by acting aggressively or try to take control of the meeting (Wahlin and Jacobsson 2017).

A third problem is about agreements and compensations. There are big differences between restorative and retributive systems in relation to this subject. According to restorative values, the parties themselves should agree on what has to be compensated, how much and in which way it should be done. It is not explicitly formulated in the Mediation Act, nor in the preparatory work, what is meant by "agreements". In practice, the agreement can be made written or spoken. Moreover, it may concern economic compensation, compensation through work or future behaviour between the parties. In our present and previous research, we have found that the attitudes to agreements varies a lot among mediators in the municipalities (Jacobsson et al. 2013; Wahlin and Jacobsson 2017). It is, for example, possible that the offender experiences double punishment if s/he has agreed to give economic compensation during mediation, and later on, at the trial process, is ordered to pay damages by the court. It is also possible that the offender gets a more lenient punishment (see below).

A broken agreement can have negative economic consequences for the victim, as well as emotional, since it can be a sign that the offender's regret was not real. If the victim wants to go on with the process, s/he can sue the offender in a civil process (Socialstyrelsen 2012; Brottsförebyggande rådet 2007). The mediator has no duty to follow-up the agreement. The fact that an agreement is not fulfilled, can, however, have legal effects, in a civil process as well as in a criminal process. The prosecutor should, therefore, at least in some cases, get a notification of how the agreement has been completed. In practice, mediators deal with this issue in different ways, some mediators always announce this, others sometimes or never (Wahlin and Jacobsson 2017). Hence, if it has come to the mediator's knowing that the offender has not fulfilled his commitment, the mediator shall inform the prosecutor, unless it is unnecessary (prop. 2001/02:126).

A fourth problem is if and in such case how the offender's willingness to mediate should be taken into account. As been described, in Sweden mediation is *complementary* to the criminal proceedings, i.e. that it is possible to influence the retributive system with restorative values, but mediation could also be seen as an *alternative punishment* or as *an alternative to punishment* (Daly 2000). This is due to the fact that the prosecutor should, according to section 17 of the Young Offenders Special Provisions Act (Lag 1964:167 med särskilda bestämmelser om unga lagöverträdere), take the offender's willingness to mediate into account when deciding whether to prosecute or not. Also, according to Chapter 29, section 5 of the Penal Code (Brottsbalk 1962:700), the court can take mediation into account in their choice of sentence. It seems to be a problem also that the application of these rules differs. Mediators in a study (Wahlin and Jacobsson 2017) claimed that the police did not refer cases to the mediation offices, because they believed that offenders should be punished by the state and that their will to mediate could lead to a milder or no punishment. As far as we know (see also Jacobsson et al. 2013; Socialstyrelsen 2012), it is, however, uncommon that prosecutors take the offender's will to participate in mediation into account when they determine the sentence, but this differs – some prosecutors often take this into account, while others do not (ibid.). In other words, young offenders have different possibilities to get lower penalty in the criminal proceeding.

A fifth problem is that, according to the mediators, many of the offenders did not want to confess (Wahlin and Jacobsson 2017). As described above, according to the fifth and sixth sections in the Mediation Act, the suspects must have acknowledged the act, or at least involvement in it, and the mediation should be implemented as soon as possible—in practice before trial. This stands in contrast to rule of law principles and international standards, for example, article 11(1) of the Universal

Declaration of Human Rights (UN), according to which: "Everyone charged with a penal offence has the right to be presumed innocent until proved guilty according to law in a public trial at which he has had all the guarantees necessary for his defense". The fact that the laws are interpreted differently by mediators, police officers, prosecutors and judges contributes to legal uncertainty for young offenders. Mediation can be considered as a complement to trial or punishment, as an alternative to punishment or as an alternative punishment. There is no common legal strategy. It is, instead, up to individual professionals to assess.

It is not only the formal technical construction of the legislation that the act is constructed as a framework legislation that is problematic, there are also organisational problems. As described, since 2008, all municipalities are under the obligation to offer mediation to offenders below the age of 21. As also have been described, there are, however, a large variation in mediation activity among municipalities. The municipalities are free to organise mediation their own way. Some municipalities have mediation offices, others buy these services from other municipalities, and some do not have any mediation services at all (Wahlin and Jacobsson 2017). There are also differences between mediation offices, i.e. how they co-operate with other organisations. Some municipalities have given priority for mediation. They have mediators working full time and special mediation training programmes. Their mediators have time to create well-functioning activities, and co-operation with authorities, like the police, the social services, prosecutors and probation offices. In other municipalities, social workers mediate as a part of their employment schedule. Other municipalities recruit laymen mediators when needed (ibid.).

This means that several offenders, and victims as well, are not getting the chance to mediate at all. This causes legal uncertainty.

One of the main reasons can be the absence of a national co-ordinator. This is something that has been brought to discussion. In the government commission (SOU 2000:105) that preceded the Mediation Act, there was a proposal that the National Board of Health and Welfare should be a national co-ordination unit and responsible for training, quality assurance and methodology development. But the National Board of Health and Welfare considered that mediation is just one of several methods social services can use to support offenders and victims and that it, therefore, should be included in the regular social services activities. Despite this fact, the Swedish government gave the National Board of Health and Welfare the task to be a supervisory authority, a mission that was reluctantly accepted. In 2012, the National Board of Health and Welfare made a review of the mediation services in Sweden. In their report, they concluded that mediation does not work as conceived and that there was a need for a co-ordinator at a national level. This was a statement that BRÅ already made when they ended their government assignment 4 years earlier. The National Board of Health and Welfare also underscored a lack of knowledge about mediation in the judiciary, and a climate of distrust reigning. In June 2013, the National Board of Health and Welfare's responsibilities concerning mediation were replaced by the Health and Social Care Inspectorate (Inspektionen för vård och omsorg, IVO). The IVO's responsibility is mainly to follow-up and check notifications and exercise risk analysis. When it comes to mediation, nothing has been done at all. This may be because the inspectorate has not received any notifications or because of their priorities. In conclusion, there is no overarching authority responsible for VOM in Sweden today. Instead, it is up to the municipalities to decide how they want to give priority to these activities.

7 The Future of Victim Offender Mediation in Sweden

We have in this article highlighted and discussed some circumstances that can explain why the interest in VOM is decreasing in Sweden. In addition to these issues, there are also other problems. Earlier studies have shown that criminal policy concerning young people in Sweden today mainly is about more control and more recourses to the police (Edvall Malm 2012). Our conclusion is as follows: if the state and municipalities do not change their criminal policy and show more interest in VOM and restorative justice, then this activity will probably disappear. But if the state would show more interest in VOM and wants to develop these activities, then there are some issues to consider.

Since Norway, Finland and Denmark have seemingly well-functioning mediation organisations, it would be possible to find inspiration from them, both when it comes to legislation and how to organise VOM on different levels. These countries, unlike Sweden, have national and regional co-ordinators. One important issue to consider is if and, if so how, another type of organisation in Sweden can support the quality and development of VOM.

Another issue to consider, in relation to experiences from other countries, is if VOM should be regarded as a *complement* to the traditional legal system or as an *alternative punishment* or an *alternative to punishment*. In Norway, for example, the intention is that mediation should be an alternative to punishment used in less serious crimes (Larsson and Dullum 2001). This is also an ideological question that can be discussed in relation to rule of law principles and international standards.

Another important issue is when and in which crimes mediation should be present. According to our study (Wahlin and Jacobsson 2017), many of the mediation offices in Sweden do not mediate in cases with more severe offenses because of statements in the government bill (prop. 2001/2002:126). However, we should add that there are restorative advocates claiming that mediation works best in more serious crimes (see, for example, Strang et al. 2013), and several countries have developed such kind of mediation. In Denmark, for example, a report on restorative justice and sexual violence was published as a project funded by the European commission (Mercer and Sten Madsen 2015). Furthermore, a recently published anthology discussed legal and therapeutic aspects (Zinsstag and Keenan 2017). We are not proposing that mediation in sexual offences or in more serious crimes is something to be recommended, but we welcome a serious debate about when and how it is most adequate with VOM in Sweden and the importance to get both further knowledge and inspiration from other countries that have more experience.

References

Braithwaite J (1999) Restorative justice: assessing optimistic and pessimistic accounts. In: Tonry M (ed) Crime and justice: a review of research, vol 25. Chicago University Press, Chicago, pp 1–127

Brottsförebyggande rådet (1999) Rapport 1999:14 Medling vid brott – gärningsmännen berättar. Brottsförebyggande rådet information och förlag, Stockholm

Brottsförebyggande rådet (2000) BRÅ rapport 2000:2 Medling vid brott – brottsoffren berättar. Brottsförebyggande rådet information och förlag, Stockholm

Brottsförebyggande rådet (2005) Rapport 2005:14. Medling vid brott i Sverige på 2000-talet. Brottsförebyggande rådet information och förlag, Stockholm

Brottsförebyggande rådet (2007) Medling vid brott. En handbok. Brottsförebyggande rådet information och förlag, Stockholm

Brottsförebyggande rådet (2008a) Medlingsverksamhetens utbredning. Brottsförebyggande rådet information och förlag, Stockholm

Brottsförebyggande rådet (2008b) Medling i går, i dag och i morgon. En kort skrift om medling vid brott, Nätrapport

Council of Europe (1999) Recommendation No. R (99) 19 of the Commitee of Ministers to Member States Concerning Mediation in Penal Matters

Daly K (2000) Revisiting the relationship between retributive and restorative justice. In: Strang H, Braithwaite J (eds) Restorative justice: philosophy to practice. Ashgate/Darmouth Publishing, Aldershot, pp 33–54

Edvall Malm D (2012) Det socio-polisiära handlingsnätet. Om kopplingar mellan polis och socialtjänst kring ungdomars kriminalitet och missbuk. Doctoral dissertation, Umeå University, Umeå

Folger JP, Bush RAB (1996) Transformative mediation and third-party intervention: ten hallmarks of a transformative approach to practice. Conflict Resolut Q 13(4):263–278

Hollander A (1985) Omhändertagande av barn. En studie av baranavårdsmål i förvaltningsdomstolarna 1974, 1977 och 1982. Aktuell juridik förlag, Stockholm

Johnstone, G. (Ed.). (2003). A restorative justice reader: Texts, sources, context (pp. 1-18). Willan Publishing, Devon

Jacobsson M, Wahlin L, Andersson T (2012) Victim-offender mediation in Sweden: is the victim better off? Int Rev Victimol 18(3):229–250

Jacobsson, M., Wahlin, L., & Andersson, T. (2013). Den svenska medlingsmodellen: till nytta för brottsoffret?. Gleerups Utbildning AB.

Larsson P, Dullum J (2001) Fra samfunnstjeneste til samfunnsstraff. Utviklingen i bruken av samfunnsstraffer og konfliktråd i Norge. Nordisk Tidsskrift for Kriminalvidenskab 88 (2):154–168

Marklund L (2011) Ett brott – två processer: Medling vid brott och unga lagöverträdare i straffprocessen. Uppsala universitetstryckeri. Doctoral Dissertation, Uppsala University

Mercer V, Sten Madsen K (2015) Doing restorative justice in cases of sexual violence. A practical guide. In: Keenan M, Zinsstag E (eds) Daphne 2011 JUST/2011/DAP/AG/3350. University of Leuven, Leuven

Prop. 2001/2002:126. Medling med anledning av brott

SOU 2000:105. Medling vid ungdomsbrott

Strang H, Braithwaite J (eds) (2001) Restorative justice and civil society. Cambridge University Press, Cambridge

Strang H, Sherman LW, Mayo-Wilson E, Woods D, Ariel B, Strang H (2013) Restorative Justice Conferencing (RJC) using face-to-face meetings of a systematic review. Campbell Syst Rev 12

Tärnfalk M (2014) Professionella yttranden: en introduktion till socualt arbete med unga överträdare. Natur & Kultur, Stockholm

Socialstyrelsen (2009) Barn och unga som begår brott. En handbok. Socialstyrelsen, Stockholm

Socialstyrelsen (2012) Medling vid brott avseende unga lagöverträdare. Socialstyrelsen, Stockholm

Wahlin L Jacobsson M (2017) Medling vid brott. En enhetlig svensk modell? Report: Allmänna
    Barnahuset
Zehr H (1990) Changing lenses: a new focus for crime and justice. Herald Press, Scottdale
Zehr H (2002) The little book of restorative justice. Good Books, Intercourse
Zinsstag E, Keenan M (2017) Restorative responses to sexual violence: legal, social and therapeutic
    dimensions. Routledge, London and New York

Part II
The Mediator, Mediation Process and Outcomes

Unwrapping Court-Connected Mediation Agreements

Lin Adrian and Solfrid Mykland

Contents

Abstract Court-connected mediated agreements seem to both fulfil and fail the ideal of self-determination in mediation theory. In a study of 134 agreements from court-connected mediation, we found that the majority of agreements contain creative elements and display great variation in the provisions they contain. These results indicate that the parties play an important role in crafting the substance of their agreements. However, we also found that the wording of the agreements is characterised by legal and bureaucratic language to the extent that people without legal training find it difficult to read and understand them. The judicial language is well known for the drafters of the agreement but not the parties. Thus, court-

L. Adrian (✉)
Faculty of Law, University of Copenhagen, Copenhagen, Denmark
e-mail: lin.adrian@jur.ku.dk

S. Mykland
The Norwegian Land Consolidation Court, Bergen, Norway
e-mail: Solfrid.Mykland@hvl.no

© The Author(s) 2018
A. Nylund et al. (eds.), *Nordic Mediation Research*,
https://doi.org/10.1007/978-3-319-73019-6_6

connected mediation seems to fail aspects of self-determination when it comes to drafting agreements. We draw on new-institutional theory when we explore and explain this apparent contradiction within the court-connected mediation practice.

1 "The Black Box" of Mediated Agreements

The content of agreements reached in mediation is largely a black box. Only a few studies have examined what the agreements are about and none of these have done so on the basis of the agreements themselves (Wall and Dunne 2012; Adrian and Mykland 2014). In this article, we aim to fill this gap by using 134 agreements reached in court-connected mediation as a basis of analysis. We present a content analysis from three different analytical perspectives: we analyse the *content* of the agreements, their *level of creativity* and the *linguistic characteristics* of the agreements.[1] The purpose of our analysis is to examine whether agreements reached in court-connected mediation reflect party self-determination.

Court-connected mediation is becoming an established feature of the civil court system in many countries. The resolution of conflicts through mediation is founded on a philosophical and theoretical basis that is quite different from conflict resolution through litigation (Vindeløv 1997) with party self-determination as an essential feature (Welsh 2001; Kovach 2004).[2] Self-determination in mediation reflects the idea that the parties, so-to-speak, own their own conflict (Christie 1977) and can influence the process of conflict resolution and decide the outcome. In our understanding, self-determination in mediation is the right of the parties to participate actively, as well as an obligation to do so.[3] The core idea of self-determination in a court-connected mediation setting is seeing the parties as the central actors. They make decisions about how to proceed as opposed to litigation where the lawyers act on behalf of the parties and the process is determined by procedural rules. They can also make tailored outcomes in mediation if they wish. In litigation, a ruling is tied by the legal claims and application of the law as expressed in statues, precedent etc. In mediation, the parties can bring other issues than those of the court case to the table—legal as well as non-legal. Moreover, they are not bound by the law in their dispute resolution and can fit their agreements to their particular circumstances.

In this article we focus on the outcome of court-connected mediation. We explore whether mediated agreements reached in a court setting reflect party self-

---

[1] The results the three analysis have been published in *Negotiation Journal*, *Retten i Sproget* and *Kart og plan*, respectively (Adrian and Mykland 2014; Mykland and Adrian 2015, 2017). This article reworks and combines our previous work with additional analysis and a new discussion.

[2] The understanding and role of self-determination differs in mediation models (e.g. Bush and Folger 2005; Friedman and Himmelstein 2008).

[3] See Adrian (2012) for a more thorough explanation of the concept of self-determination in mediation.

determination. We begin by outlining previous research regarding the content of mediated agreements. We go on to present the context of court-connected mediation in Norway and Denmark and the methodology of our study. The bulk of the article presents the results of our analysis. We conclude with a discussion of our findings.

2 State of The Art

Over the past four decades, a large body of literature, studies and evaluation reports regarding mediation, in general, as well as court-connected mediation, in particular, have emerged (e.g. Eisenberg 2015; Wall and Dunne 2012; Roepstorff and Kyysgaard 2005; Kjelland-Mørdre et al. 2008). Among others, studies consistently show that parties are very satisfied with court-connected mediation (Wall and Dunne 2012; Wissler 2004; Knoff 2001) and that cost and time is saved when cases settle in mediation (Adrian 2016; Pel and Combrink 2011). In addition, we know that compliance with a mediated agreement seems to be higher than with court orders (Charkoudian et al. 2017; Lawrence et al. 2007) and that mediation seems to repair the relationship of the parties less than observers anticipate (Relis 2009; Roepstorff and Kyysgaard 2005; Golann 2002). Mediation seems to fulfil its goal of settling disputes in many instances, although settlement rates vary a great deal (Adrian 2016; Wall and Dunne 2012; Wissler 2004).

Only few studies have looked at the content of mediated agreements (for a review, see Adrian and Mykland 2014). In North America and Canada, these studies have been inconclusive with regard to the extent to which agreements are tailored to the interests and needs of the parties and not limited by the legal claims of the case (Adrian and Mykland 2014). None of the studies have examined the mediated agreements themselves but are based on interviews, questionnaires and observations. In a Finnish study, Ervasti used the same methodology as we did (described below) and found that in about 20% of the mediated cases a solution included elements outside the claims of the court-case (Ervasti 2014). A very preliminary look at the content of Danish court-connected agreements from the present study revealed that elements beyond those of the court cases seemed to cover a broad spectrum of issues (Adrian 2012). In summary, our knowledge of the content of agreements made in court-connected mediation is rudimentary.

3 Court-Connected Mediation and Its Legal Framework

Judicial settlement efforts have been part of civil litigation in Norway and Denmark for centuries.[4] In Denmark, it is known as "forligsmægling" and is regulated in sections 268–270 of the Administration of Justice Act. In Norway, it is known as

---

[4]For a more thorough description of judicial settlement efforts, see Adrian (2016).

"mekling" and is regulated in the Dispute Act, sections 8–1 and 8–2. Such settlement efforts are part of the regular litigation process and rules of procedure apply. Judicial settlement is performed by one or more judges who, so-to-speak, act "in robe", including typically making a ruling if settlement efforts fail.

Agreements made in *court-connected mediation* are the result of a different process. In Norway, court-connected mediators are primarily judges whereas both judges and lawyers act as mediators in Denmark. However, their role is to facilitate a process that enables the parties to come to an amicable agreement of their own and their approach to mediation is largely facilitative (Vindeløv 2012; Kjelland-Mørdre et al. 2008; Riskin 1996). If the case is not settled, it continues in the litigation track. If the mediator is a judge, as is most often the case in Norway and in about one-half of the cases in Denmark, the case is passed on to another judge for continued litigation.[5] In court-connected mediation, the court-case is paused and the general rules of procedure do not apply. Instead, this activity is governed by its own set of rules, which for Norway is the Dispute Act, Chapter 8, sections 8–3 to 8–7, and for Denmark, the Administration of Justice Act sections 271–279.[6]

The purpose of court-connected mediation is to provide more satisfactory results in court cases than is often possible in litigation by assisting disputing parties in finding tailor-made solutions to their disputes based on their interests and needs. In other words, instead of a judge making a ruling or suggesting a settlement, the parties are supposed to find an amicable solution themselves. As stated in the preparatory work for the Norwegian Dispute Act:

> ... the purpose of judicial mediation is to facilitate a way for the parties to get to a joint agreement before the dispute is handled through a traditional judicial approach. The mediator must seek to get insight in the parties' underlying interests and needs, and stimulate a dialogue that can promote understanding and joint agreement (NOU 2001:32 pt 3.0).

Similarly, the Danish Minister of Justice has stated that court-connected mediation gives parties in civil court-cases:

> ... an opportunity, if they wish, to settle the dispute in another way than traditional judicial settlement efforts, that are based on the law, or a ruling. Court-connected mediation can pave the way for a negotiated agreement that is experienced as more satisfactory for both parties as the parties can influence the process and the underlying interests, needs and future of the parties can be taken into account (Lovforslag nr. 17 from 28. November 2007).

An agreement reached in court-connected mediation ends the court case and can be entered into the court records at the parties' request. If so, it gets the status of a judicial settlement and becomes enforceable and publicly accessible. If it is not entered into the court records, it is legally binding like any other contract and subject

---

[5]In Norway, a mediator is technically permitted to serve as judge following a court-connected mediation at the parties' request if the judge finds it unobjectionable (Dispute Act section 8–7). The preparatory work states that the judge cannot serve as a judge if a caucus (separate meeting) has been used during the mediation. To our knowledge mediators very rarely, if at all, go on to act as judges.

[6]For more on the difference between the two types of settlement activities, see Adrian (2016).

to contract law. In Denmark, there are no formal requirements of judicial settlements, see Administration of Justice Act, chapter 26. In Norway, on the other hand, there are formal requirements of settlements in the Dispute Act, section 19–11. The court must ensure that the agreement states exactly what the parties' have agreed to and the parties must sign the settlement. In addition to this very limited legal regulation of agreements reached in court-connected mediation, Nordic mediation literature provides a number of practical suggestions regarding drafting and content of mediated agreements (e.g. Kjelland-Mødre et al. 2008; Vindeløv 2012).

We examine agreements that originate from court-connected mediation in this article. Even though they are a result of a settlement activity tied to the court, they originate from a process that is fundamentally different from regular judicial settlement efforts, as demonstrated in this section. In addition, the parties choose whether the agreement's legal status is that of a judicial settlement or a contract. This choice may affect the content of the agreement in Norway, as there are a few formal requirements that must be fulfilled in order for the agreement to obtain status as a judicial settlement. However, the formal requirements are very limited. We have found that it does not influence the agreement in ways that affect the result of our analysis in this study.

4 Methodology

We have analysed 134 written agreements, as well as complaint and answer reached in court-connected mediation of civil cases: 92 from Norway and 42 from Denmark.[7] We have made a joint rather than a comparative analysis of the settlements based on the following three arguments: Firstly and most importantly, we have run a number of statistical analyses when possible to check for potential differences in the data explained by nationality and none revealed any significant differences (Adrian and Mykland 2014). Secondly, the set-up and regulation of court-connected mediation is very comparable in the two countries, and they are embedded in similar civil justice systems.[8] Lastly, the languages are so similar that we can analyse the data without translation, including conducting linguistic analysis.

There is great variation in mediation activities across courts. Hence, instead of random sampling of participating courts, where we might include courts with hardly any mediation activity at all, in both countries we used "purposive sampling" and thus requested mediated agreements from courts with an extensive mediation practice (Frankfort-Nachmias and Nachmias 1996). We obtained settlements, as well as claim and answer, from four courts of first instance in Norway and four courts of first instance and one appeals court in Denmark. The settlements were randomly chosen

---

[7]We did not include cases involving child custody and visitation in our sample because these cases have different characteristics, both procedurally and substantively, than other civil cases.

[8]For an in depth comparison of the similarities and differences in court-connected mediation in the two countries, Adrian (2012).

in the sense that we got all agreements from a certain starting date until we had a predetermined amount in each court. The Norwegian courts were identified by the Norwegian Council for Court-Connected Mediation, and, in Denmark, courts that had participated in a pilot project of court-connected mediation were chosen. In Norway, the data was collected in 2008 (Mykland et al. 2009) and in Denmark from 2008 to 2009 (Adrian 2012). There has not been any changes in the judicial framework for the court-connected mediation in either country, nor significant changes in practice since our data-collection.[9]

As described in the introduction we have conducted three different analyses:

For our qualitative *content analysis*, we started by identifying elements of agreement in 10 randomly selected agreements individually and gave each element a label. Afterwards, we made a comparison of the elements and agreed on the labels. Subsequently, we each labelled approximately one-half of the agreements.

For our quantitative *creativity analysis,* we developed a five-point scale and coded the agreements accordingly.[10] Initially, we each coded the same 20 randomly selected agreements. After the coding, we compared and discussed our coding and resolved our differences. Subsequently, we each coded half of the remaining agreements. We also categorised the types of parties in the cases, the duration of the mediation, the type of dispute and the monetary amount.[11]

For our qualitative and quantitative *linguistic analysis*, we started inductively by reading all the agreements for linguistic patterns and found frequent use of judicial and bureaucratic language.[12] Subsequently, we developed a coding system and systematically coded our material for legal words and expressions and the different elements of bureaucratic language. We coded about one-half of the agreements each. In addition, we ran a readability test.

In all three analysis, we each kept a logbook in the coding process. When we noted uncertainty about a code, we discussed it and came to a solution. To the extent that it affected previous coding, we went back and re-coded.

In the presentation of our findings regarding content and linguistic characteristics below, we find it important to show how the agreements are written. Consequently, we use a show-and-tell technique where we include many examples of our data (Golden-Biddle and Locke 1997). This makes our research process more transparent and allows us to present our unique data in some detail.

---

[9]We are both in continuous contact with the court-system and court-connected mediators through trainings, lectures etc. and as part of this, we have seen agreements produced since our data-collection and they are similar to the agreements in our dataset.

[10]This analysis was based on 129 agreements. We had to exclude the rest of the cases, as we did not have both the complaint and answer, which was necessary to conduct this analysis.

[11]For more detailed information regarding research methodology, see Adrian and Mykland (2014).

[12]For more detailed information regarding research methodology, see Mykland and Adrian (2015).

5 The Substance of the Agreements

The first analysis that we present concerns the substance of the agreements. We identified a total of 36 different types of provisions across the agreements such as monetary elements, work elements, payment plans, practicalities etc. Based on our knowledge of litigation and mediation, we organised these elements into three main categories:

1. Substantive issues,
2. Procedures, and
3. Safeguarding

Substantive issues are the core elements of the agreements. This is what the parties agree to pay, deliver, exchange, do etc. These substantive issues are supported by a number of items in the agreements that regulate *procedures* on how the core elements will be accomplished—for example, a plan on how a right will be exercised or an amount of money paid. The last category, *safeguarding*, are elements that in one way or another serves as a kind of "scaffold" supporting that the substantive issues will be met, such as conditions and deadlines. Each of these categories and the elements belonging to it will be presented in turn below.

5.1 Substantive Issues

Unsurprisingly, many of the substantive provisions in the agreements relate to the dispute as it is presented to the court. However, when comparing the claim and answer in a case to the agreement, we see that the matter is often resolved in other ways than they would be in a ruling and, additionally, the agreement often contains elements that were not part of the original claim. The claim in a case may, for example, be for an amount of money or transfer of title to a piece of land, but some of the substantive components of the agreement reflect a resolution of the claim in another way than the demands in the court case suggest or do not stem from the claim altogether. This is explored further in our creativity analysis in Sect. 6.

The vast majority of the agreements (90 %) include provisions about *money* in some way. The most common way is through payment or compensation. This is to be expected, as a great deal of the legal claims in our study—as well as in litigation in general—are monetary claims. What is interesting is the variation in the way money is dealt with. We see many examples of provisions including money that are different from simply passing on an amount from A to B. For example, debt can be waived or assumed, mortgage debt paid for, a loan divided, an amount earmarked for education, or as we see in the agreement below, a property serves as lien for someone else's loan:

Magnus Larsson assents to the property gnr. 47 bnr. 85 being used as mortgage for a real estate loan that Elisabeth Larsson might need up to kr. 1.000.000 (approximately euro 105 000). (mediation 81)[13]

The substantive elements in the agreements can also pertain to *property* and *things*. Parties in mediation make deals about property that are not solely about property rights and financial compensation. They reach agreements on how to share jointly owned property, agreements on how to divide up property or how to handle inherited property. They also make agreements about things. The latter, for example, occurs in the following manner:

> The property is to be taken over including the chattels and appurtenances therewith on the date of the property transfer, as Helle Hansen is entitled, up until 1.12.2007, to remove whatever chattels she wishes, with the exception of the garden tractor, which is to be taken over by the buyer. (mediation 26)

In about 10% of the cases, parties agree on performing some kind of *work*. The original claim is usually about compensation for work not performed or work performed in an unsatisfactory manner. Instead of resolving the dispute with money, the parties in mediation—sometimes in combination with money—agree to repair a wall, change a door or make a new architectural drawing. The following is an example of a repair on a building:

> However, Ark Building and Housing AS must inspect/repair the house's mouse guard as well as take care of repairing the wall behind the mailbox stand. (mediation 12)

A substantive theme that we find in Norwegian agreements exclusively is that of *letters of recommendation*. In Norway, issuing letters of recommendation is a normal practice when an employment ends, while this is not the case in Denmark. In about one-half of the disputes pertaining to dismissals in Norway, we find provisions regarding this. In some case, the wording of the certificate is worked out in the mediation and included in the settlement in full or part. An example of such a wording in an agreement is the following agreed upon addition to an already worked out recommendation:

> KL draws up a new letter of recommendation before 02.12.09 with the following addition as a new section 3: TH is easy to cooperate with and has had a friendly relationship with the shop's employees. She is committed and eager to work. (mediation 134)

The last theme that we will address concerns *relationships*. One might argue that reaching an agreement in a mediation is in itself a relational expression. The parties choose to end the conflict in a more amicable matter than taking the case through an ordinary court process. We find explicit relational elements in almost 10% of the agreements. These are provisions that directly or indirectly encourage the parties to put the conflict behind them and look forward or expressions of regret:

---

[13]Names, places etc. have been changed in this and all other examples of text from agreements for confidentiality reasons.

> The parties agree to disregard the statements that have led to a strained relationship. These statements shall be considered forgotten. (mediation 35)

> Machet Kitchenware acknowledges that Marion Tønnesen was wrongfully excluded from her workplace as of 3.11.08 and that she subsequently was wrongfully dismissed effective from 15.12.08... Machet Kitchenware regrets the personal strain this has entailed for Marion Tønnesen. (mediation 60)

The first example shows how the parties want to put the conflict behind them. They acknowledge the effect of their actions on their relationship and want to erase this effect. Provisions like this express the importance of resolving a dispute in a way that removes the strain on the relationship. This seems to be of value to the parties independent of whether the relationship is ongoing or not. In the second example, we see a direct expression of regret concerning the effects of an action on one of the parties. In this case of dismissal the parties were hardly going to have an ongoing relationship but even so repairing the harm done seems important. Interestingly, the word "regret" is used in this and other examples, whereas the words "apologise/ apology" do not appear in any of the agreements. The words are synonymous but have different overtones. To apologise for something seems like a more sincere acknowledgement of having made a mistake than to regret something.[14]

In general, parties are probably more likely to address relational matters during a mediation than we see reflected in our sample of agreements. The parties may talk about relational issues and leave such matters out of the drafted agreement. One reason may be that a provision regarding relationship are considered foreign elements in a document with a legal status; another that parties fear that it could be a sign of distrust to formulate this in the agreement and thereby a cause of conflict escalation rather than the opposite.

5.2 Procedures

Over one-half of the agreements include procedural elements that regulate how the central parts of the agreement will be accomplished. The procedure-related aspects include details concerning how something shall be paid (payment plans), how something shall be done or executed (action plans), and, finally, what we might call simple practicalities.

Below is an example of a payment plan:

---

[14]Professor Erik Hansen, SprogbrevetDR nr. 90, 1994. http://sproget.dk/raad-og-regler/artikler-mv/ sprogbrevet-dr/sprogbrevetdr-nr-90/undskyldning.

1. Building Corp AS shall pay the sum of Kr.500, 000,- (approximately euro 56, 000) to Best Invest AS, Peter Eiendom AS and Krp Invest AS represented by legal counsel Anita Hansson.

2. Kr.250,000,- is due for payment by 15 September 2008 at the latest, and the remaining Kr.250,000,- (approximately euro 28, 000) by 26 February 2009 at the latest.

3. A bank guarantee for correct payment of the latter amount is to be provided in SEB no later than 15 September 2008. The guarantee is to be provided as an on-demand guarantee.

4. In the event the first payment and bank guarantee have not been provided by 15 September 2008, Building Corp AS shall transfer the physical half of cadastral number 19, title no. 34 in Bergen that is located closest to building no. 5 to Best Invest AS, Peter Eiendom AS and Krp Invest AS. (mediation 90)

The payment plan lays out instalments and dates they are due as well as the details of a bank guarantee. To top it off, the agreement outlines an alternative in case the bank guarantee is not provided. In about one-third of the agreements, we find these kinds of payment plans. The level of detail varies, but common to all of them is the elaboration concerning how the payment is to be made, such as through instalments, by providing guarantees or setting various deadlines.

In about one-quarter of the agreements, we find plans for how something other than the payment of money must be carried out. We have labelled these "action plans". Common examples of action plans are details regarding how an agreed upon work must be performed, plans regarding real estate use and plans for terminating employment. Below is an example of an agreement on repairing in a building:

Vinterbyg shall conduct the following inspections/improvements in the claimants' residences:

a) The ventilation slot for ventilation above the roof in the rafter framework of all dwellings shall be inspected. The ventilation slot must measure 50 mm. If it is less than this, it shall be repaired. The deadline for completion of the repairs is 1 September 2008. . . .

b) Air leaks in flats 9B and 27B shall be repaired by 15 September 2008. The results shall be documented via conducting air resistance measurement where an air leak factor of up to 4 with a 10% measurement uncertainty is acceptable. Flats 11B and 11B shall be repaired in the same manner, but are not to be inspected

c) Streetlights are to be repaired by 1 November 2008 - cf. report from NTE of 19 May 2008. . . (mediation 103)

Instead of merely agreeing on a repair, the parties set a standard for when repair is necessary and the standards the repair must meet. This agreement also illustrates how action plans can include deadlines, i.e. safeguarding the agreement—a theme we will return to in detail below.

What we labelled simple practicalities are found in three-quarters of the agreements. This category encompasses a wide variety of elements that coordinate mundane practicalities after the mediation meeting has ended. In this category, we find a myriad of different items, e.g. account numbers into which a payment is to be deposited, who informs the court of the agreement, who informs the land registry of ownership changes, who cancels guarantee commitments, printing and photocopying tasks and so forth. Here are two examples:

> Mohammad Salid takes over the property and the encumbrances. He obtains the bank's acceptance that Helen Soderman is no longer co-responsible for the loan. (mediation 37)

> When the amount is paid, the case is dismissed by plaintiff's laywer, who receives a copy of this letter which at the is signed by both parties. (mediation 23)

We include two procedure-like elements in our procedures category. They directly relate to overcoming obstacles that can occur when the parties try to reach an agreement: objective criteria and delimitation of substantial elements (in 4 % and 7 % of the agreements). Objective criteria help parties get to an agreement by getting assistance from an external standard, for example:

> The plaintiff shall see to it that the dishwasher is adjusted/inspected so that it works in a manner that can be approved by the Veterinary and Food Administration. (mediation 23)

Using objective criteria is a well-known instrument in the negotiation literature (Fisher et al. 1991) and it facilitates agreement on content in a roundabout way by agreeing on a criterion for resolution that is independent of the parties and hence objective, such as approval by an authority, as we see in the example.

Parties may also reach agreements in mediation by postponing resolution of parts of the dispute. They may decide to resolve certain issues after the mediation or they may refer the unsettled part of the dispute for the court to decide:

> The parties shall before [an agreed upon] remodeling begin agree in writing on how the costs for materials and labour are to be distributed. (mediation 111)

> The parties disagree on whether the marital agreement signed on 17 April 2002 is valid. The trial for hearing the issue is scheduled for 1 November 2008. (mediation 57)

Some of the agreements combine postponing parts of the negotiation until after the mediation with the option of referring the matter to the courts if they do not reach agreement, such as in the following example:

> The question of a possible price rebate for reduced water pressure shall be further clarified between the parties. If agreement is reached, the case shall be settled on this point, too, and thereby in its entirety. In the event agreement is not reached, this point of contention will become the object a hearing at the trial set for 14 March 2008. (mediation 66)

5.3   Safeguarding

The settlements have different kinds of safeguarding mechanisms. The purpose of these are at least twofold: (1) to make sure the settlement is complied with and (2) to prevent future conflict in the case. A majority of the settlements are entered into the courts records (86 %), which automatically serves as a form of safety mechanism, as it makes the agreement enforceable. However, in addition to this we see a rich variety of other the forms of safety mechanisms that the parties incorporate in their agreements.

One kind of safeguarding mechanisms is the uses of deadlines. As appears in the examples from agreements in the section above, the use of deadlines is widespread (in 82 % of the agreements). We see how lumps of money must be paid in full or in instalments within certain deadlines, how work must be performed before a certain day and other types of obligations that must be met within set deadlines.

Another kind of safeguard mechanism is the use of conditions (in about 1/3 of the agreements). A typical example is that either the agreement, as such, or parts of it is contingent on something else, see:

> Payment is dependent on Pernille and Mogens Grandahl and family vacating the cabin before 1.10.2008. (mediation 2)

> The settlement is contingent on effective payment. (mediation 13)

A third kind of safeguarding are phrases indicating that settlement constitutes "full and final decision". In over 2/3 of the agreements, we find variants of this—either as a general "full and final" provision or as a "full and final" provision relating either to the court case or to all aspects of the dispute. See examples of all three types:

> As full and final settlement. . . (mediation 133)

> The parties have no further claims against one another in conjunction with the case. (mediation 118)

> For full and final decision regarding all claims between the parties. (mediation 30)

A final safeguarding mechanism are the "what ifs." "What ifs" are decisions about what is going to happen if the agreement or parts of it are not fulfilled. We find them in just under one-fifth of the agreements. These decisions do not assure compliance, but they safeguard that the parties know what is going to happen in such a situation.

6   Creativity in Court-Connected Mediation

Another way of approaching the content of the agreements is to explore their level of creativity. In the previous section we laid out what types of elements the agreements contain through a qualitative and quantitative analysis. In this section, we use quantitative measures to capture the potential added value in mediated solutions. We consider added value a sign of creativity and apply a "creative product perspective" (Carnevale 2006). We define a product as creative when it has interest, novelty and value (Simon 2001, p. 208). With this understanding of creativity, we categorised agreements as creative when they contained one or more substantial element that was not part of the claims in the court case, nor would automatically be included in a ruling (like, for example, payment of interests at standard rates, usual division of legal costs, usual deadlines for fulfilment and the various "full and final" provisions). We developed the following five categories and placed the agreements accordingly:

1. Only one party's claim was met in the agreement.
2. The parties' agreement fulfilled neither party's claim, but was somewhere in between.
3. The agreement contained one element outside the claims in the case.
4. The agreement contained two to four elements outside the claims in the case.
5. The agreement contained five elements or more outside the claims in the case.

One could question whether it is meaningful to consider an agreement creative with only one extra element. However, the scale intends to capture all levels of creativity and designing the scale the way we have chosen to do, creativity can both be present or absent, and, more importantly, creativity can be graduated in that it can be present to a smaller or larger extent.

The level of creativity in our study varied a great deal, and it is interesting to take a closer look at the distribution (Table 1). Applying our scale of creativity, we found that 65% of the agreements were creative. However, there is quite a range. In about 13% of the cases, there was only one creative element, whereas in about 50% of the cases there were two or more creative elements. About 25% qualify as very creative in that the parties agreed to five or more elements outside the claims in the case.

In 35% of the cases in our study, we found no creativity in the outcomes. The agreements constituted a compromise between the parties' claims (31%) or, rarely, one of the parties' claims was met (3.9%). Since this is a document analysis and we were not present in the mediations resulting in these agreements, we do not know whether this is caused by the absence of creative potential in the case or whether the mediator and the parties have been unsuccessful in releasing potential creativity. Nor do we know whether the parties agreed to creative elements but omitted these from the written agreements. However, we consider the latter very unlikely, as we did not see this happen in any of the court-connected mediation processes that we have observed in two other studies of court-connected mediation (Adrian 2012; Mykland 2011).

This analysis of our agreements reflect our interest in exploring whether creativity in court-connected mediation is a myth or a reality. In academic, as well as promotional literature, the potential for creating solutions that meet the parties'

Table 1 Distribution of creativity within the five categories

	Frequency	Percent
One party's claim is met	5	3.9
Between claims	40	31.0
One extra element	17	13.2
2–4 Extra elements	34	26.3
5+ Elements	33	25.6
Total	129	100.0

needs instead of focusing on rights is often highlighted as an asset in connection with court-connected mediation. Based on our results we can conclude that creativity in court-connected mediation is both a reality and a myth. As demonstrated, some agreements display a lot of creativity and some no creativity at all. With one-third of the cases without creative outcomes there seems to be a potential for creativity in more cases, as well as for a higher level of creativity in the cases with very minor or more moderate creative outcomes.

To explain and understand these findings we need to know more about the process and other factors that affect creativity. The factors that were available for our analysis were limited to the type of disputant, the amount of time spent in mediation, the type of case and the amount in dispute. We refer interested readers to *Creativity in Court-Connected Mediation: Myth or Reality?* (Adrian and Mykland 2014) for our findings with regard to these variables.

7 Linguistic Analysis

As we conducted our analysis of substance and creativity, we found the agreements strikingly similar in structure and language. This motivated us to do a third analysis of our material: an examination of the "verbal wrapping" of the mediated agreements. We focused our investigation on examining whether the agreements reflect a standard linguistic practice and, if so, what the characteristics of this standard practice are. In the tradition of critical discourse analysis and among others Fairclough, we understand language as not just a neutral tool that depict a reality (Fairclough 1992). Rather, we understand language as a social practice that plays a role in shaping our perception of identities, roles, social relations etc. (Jørgensen and Phillips 1999; Tønnesson 2008). Hence, we can learn something about a practice by studying the discourse used in that practice.

Nordic mediation literature has different approaches as to who should write the agreement. Some find that agreements are naturally written up by the court-connected mediator (e.g. Kjelland-Mødre et al. 2008), while others find that the parties and their advisors should do the writing (e.g. Jørgensen and Lavesen 2016). In all of the mediations in our observational studies of court-connected mediations meetings mentioned above (Adrian 2012; Mykland 2011), either the mediator or the parties' lawyers authored the agreement. Based on these observations combined with the linguistic appearance of the agreements in our dataset laid out below, it seems safe to assume that either the mediator or the lawyer drafted the mediated agreements that we analyse.

7.1   Framing and Stereotyped Expressions

Many of the agreements in the study are "framed" by similar opening and closing linguistic phrases. Typical opening phrases are "as an amicable settlement", or "in full and final settlement", or "Mr. Grey pays Mrs. Grey in full and final settlement". Recurring patterns found in closing phrases are, for example, "each party pays their own costs" and "the parties demand that the case is dismissed as settled in full and waive the announcement of the dismissal decision."

Repeated use of phrases are referred to as stereotyped expressions (in German "Routineformeln") in linguistic theory (Kopaczyk 2013; Kjær 1997) and when stereotyped expressions appear in the same position in different texts, they are so-to-speak fixed (Kjær 1997). Many recognise this phenomenon from fairy tales that start with *once upon a time* and often end with *they lived happily ever after.* Fixed stereotypical expressions serve as rules for a particular genre. They homogenise texts and make them immediately recognisable. Our finding of consistent use of fixed stereotyped expressions suggests that the wording in the mediated agreements is not individual and random but rather the result of unwritten rules that the drafters follow. Our findings also suggest that mediated agreements constitute a genre with its own rules, the so-called genre conventions (Bhatia 2004). Interestingly, this is the case despite the fact that the agreements are not public, they do not follow predefined templates and are not outlined in textbooks or books of mediation practice.

7.2   Legal Language

The agreements are typically titled *settlements* instead of agreements. The parties are often referred to as *plaintiff* and *defendant* instead of by their names and their disagreement is often referred to as *the case*. If more persons are responsible for a payment, they are to pay *in solidum*. The parties often *pay their own costs in the proceedings* and the agreements are at times *submitted to the court record*. The agreements are full of these and other legal expressions.

These legal expressions are foreign for many laypersons and constitute a form of coded language that carries meaning for the professionals in the room but not necessarily for the parties. *In solidum*, for example, means each person is responsible for the payment in full and has to pay for the other person, too, if he or she does not honour the payment. And when the parties *pay their own costs in the proceedings* they have to pay for all expenses that they have incurred, such as court filing fees, lawyer fees, expert appraisals, lost earnings etc. The parties may have difficulty subtracting this meaning from the agreements and may, at times, enter into agreements where they do not fully understand the consequences depending on what kind of explanations they get from the mediator and/or their lawyers, if they bring one.

7.3   Bureaucratic Language: "Kancillisprog"

The language of the Danish and Norwegian public administration is influenced by a merger of Danish, Latin and German traditions that evolved in the public administration during the absolute monarchy (1660–1848) (Andersen 2015). This "language" has its own name *kancillisprog* (often translated into English *legalese or officalese*). It is not legal lingo but rather a way of writing that is widespread in all areas of public administration, including the courts in both countries to this day. "*Kancillisprog*" consist of a number of features that in combination makes a text difficult to read and understand: verbal nouns (gerunds), passive voice, "paper words", inversed word order, long words and long sentences. We find all of these features in the agreements.

Firstly, the texts contain many verbal nouns. Verbal nouns are verbs that are made into nouns, for example, pay and treat transformed to payment and treatment. Secondly, the passive voice is prevalent. An amount is paid or a house is put up for sale instead of the active form where a subject pays or puts a house up for sale. Thirdly, words and expressions that are used in written language only, so-called paper words, appear often in the agreements: Parties have to "clarify" instead of find out, "receive" instead of get, and this becomes "the present". A fourth feature is a complicated sentence structure with inverse word order, interposed sentences, and central ideas that are put at the end of a sentence instead of up front. The following is an example:

> As full and final settlement of the case, with the exclusion of a potential rebate for reduced water pressure, Mai and Mons Haugen and MaksiVanngruppen Ldt. pay one for all and all for one, kr. 93.000 – ninety three thousand (approximately euro 10 000). (mediation 66)

The central point of the sentence is that Mai and Mons Haugen together with MaksiVanngruppen Ltd. pay an amount of money, but this point is placed at the end of the sentence instead of in the beginning. Also, there is an interposed sentence "with the exclusion of a potential rebate for reduced water pressure".[15]

The features described combined with long words and long sentences make these agreements difficult to read—at least for a layperson. We measured this quantitatively by running a readability index. We used the LIKS test (Björnsson 1968), which is based on number of words per sentence and the share of words over seven letters. The agreements had on average a LIKS of 53, which puts them in the category of "difficult texts" for the normal adult reader (Hansen 1993).

One might think that the difficult language is used with regard to legal elements of the agreement only, but this is not the case. Also interpersonal utterances and everyday activities are formulated in this stilted language. For example, in a case where the parties agreed that those who did not own land in a particular area could borrow a

---

[15]In Norwegian the verb "pay" is placed before the subjects, Mai and Mons Haugen etc. but this is lost in the translation into English.

key from the landowner in order to access a certain road. This was expressed as follows in the agreement:

> Loan of a key for those without right of using the road according to this agreement must take place after agreement of the landowner. (mediation 3)

7.4 Hidden Subjects

The widespread use of passive voice contributes to a last linguistic feature of our analysis: the hidden subjects. When "an amount is paid" or "a tractor delivered" the agent becomes obscure. This happens in other ways, too. Personal pronouns are very rare and the parties are typically referred to by their names only once, if at all. Instead, they are referred to by their legal status such as plaintiff, defendant, a rights owner or land owner. Also, the recipient of something is often absent in the wording. The parties to the agreements probably know who is doing what, but action and the responsibility is obscured by this wording. According to Jørgensen and Phillips (1999), the passive sentences deprives the "agent responsibility by emphasising the result and ignoring the actions and processes leading to them".

In sum, our linguistic analysis demonstrates how these agreements mimic legal writing. They are written in a professional language that is difficult to understand for others than legal professionals.

8 Discussion

In our study, we have explored the content of mediated agreements, the creativity in the agreements, and, finally, the language in which the agreements are written. In this section, we discuss how the results of the analysis relate to party self-determination. Our linguistic results are contradictory to what we could expect when drawing on mediation theory only. Hence, we discuss in some detail how new-institutional theory might shed some light over these findings.

First of all, we have found an extraordinarily variation of different themes in the content of the agreements. The provisions of each agreement seem to relate specifically to the circumstances of that particular case. This variation in substance can be interpreted as an expression of self-determination. The disputing parties are the ones that know the specific circumstances the best, and it is most likely that they brought the variations to the table rather than any of the other actors present (e.g. the lawyers or mediators). This is also our experience based on observations of court-connected mediation processes (Adrian 2012; Mykland 2011). The variation demonstrates that the parties are probably encouraged to bring items to the discussion, and they are included in designing the content of the outcome. We see that both the substantive elements, procedural elements and safeguarding elements seem to be tailored to the parties dispute. In the substantive elements, for example, we see many elements besides the monetary issues that are at the core of the civil case, such as performance of work exchange of things, divisions of property etc. We also see this in the procedural elements where there is a bulk of practical descriptions regarding how to fulfil the agreement.

Secondly, we find traces of creativity in about 65% of the agreements studied. Hence, it is safe to conclude that many court-connected mediations result in creative agreements. However, we believe that there were more creative potential in the cases. About one-quarter of the agreements studied were highly creative, but the rest of the agreements had a lesser and more marginal degree of creativity. Nevertheless, the creative touch, independent of amount, can be interpreted as a sign of self-determination in the agreements. In order to reach creative solutions, interests and needs have probably been brought to the mediation and, in some cases, also other issues than the legal claims. This is probably based on knowledge that only the parties possess and occurs based on the involvement of the parties in the resolution of their own conflict.

Results from these first two analyses are, therefore, in line with what one could expect from mediated settlements based on mediation theory regarding self-determination. They appear tailored to the case and reflect the involvement of the parties in the outcome of the conflict. The result of our linguistic analysis is different.

The principle of self-determination relates to process and outcome. Our understanding of self-determination includes influencing the way the agreement is formulated and includes being able to read and understand one's own agreement. Our linguistic analysis shows that the latter is hardly the case and one can seriously question whether the parties have influenced the way the agreement is drawn up. The wording of the agreements is so highly judicial and bureaucratic that they are hard to read and understand, at least for laypersons who are not educated within the judicial domain. Also, the agreements exhibit extensive use of standard phases and appear quite scripted in their set-up. This, in combination, suggests that when it comes to formulating agreements, self-determination of the parties' seemingly ends. Rather, the professionals take over and the tailor-made aspects of the agreements seem to stop at the formulation of these.

Court-connected mediation is a curious practice because it happens within the court system—a well-established institution with a well-known practice regarding both the process and the outcome. The judicial practices are institutionalised during literally hundreds of years. When court-connected mediation was introduced in the 1990s in Norway and 2000s in Denmark, an interesting situation arose: legal professionals should offer and carry out a new process, namely court-connected mediation, but do so within the well-established judicial system. They were supposed to act differently and do so based on a new ideology of conflict resolution. The professionals needed new practices to fulfil their new role and scope.

To explain and understand how practices in an organisation develop, the new-institutional theory from organisational theory might be helpful. Since the 1970s this theoretical perspective has been widely used to understand the mechanisms that works in and within organisations (e.g. DiMaggio and Powell 1983; Gooderham et al. 2011; Marano et al. 2017). This perspective explains, among others, how organisations develop practices (Meyer and Rowan 1977), and how they mimic one another to be viewed as legitimate (Di Maggio and Powell 1991). Organisations "borrow" the legitimacy of others by, for instance, using procedures that the others already perform more or less unconsciously without evaluating the efficiency or how suitable they are in the new domain (Meyer and Rowan 1977).

What we find in the mediated agreements are visible (and large) "footprints" of the judicial language including standard phrases that mimic legal documents. The professionals probably draw on well-known practices with regard to this part of the mediation process instead of developing new practices. The use of legal and bureaucratic language may serve other purposes as well. It may lend legitimacy to agreements reached through this rather new and different process. Additionally, it may lend legitimacy to the process itself. Mediation is often referred to as a form of alternative dispute resolution giving associations to alternative medicine and other alternatives that are performed on a questionable basis, at least seen from the perspective of the established. Using bureaucratic and legal language may contribute to portray this alternative as an acceptable practice.

When the judicial footprints becomes too visible in the mediation outcome, it may challenge the parties' self-determination and, of course, also the tailor-made ideal of the agreements. The judicial concepts and phrases are typically not familiar to the parties and they may alienate the parties from their own agreements. When we find many standard phrases across different agreements, it seems unlikely they have been negotiated and decided on by the parties in each case. Rather, it seems as if they have been added to gain value or legitimacy by mimicking other legal genres.

From a mediation as well as a judicial perspective, agreements need to be clear and understandable. In mediation, this is necessary so that the parties can use the agreement to be reminded of their solutions and control that they are fulfilled. In court, this is necessary so that the agreement can be subject to enforcement. The latter is met by judicially written agreements, but not the former.

We question parts of the current practice based on our findings. It seems that the court-connected mediation process enables the parties to be creative and come forward with a great variety of themes to end their conflict. It also seems that agreements are tailored to and by the parties. Nevertheless, the judicial language of the mediated agreements challenge self-determination in court-connected mediation in at least three ways: Firstly, the parties are not the central agents in drafting the agreements. Secondly, they probably do not understand their own agreement in full, and, thirdly, some elements of the agreement are probably added by the professionals (the lawyers and the mediator), without the parties fully understanding the implications.

We argue that there should be more focus on the implications of these practices. The main goal in mediation is to develop robust agreements that are based on the interests and needs of the parties. Our analysis suggest that the agreements are robust with regard to their content, but not with regard to wording. We call for critical reflections on this practice.

References

Adrian L (2012) Mellem retssag og rundbordssamtale – retsmægling i teori og praksis. Jurist- og Økonomforbundets Forlag, København

Adrian L (2016) The role of court-connected mediation and judicial settlement efforts in the preparatory stage. In: Ervo L, Nylund A (eds) Current trends in preparatory proceedings: a comparative study of Nordic and former communist countries. Springer, Cham, pp 209–231

Adrian L, Mykland S (2014) Creativity in court-connected mediation: myth or reality. Negot J 30 (4):421–439

Andersen P (2015) Kancellisprogets fødsel. In: Kjær AL, Adrian L, Cederstrøm CB, Engberg J, Gabrielsen J, Rosenmeier M, Schaumburg-Muller S (eds) Retten i sproget. Jurist- og Økonomforbundets Forlag, København, pp 73–88

Bhatia VK (2004) Worlds of written discourse. Continuum, King's Lynn

Björnsson CS (1968) Läsbarhet. Lärarbiblioteket, 99-0346315-4. Liber, Stockholm

Bush R, Folger J (2005) The promise of mediation. Jossey-Bass, San Francisco

Carnevale PJ (2006) Creativity in the outcomes of conflict. In: Deutsch M, Coleman PT, Marcus EC (eds) The handbook of conflict resolution, 2nd edn. Jossey-Bass, San Francisco, pp 414–435

Charkoudian L, Eisenberg DT, Walter JL (2017) What difference does ADR make? Comparison of ADR and trial outcomes in small claims court. Confl Resolut Q 35(1):7–45

Christie N (1977) Conflicts as property. Br J Criminol 17:1–15

Di Maggio PJ, Powell W (1983) The iron cage revisited: institutional isomorphism and collective rationality in organisational fields. Am Sociol Rev 48:147–160

Eisenberg DT (2015) What we know and need to know about court-annexed dispute resolution. S C Law Rev 67:245–265

Ervasti K (2014) Court-connected mediation in Finland: experiences and visions. In: Ervo L, Nylund A (eds) The future of civil litigation. Springer, Cham, pp 121–135

Fairclough N (1992) Discourse and social change. Polity Press, Cambridge

Fisher R, Ury W, Patton B (1991) Getting to yes: negotiating agreement without giving in, 2nd edn. Houghton Mifflin, Boston

Frankfort-Nachimas C, Nachimas D (1996) Research methods in the social sciences. St. Martin's Press, New York

Friedman G, Himmelstein J (2008) Challenging conflict: mediation through understanding. American Bar Association, Chicago

Gooderham P, Navrbjerg SE, Olsen KM, Steen CR (2011) Arbeidslivsregimer i Danmark og Norge – går de hver sin vei? Tidsskrift for Arbejdsliv 13(3):30–44

Golann D (2002) Is legal mediation a process of repair-or separation? An empirical study, and its implications. Harv Negot Law Rev 7:301–336

Golden-Biddle K, Locke KD (1997) Composing qualitative research. Sage Publications, Thousand Oaks

Hansen E (1993) Ping- og pampersprog. Hans Reitzels Forlag, København

Hansen E (1994) Sprogbrevet DR nr. 90: Undskyldning. http://sproget.dk/raad-og-regler/artikler-mv/sprogbrevet-dr/sprogbrevetdr-nr-90/undskyldning. Accessed 30 June 2017

Jørgensen LØ, Lavesen M (2016) Mediation – ret og rammer, 2.udg. Karnov Group, København

Jørgensen MW, Phillips L (1999) Diskursanalyse – som teori og metode. Roskilde Universitetsforlag, Frederiksberg

Kjelland-Mødre K, Rolland ANH, Steen KS, Gammelgard P, Anker C (2008) Konflikt, Mekling og Rettsmekling. Universitetsforlaget, Oslo

Kjær AL (1997) Thi kendes for ret – om lemmata og eksempler i juridisk fagleksikografi. Hermes J Linguist 18:157–175

Knoff RH (2001) Raskere? Billigere? Vennligere? – Evaluering av prøveordning med rettsmekling. Rapport fra Justisdepartement, Olso

Kopaczyk J (2013) The legal language of Scottish Burghs: standardization and Lexical Bundles 1380–1560. Oxford University Press, Oxford

Kovach KK (2004) Mediation – principles and practice, 3rd edn. Thomson/West, St. Paul

Lawrence A, Nugent J, Scarfone C (2007) The effectiveness of using mediation in selected civil law disputes: a meta-analysis. Canada Department of Justice, Canada

Marano V, Tashman P, Kostova T (2017) Escaping the iron cage: liabilities of origin and CSR reporting of emerging market multinational enterprises. J Int Bus Stud 48(3):386–408

Meyer JW, Rowan B (1977) Institutionalized organizations: formal structure as myth and ceremony. Am J Sociol 83(2):340–363

Mykland S (2011) En studie av mekleratferd i norske rettsmeklinger, (PhD Dissertation). Norges Handelshøyskole, Bergen

Mykland S, Adrian L (2015) Alternative løsninger i juridisk språkdrakt – språklige kjennetegn ved rettsmeklingsavtaler i Norge og Danmark. In: Kjær AL, Adrian L, Cederstrøm CB, Engberg J, Gabrielsen J, Rosenmeier M, Schaumburg-Muller S (eds) Retten i sproget, Samspillet mellem ret og sprog i juridisk praksis. Jurist- og Økonomforbundets Forlag, København, pp 73–88

Mykland S, Adrian L (2017) Rettsmeklingsaftaler – rammer, detaljeringsgrad og innhold. Kart og Plan 77:347–359

Mykland S, Rognes J, Sky PK, Hoddevik CL, Laskemoen LM (2009) En studie av rettsforlik i norske tingretter – om konflikttransformasjon i rettsmeklingsprosessen. Kart og plan 69:236–244

Pel M, Combrink L (2011) Referral to mediation by the Netherlands judiciary. Judiciary Q 30:25–52

Powell WW, DiMaggio PJ (eds) (1991) The new institutionalism in organizational analysis. University of Chicago Press, Chicago

Relis T (2009) Perceptions in litigation and mediation: lawyers, defendants, plaintiffs, and gendered parties. Cambridge University Press, Cambridge

Rett på sak – Lov om tvistløsning n.d.(tvisteloven). NOU 2001:32

Riskin LL (1996) Understanding mediators' orientations, strategies, and techniques: a grid for the perplexed. Harv Negot Law Rev 1:7–51

Roepstorff J, Kyvsgaard B (2005) Forsøg med retsmægling – en evalueringsrapport. Justitsministeriets Forskningsenhed, København

Simon HA (2001) Creativity in the arts and the sciences. Canyon Rev Stand 23:203–220

Tønnesson J (2008) Hva er sakprosa. Universitetsforlaget, Oslo

Vindeløv V (1997) Konflikt, Tvist og Mægling – Konfliktløsning ved Forhandling. Akademisk Forlag, København

Vindeløv V (2012) Reflexive mediation. Djøf Publishing, København

Wall JA, Dunne TC (2012) Mediation research: a current review. Negot J 28(2):217–244

Welsh NA (2001) The thinning vision of self-determination in court-connected mediation: the inevitable price of institutionalization? Harv Negot Law Rev 6:1–96

Wissler RL (2004) The effectiveness of court connected dispute resolution in civil cases. Confl Resolut Q 22(1–2):55–88

Custody Mediation in Norwegian Courts: A Conglomeration of Roles and Processes

Camilla Bernt

Contents

C. Bernt (✉)
Faculty of Law, University of Bergen, Bergen, Norway
e-mail: camilla.Bernt@uib.no

© The Author(s) 2018
A. Nylund et al. (eds.), *Nordic Mediation Research*,
https://doi.org/10.1007/978-3-319-73019-6_7

Abstract In this article, I critically examine the judicial settlement scheme in custody and contact cases in Norway. The scheme is called mediation by the legislator, but it takes place as an integrated part of preparatory hearings in district courts. In most cases, an expert, typically a psychologist, is appointed to assist the judge. The role of these third parties varies but often they co-mediate. However, the expert can also be appointed as a mentor to the parents if they enter into interim settlements. If the case is not settled in the preparatory phase, the expert may provide the court with an evaluation of the quality of care each parent has to offer and the best interests of the children. The judge, on the other hand, is meant to preside over the main hearing should the settlement efforts not succeed and must, therefore, not say or do anything that is liable to impair his or her impartiality. The judge and the expert often use fairly evaluative techniques when promoting settlement. This so-called mediation scheme and the procedural rules and practices connected with it have been criticised, in particular, for the use of a single expert in several roles and for the unpredictable process that ensues from preparatory hearings with multiple purposes. A main concern is that there is an undue settlement pressure. At the end of this article, I propose amendments of regulation and practice.

1   Introduction

It is an undisputed fact that escalated conflict between parents is stressful and potentially harmful for the health and wellbeing of children. Therefore, it is paramount that there are systems in place to ensure that disputes concerning custody and contact are handled in a manner that provides sound and durable arrangements that are in line with the best interests of the children. Disputes need to be handled at an early stage and in a manner that does not escalate the conflict between the parents.

In Norway, all separating spouses and co-habitants with children under the age of 16, and parents intending to instigate legal proceedings concerning custody or contact are required to attend a one-hour mediation session. Additionally, they may be offered up to six hours of voluntary mediation in addition to this (The Children Act section 54).[1] This mediation scheme is further described by Anna Nylund in another article in this volume (Nylund 2018). However, although most parents manage to reach a custody arrangement out of court, a considerable number of custody disputes are brought to court. In 2014 and 2015, cases concerning custody

---

[1]Mediation for separating spouses and cohabitants is prescribed in The Marriage Act of 4 July 1991 no 47 Section 26, cf. Act relating to Children and Parents [The Children Act] of 8 April 1981 no 7 section 51 and the Family Allowance Act of 8 March 2002 no 4 Section 9, fifth paragraph. As regards the requirement for mediation before the commencement of legal proceedings, see The Children Act Sections 51 and 56 second paragraph.

and contact amounted to 16 per cent of all civil disputes in the district courts (The Norwegian Courts Administration 2014, 2015).

In 2004, amendments were made to The Children Act with particular focus on the preparatory stages of the trial in parental disputes concerning custody and contact rights. A main goal was to facilitate settlement, and a specific dispute resolution scheme was introduced where the presiding judge mediates, most often together with a psychologist (The Children Act sections 59 and 61 and Ot. prp. no. 29 2002–2003).

This judicial settlement scheme is much debated. On the one hand, the benefits of amicable settlement compared to a distressing trial are widely recognised. In a trial, the parents inevitably escalate the conflict by emphasising their own qualities as parents, while highlighting the other's shortcomings.

On the other hand, several concerns are raised: Firstly, some are worried that the settlement efforts lead to settlements that are not in the best interests of the children and that settlement is reached in cases that should not be mediated, due to specific concerns regarding substance abuse, physical and psychological abuse, or the mental health or capabilities of one or both parents (Breivik and Mevik 2012; Nylund 2012; Haugli and Nordhelle 2014). Secondly, the structure, regulation, and practice of the judicial settlement scheme is criticised, with particular regard to the fact that the so-called mediation is an integral part of the preparatory hearings of the trial, which are led by the presiding judge.

The use of the term 'mediation' is debatable where the third party is also the presiding judge. In Norway, the term mediation is used for this process in all sources and is also used for judicial settlement efforts, in general, in The Dispute act section 8-2. This use of terminology is not discussed in the preparatory works or official guidelines. From a mediation-theory point of view, is important to distinguish between mediation, where the third party does not have the power to adjudicate, and settlement efforts where the third party will determine the outcome should the parties not reach a full settlement. This lack of distinction between the adjudicator and mediator is one of the reasons why there have been some concerns regarding the settlement efforts in preparatory hearings. The fact that the third party is also the presiding judge may place substantial pressure on the parties to settle in these cases.

This issue is amplified by the fact that the expert who aids the judge in the preparatory hearings—and who is often given an active role as a co-mediator, or sometimes even as the sole mediator—frequently has other roles in the same case. Most importantly, if the case is not settled, the expert may serve as a court appointed expert for the purposes of the main hearing (expert evaluator), providing the court with an expert opinion on the quality of care each parent has to offer and the best interests of the children. It is argued that this combination of roles on part of the judge and the expert places too much pressure on the parties to settle (Nordhelle 2011; Nylund 2011, 2012; Breivik and Mevik 2012).

In terms of terminology, choosing another term than mediation to describe the settlement efforts of the presiding judge and the expert is a two-edged sword. For those who are well versed in dispute resolution terminology and theory, it clarifies the type of dispute resolution process.

On the other hand, using another term other than mediation to describe the process can serve as a wild-card to allow processes and techniques that are at odds with important mediation principles. In my experience, it is sometimes argued by experts or judges that it is appropriate for the experts to evaluate extensively during the judicial settlement efforts because they are *not mediating*.

Although judicial settlement efforts are not mediation in the pure sense, the process bears more resemblances to mediation than adjudication. Both are assisted negotiation processes, and in both processes the decision of whether to settle lies with the parties. In both processes there is typically a lack of the legal safeguards that govern adjudication, such as formal presentation of evidence, the adversarial principle, the right of appeal and so forth. This is particularly the case when the settlement efforts occur at the preparatory stages of the trial, which is the case in custody disputes in Norway. Therefore, when discussing the contents of the dispute resolution process, I find it useful and appropriate to use the term 'mediation', and the judge and expert will sometimes be referred to as 'mediators'. When referring to the institute as such, I will, however, use the term 'judicial settlement efforts' or settlement efforts.

In my PhD thesis I analysed and critically reviewed the legal framework for the role of the mediator in the mediation schemes currently in place in Norwegian courts (Bernt 2011). One of these is the mediation scheme for custody cases. I particularly focused on the judge as a mediator. I have explored the roles of the *expert* further in the extensive article *Sakkyndige i barnelovssaker for domstolene: roller og rettssikkerhet* (Experts in Court Disputes Concerning Custody and Contact Rights: Roles and The Rule of Law) (Bernt 2014). In this article, I will present some of my main points and conclusions regarding the judicial settlement scheme in the two mentioned publications with some updates.

The article combines legal analysis with a critical evaluation of the rules and practices based on a rule of law perspective, and conflict and mediation theory. I have not conducted systematic empirical studies of mediation practices. However, I have obtained experience and increased knowledge of the practices and issues of the mediation scheme through observations of mediations, combined with informal conversations with judges and experts as well as plenary discussions in workshops and working groups where both professions have been represented.

Firstly, the concerns and considerations motivating the amendments to The Children Act in 2004 will be presented (Sect. 2), followed by an overview of the procedural rules for custody cases, with particular focus on those rules affecting the judicial settlement efforts (Sect. 3). Then, the different roles of the expert in such cases will be described (Sect. 4). I will then proceed to take a closer look at the role of the judge and the expert in the settlement efforts in cases concerning custody and contact. I start by discussing why evaluation is so common in such cases (Sect. 5), and some concerns regarding an evaluative mediator role in these cases will be highlighted (Sect. 6), followed by a question raised by some lawyers and psychologists when argued for a facilitative mediator role: What is the point of having judges, psychologists and other experts as mediators if they are not supposed to offer their opinions and advice (Sect. 7)? Secondly, how can a good mediation process that provides durable outcomes that are in the best interests of the children be achieved without evaluation (Sect. 8)? I will then proceed to look at the interaction and cooperation between the judge and the expert in the mediation process and highlight some potentially problematic aspects (Sect. 9). I will conclude on the issue of legislative amendment (Sect. 10).

2 Legislative Considerations: The Main Objectives Behind the Current Regulation

In 2004, a number of amendments to the procedural rules for parental court disputes regarding custody and contact entered into force. The main purpose was to design the court proceedings in a manner that would enable processes and outcomes that would serve the best interests of the children better. The amendments included an increased focus on amicable settlement where appropriate, *inter alia* a duty for the court to consider and, if appropriate, facilitate settlement efforts, and the introduction of a specific dispute resolution scheme in preparatory hearings, called 'mediation'. Furthermore, the Ministry wished to enable an increased and more varied use of experts (such as psychologists) in these cases (Ot. prp. no. 29 2002–2003). Traditionally experts were appointed in certain cases to conduct investigations and provide the court with an evaluation of the quality of care each parent had to offer and the best interests of the children, but such evaluation is costly and often leads to delay (Ot. prp. no. 29 2002–2003). The Ministry proposed that experts should also be assigned other tasks, such as aiding the judge in the preparatory stages of the trial, for instance, in settlement efforts. The purpose of the changes was to achieve good quality and durable settlements where appropriate, and to strive for a quick and effective process in the best interests of the children (Ot. prp. no. 29 2002–2003).

3 Overview of the Procedural Rules for Custody and Contact Cases

After the amendments in 2004, the Children Act section 59 states that the judge must handle the case as efficiently as possible. In the preparatory works it is however emphasised that a quick handling of the case must not hinder the use of more time where needed. For instance, the parents may agree to an interim settlement after the first preparatory hearing, to be renegotiated by the parents in another preparatory hearing, sometimes even followed by another interim settlement, with a subsequent preparatory hearing thereafter. Furthermore, in some cases, there is a need to appoint an expert to conduct investigations of the quality of care each parents have to offer, and the needs of the child (See: The Children Act section 61, first subsection, no. 3) (Ot. prp. no. 29 2002–2003). When the interest of a speedy process is in conflict with the best interests of the children, the best interests of the children must always prevail (Holgersen 2008).

In section 59, subsection 2, the judge is instructed, on every stage of the process to "consider, whether an amicable settlement between the parties is possible, and to facilitate this". This is primarily a duty to *consider* whether amicable settlement is possible, but if this seems to be the case, a duty to *facilitate* settlement follows (Backer 2008). Although it is not stated in section 59, the judge must not only consider the possibility of the parties reaching an amicable settlement, but also whether settlement efforts are appropriate, considering the circumstances of the case and the characteristics of the parties. If one of the parties is unable to take care of his or her interests in such a process, for instance, because of his or her mental capabilities or a history of physical and psychological abuse from the other party, settlement should not be attempted. The same applies where there is a considerable risk that the settlement efforts will result in a settlement that is not in the best interests of the children, for instance, where there is information in the case suggesting considerable concerns regarding the quality of care one of the parents has to offer and which have not yet been investigated.[2] To increase the awareness that amicable settlement is not appropriate in all cases, section 61 no. 1 was amended in 2013, adding that the case must be suitable for 'mediation' (Prop. 85 L 2012–2013 and Act 21 June 2013 no. 62 (in force 1 January 2014)). However, even before this amendment, a restrictive interpretation of section 59 subsection two was necessitated by the fundamental rights of access to justice and fair trial and the overriding principle of the best interests of the children (The Children Act section 48, c.f. the Dispute Act 17 June 2005 no. 90 section 1-1, The European Convention of Human Rights article 6 no. 1 and The International Covenant on Civil and Political Rights article 14 no. 1).

In The Children Act 61, procedural rules for custody and contact cases are given, supplementing the general rules of procedure in the Courts of Justice Act and the Dispute Act. Section 61 no. 1 states that the court, as a main rule, shall summon the parties to one or several preparatory hearings to, among other things, clarify the issues of dispute between the parties, discuss the further handling of the case, and possibly mediate. Furthermore, different possible tasks for court appointed experts are described: The court may appoint an expert to partake in the preparatory hearings, and may also ask the expert to talk to the parents and/or the children before or in-between preparatory hearings, as well as conduct certain investigations to clarify the facts of the case, unless the parents object to it. The parties must be consulted on which tasks should be assigned to the expert.

No. 3 states that, when needed, the court should appoint an expert to conduct a traditional *evaluation* on one or several of the issues of the case. The expert's report will be, in most cases, given considerable weight as evidence and will typically be

---

[2]This does not mean that mediation or similar processes cannot be used in cases where there are concerns regarding the quality of care one of the parents has to offer. The point is that settlement must not be reached where the parents do not take these concerns seriously or where there is such power imbalance between the parties that the parent whose quality of care is questioned may become the custodial parent.

the most important piece of evidence in the case (The Ministry of Children and Equality 2015; Koch 2000).

Such reports may be prepared and presented prior to a preparatory hearing and used as a basis for settlement efforts in the case—or for deciding that such a process will not be appropriate. However, to my knowledge, investigations pursuant to section 61 no. 3 at such an early stage are rare, since they are time consuming and very costly. Unless settlement is considered out of the question or unsuitable, or there is considerable doubt about the suitability of settlement, investigations pursuant to section 61 no. 3 will typically not be conducted before the settlement avenue has been explored. Instead, more limited and less formal investigations will sometimes be conducted, pursuant to section 61 no. 1.

Section 61 no. 4 states that the court may talk to (hear) the children, c.f. The Children Act section 31, and may appoint an expert or another suitable person to assist, or to complete this task alone. In practice, it varies how this is done. Some judges prefer to delegate the hearing of the children to the court appointed expert, cf. 61 nos. 1 and 3. Others prefer to talk to the children together with the expert. Some judges talk to the children alone. The new national guidelines for custody cases have no recommendations or discussion about the different alternatives (The Norwegian Courts' Administration 2016).

The option of entering into interim settlements is a core element of the current procedure in custody and contact cases. The Children Act section 61 no. 7 states that the court may give the parties the opportunity to enter into interim settlements for a set period of time. The court may appoint an expert or another suitable person to serve as a mentor to the parties in the interim period.

The purpose of this option is to enable amicable settlements in cases with a high level of conflict and insecurity on part of the parents as to how the arrangement will work. It is based on the assumption that agreeing to an interim settlement will be considered less drastic by the parents than a traditional settlement, which makes settlement more likely. Furthermore, a trial period may be useful to evaluate what arrangement works best for children and parents.

The option of interim settlements was tested during pilot schemes in some courts, with good results. The option of having a mentor is seen as an incentive to reach interim settlements, and may improve the likelihood of a permanent settlement (NOU 1998: 17 with endorsement in Ot. prp. no. 29 2002–2003). A party is not bound by the agreed trial period and may, at any time, demand that the interim settlement ceases, with the consequence that the court proceedings continue towards a main hearing (Backer 2008; Ot. prp. no. 29 2002–2003).

As mentioned, the attempts to facilitate amicable settlement take place as an integrated part of the preparatory hearings of the trial, which are led by the presiding judge. It is stated in the preparatory works that as a main rule, the judge should conduct settlement efforts in a manner that is not liable to impair his or her impartiality as a presiding judge. Thus, the judge who facilitates settlement is, as a main rule, supposed to adjudicate the dispute in case of none or only partial settlement (Ot. prp. no. 29 2002–2003). It is emphasised that the issue of the judge's impartiality must be determined in each case and that in some cases the judge may have to recuse himself or herself from the case after the settlement efforts (Ot. prp. no. 29 2002–2003).

The question of whether the role of 'mediator' and/or mentor can or should be combined with the role of expert evaluator pursuant to The Children Act section 61 no. 3 is debated. The Dispute Act section 25-3, subsection three states that the same rules of impartiality and recusal apply for experts as for judges. However, it is debated whether the roles of 'mediator' and mentor constitute—or should constitute—grounds for recusal as such. Some courts and judges normally use the same expert in all roles, some determine this on a case-by-case basis, with regard to whether one or both parties have raised the issue of appointing a new expert, and some always change experts. Some experts say that they find the combination of roles problematic, and some even have a conveniently fully booked schedule when the court asks them to do the expert evaluation.

The issue of whether there should be a new presiding judge for the purposes of the main hearing is also debated. Some judges preside over the main hearing as a main rule, unless there are special circumstances that require a new judge, others recuse themselves in some cases, whereas others do so in every case they have mediated in. There has been a shift in opinions, where an increasing number of judges believe that another judge should preside over the main hearing (The Norwegian Courts' Administration 2016).

The question of whether to change judges, of course, also depends on the process. If the judge has taken part in caucuses (separate meetings) with the parties, he or she cannot preside over the main hearing (The Dispute Act section 8-2 (1) and The Children Act section 59). If the judge has proposed settlements, given the parties advice or in other ways voiced opinions that are liable to impair his or her impartiality, he or she must also recuse himself or herself (The Dispute Act section 8-2 (1)). Another issue to consider is the nature of the communication between the expert and the judge out of the earshot of the parties in course of the process. This will be described and discussed further towards the end of the article (Sect. 9).

The threshold for proposals, other statements and conduct that are grounds for recusal are, however, not very clear (The Norwegian Courts' Administration 2016). There are no precedents on this threshold in custody and contact cases. In practice this issue seems to be viewed as more than a pure legal matter: The matter of trust—or lack thereof—in the judge from one or both parties is an important factor, even where the conduct and statements of the mediating judge may not constitute grounds for recusal. An important concern is that a lack of trust in the judge may lead to a loss of trust in the process as such, perhaps leading to a higher likelihood of a new court dispute in the future (Ot. prp. no. 29 2002–2003; Norwegian Courts' Administration 2016).

4   The Different Roles of the Expert in Custody and Contact Cases: An Overview

4.1   Which Qualifications Are Required for Experts?

As described above, (Sect. 3) The Children Act section 61 defines at least three main roles for the expert: *mediator*, *mentor* and *expert evaluator*. These roles are fundamentally different. Before an overview of the different roles can be given, it is necessary to know what qualifications are required for an expert in custody and contact cases.

The nature of the tasks assigned to the experts in custody and contact cases entails that the person appointed typically needs to have mediation skills as well as sound knowledge of the psychological issues relevant to such cases. Depending on which role(s) the expert is given in a case, he or she must have sound understanding of the particular issues and challenges of the relationship between parents and their children, as well as the needs of children and developmental psychology. Consequently, psychologists are often seen as suitable and are frequently used. However, other professions may serve as experts as well, for instance, social workers or child welfare officers. There is no legislation specifying which qualifications are required, and this is a deliberate choice by the legislator. In the preparatory works the Ministry of Children and Equality stated that the different roles of the experts call for using experts with different professions and fields of expertise. Furthermore, the supply of experts is better when required qualifications are not defined by law (Ot. prp. no. 29 2002–2003). The issue of the limited supply of experts is a recurring theme when different aspects of regulation of the use of experts are debated.

4.2   The Role of Expert Evaluator

The Dispute Act section 25-1 defines expert evidence as "an expert assessment of factual issues in the case". Traditional expert evaluations typically include talking to parents and children, home visits, and, depending on the case and terms of reference, other investigations such as talking to teachers, health care professionals and sometimes friends or family, as well as studying relevant documentation. The purpose is to contribute to the factual base for the court's decision, in other words, to serve as evidence. The expert gives his or her opinion on the questions raised by the court to him or her in the terms of reference (The Dispute Act section 25-4), based on the findings of his or her investigations. The report and oral testimony of the expert is called "expert evidence".

4.3 The Mentor Role

The role of *mentor* in an interim settlement period (The Children Act section 61 no. 7) has some similarities to the role as expert evaluator in the sense that the expert is meant to use his or her expertise to guide the parents. However, there is a fundamental difference between contributing to the factual base of the court's decision—evidence—and being a mentor. A mentor is meant to help the parents cooperate, and the parent's´ view of the mentor as a helper may affect what information they share with him or her, and their general conduct. It can be assumed that if a parent considers the expert as a mentor and does not consider the possibility that he or she might have the role of expert evaluator at a later stage, the parent may communicate more uncensored and less guarded than he or she would with the knowledge—or fear—that what is said or done may be used against him or her at a later stage.

4.4 The Mediator Role

4.4.1 Definition and Distinguishing Characteristics

The role of *mediator* is in principle fundamentally different than the roles of expert evaluator and mentor. A simple definition is that mediation is a dispute resolution process where two or more parties attempt to solve a conflict with the help of a third party. The third party does not have the power to determine the outcome of the dispute but help with the process, where *the parties themselves* identify issues of dispute, develop and consider different possible solutions and attempt to reach an amicable settlement. This definition is very inclusive and does not address the contentious issues of a *facilitative* versus *evaluative* mediator role. In the settlement efforts of judges and experts in custody and contact cases in Norway, evaluation seems to be rather common (See: for instance, Breivik and Mevik 2012).

4.4.2 Evaluation from Judges and Experts in Judicial Settlement Efforts

The issue of an *evaluative* versus *facilitative* mediator role is typically discussed with a focus on statements about legal issues made by judges or other jurists in the role of mediator. In custody court disputes, where the judge and the expert mediate, evaluation includes psychological as well as legal matters. The best interests of the children is an overarching principle in these cases, which means that psychological knowledge plays a very important part in the legal reasoning.

Evaluative statements on legal matters may vary in scope and strength. The most extreme form of evaluation is to give a prognosis on the probable outcome should the dispute be adjudicated. For example: "It is unlikely that you will get custody of the children, should the case be adjudicated." A milder variety of evaluation is when the mediator gives an opinion on a particular issue, for instance, on whether a certain rule is applicable or whether there is sufficient evidence to support a particular assertion, for instance: "I have not seen any evidence so far suggesting that William is upset after his overnight visits with his father." The mildest variety of evaluation on legal matters is to express what may be deduced from a particular source of law. For example, a precedent a party has quoted to support his or her case. "I am not convinced that this precedent is applicable here. The child in question was two years old and had mild autism, whereas your son is four and has no cognitive issues." The strength of evaluative statements also varies with regard to whether or not the mediator has given the statement with reservations or expressed uncertainty. For instance, the mediator may express qualifications regarding the extent of his or her knowledge on the legal issues in question or underline that formal presentation of evidence has not yet taken place.

Other forms of evaluation are presenting settlement proposals or evaluating the parties' proposals. In some cases, the mediator's suggestions and evaluations of the parties' proposals are expressions of the mediator's view of the legal and evidentiary matters of the case, but this is not always the case. Settlement proposals or evaluation of the parties' settlement proposals are sometimes primarily based on what the mediator sees as realistic, given the positions of the parties, or what seems to meet the interests and needs of the parties.

It is important to consider that in custody and contact cases it is likely to be more common than in most other types of civil disputes that settlement proposals and the evaluation of such are in accordance with the mediator's view of the legal and evidentiary matters of the case. The reason for this is that the court has a duty to safeguard the best interests of the children, both in terms of process and outcomes (The Children Act section 48). The child is not a party in the court dispute nor is the child a party in mediation, which means that the court must ensure that the child's interests and needs are not overlooked. Evaluative statements regarding settlement options are affected by this concern.

For *experts*, probably the most prevalent type of evaluation is statements about the needs of the children and the quality of care each of the parents have to offer, and evaluation of settlement proposals in light of these factors. There are different varieties of evaluation, similar to those varieties of evaluation of legal matters presented. The strongest form of evaluation would be to state what custody and contact arrangement he or she believes is the most optimal for the child. This is close to being a prognosis of the outcome should the case be adjudicated, since expert evaluations are such an important piece of evidence.

Regardless of the actual evidentiary impact of the expert evaluation in a case, the parties are likely to consider such evaluation in mediation from an expert as a prognosis on the probable outcome in adjudication. A more careful variety of evaluation is to express some doubts concerning a proposal that has been presented, but without divulging what custody and contact arrangement *would* be in the best interests of the children. On the lower end of the evaluative spectrum is expressing points of view on particular elements of the custody or contact arrangements proposed by a party, but which cannot be seen as support or rejection of the arrangement as such. An example of such evaluation may be expressing points of view based on experiences from other cases regarding routines and logistical arrangements for contact.

As described above, evaluation from experts and judges alike may be interpreted as a hint—or more—as to how the case would be viewed in a judgement. Evaluation may therefore affect the mediation and settlement significantly and, in some circumstances, may also entail considerable pressure to settle. This issue will be revisited later in the article.

4.4.3 A Facilitative Role in Judicial Settlement Efforts in Custody Disputes?

Since a purely *facilitative* mediator does not express such views as described above, some experts and judges express concern that a facilitative mediator role is merely the role of a moderator and not suitable for custody and contact cases, where the best interests of the children must be safeguarded. This is, in my opinion, a grave underestimation of the potential of a facilitative mediation process. Skilled facilitative mediators enable the parties to critically evaluate their own assumptions, points of view and settlement options, simply by asking good questions that require reflection and well-reasoned replies. Instead of stating opinions, the mediator facilitates the parties' reflections and enables them to draw the conclusions themselves.

The mediator can pose reflexive questions that require that the party assess his or her own points of view. For example, if a mother is determined that the father must have only limited contact with the children due to animosity between the children and the father, the mediator may ask the mother to reflect on what would happen if she became ill and had to be hospitalized for a long period of time (Example inspired by Tomm 1987). Such questions are a facilitative mediation technique, as long as the form of question rather than statement is not merely a matter of rhetoric. Leading questions may cross the line from facilitation to evaluation.

It is an important part of every mediator's role to enable the parties to evaluate their own and the other party's positions and points of view in light of the information that is given in the mediation. The mediator should, through asking questions, help the parties identify the interests and needs behind their positions, and possible and probable consequences of different outcomes. A mediator who does not ask questions that enable the parties to reflect and critically evaluate their own assumptions and positions is scarcely more than a microphone boom in the negotiations of the parties. In family cases, where the best interests of the children should be the main focus, it is normally essential that the mediators take an active role, since the conflict has been brought to court because of the parties' inability to settle out of court. However, as described above, being an active mediator does not in itself require evaluation. In (Sects. 7 and 8) the conditions, tools and possibilities of a facilitative mediator role in custody cases will be explored.

5 Why Is Evaluation so Common in the Judicial Settlement Efforts of Custody and Contact Cases?

One important contributing factor to the widespread use of an evaluative approach in judicial settlement efforts is the use of experts that are appointed not merely as mediators, but combining mediation with expert evaluations and the role of mentor. The lines between the different roles may become blurred.

When parents meet in court in need of a solution to their conflict, they meet two experts: The judge—with legal training, expertise and experience—and the expert—who most commonly is a psychologist. As mentioned, the two often conduct settlement efforts as a team. Parents, who for the most part have little experience with mediation, judicial settlement efforts and adjudication, may expect that the judge and the expert will give advice and in other ways state their opinions. Furthermore, many will expect the judge or the expert to tell the *other party* why he or she is in the wrong. This is a wish that is probably shared by many lawyers: They have failed to convince the other party of the errors of his or her ways in negotiations, and now they hope for the court's help.

Judges, psychologists and other experts typically do not primarily identify themselves as mediators. Given the expectations of the parties and the professional identities of the judges and the experts, it is not surprising that the settlement efforts can be fairly evaluative (Similar points of view are expressed by Nylund 2011).

Furthermore, judges and experts focus on ensuring that both process and outcomes are in the best interests of the children (The Children Act section 48). In my experience, evaluation is seen by many judges and experts as the most effective means to ensure this fundamental principle.

This is, however an underestimation of the potential of mediation as a conflict resolution method. Widespread use of evaluation also threatens the uniqueness of mediation and judicial settlement efforts as alternatives to adjudication.

Furthermore, it underestimates the importance of a fair and thorough process in accordance with the rule of law to ensure that the result is in the best interests of the children. As will be discussed in Sect. 6 below, evaluative mediator behaviour in a dispute resolution process, which is so closely connected to the adjudicative proceedings as the judicial settlement scheme, may be problematic in a rule of law perspective. It may put undue pressure on the parties to settle and may blur the line between mediation and adjudication in the eyes of the parties. Breivik and Mevik (2012) have examples of informants being pressured through evaluation. (For critical views of evaluation in mediation, see Kovach and Love 1998; Kjelland-Mørdre et al. 2008; Nylund 2012; Vindeløv 2007a, b, 2013).

6   Concerns Regarding an Evaluative Mediator Role in Contact and Custody Cases

For mediation that is integrated in the court proceedings, i.e. judicial settlement efforts, an evaluative mediator role raises particular concerns. Firstly, it may be in conflict with procedural safeguards—the principles of fair trial. In adjudication there are a number of procedural safeguards and rules to ensure that there is a sound basis for the court's decision. The purpose is to achieve the right outcome. For custody cases the procedural safeguards should then essentially ensure an outcome in line with the best interests of the children.

Since the outcome of judicial settlement efforts and mediation is decided by the parties themselves, the process is not subject to the same principles and rules as a trial and judgement. When settlement efforts take place at an early stage of a custody dispute, there has been no formal presentation of evidence.

If the expert gives evaluative statements in the role of mediator, such statements may be based on information and observations that have not been submitted to the court and parties in the form of a report the parties have been given the opportunity to critically examine. For this reason, it may be difficult for the parents to assess the soundness and weight of the expert's statements. This poses a risk that the parents accept arrangements that they neither view as right nor good, because of what the expert has said with the judge present. They fear that the judge and the expert have already made up their minds, meaning that they will lose if the case were to be adjudicated (Breivik and Mevik 2012).

If parties feel pressured to enter into certain settlements because there have been statements that reveal that the expert and/or the judge have already made up their minds, this may constitute a breach of the right to access to court and a fair trial before an impartial court of law (The Dispute Act section 1-1 and the ECHR article 6 no. 1). In Deweer vs. Belgium (Series A No. 35) ECJ established that pressure, which causes a party to settle rather than utilising his or her right to adjudication, may constitute an infringement of the ECHR art. 6 no.1 (NOU 2001: 32 and Møse 1999).

However, as mentioned, it is nevertheless not unusual for the expert who has mediated to be appointed as expert evaluator, c.f. section 61 no. 3. And even if there is a different expert in the latter role or if no traditional evaluation pursuant to section 61 no. 3 is done, the parties may fear that the judge is influenced by the views expressed by the expert who aided the court pursuant to section 61 no. 1.

Another issue with evaluative statements is that the settlement efforts take place as an integrated part of the court proceedings and that evaluation then may blur the line between settlement and adjudication for some parties. A survey done by *Katrin Koch* revealed that some parties were uncertain whether the expert had been appointed to conduct an expert evaluation pursuant to section 61 no. 3 or not, and some were uncertain whether the outcome of their case was a settlement or a judgement (Koch 2008).

Some might argue—and this is an actual point made by an expert when I mentioned Koch's findings—that some parents do not have the cognitive capacity to understand the difference between a settlement and a judgement, and that Koch's findings might stem from such cases. However, if the judge and expert find themselves unable to explain the difference between a judgement and a settlement to a party, it is clearly not in accordance the principle of fair trial, and also a breach of judicial ethics to mediate the case. It is an absolute requirement for mediation that both parties are mentally capable to understand what mediation is and that entering into a settlement is voluntary.

When an expert or judge takes an evaluative role in their settlement efforts, this also raises other concerns. It is a fundamental principle of adjudication that judgements should have reasons (The Dispute Act section 1-1). The written reasons guarantee clarity and certainty about the court's reasoning and also helps ensure that the conclusions are sound. If parties settle based on oral statements from the expert or the judge, there is no documentation on what has been said.

An in-court settlement cannot be appealed. Consequently, the only option for a parent that regrets the settlement and believes that it is based on wrong premises, but is unable to convince the other party to enter into a new custody and contact arrangement, is to file another lawsuit (The Children Act section 64).

Summing up, the judicial settlement process lacks some fundamental legal safeguards that are in place in adjudication, in other words, the formal presentation of *evidence, the adversarial principle, reasoned judgements, and the right of appeal.* These principles are not in place in mediation or judicial settlement efforts because settlements are based on party autonomy. If the judge or the expert expresses points of view or prognoses, and thus affects the settlement of the parties, elements from adjudication are introduced to the process of judicial settlement efforts, without the legal safeguards in place for adjudication.

Evaluation is particularly problematic when it indicates that the judge and the expert have already decided what the outcome of the dispute should be. In such instances, the judge and the expert must be recused from the further handling of the case.[3]

However, statements that will not constitute grounds for recusal—for example, because of reservations made or because they only relate to single issues—may also be problematic. Such statements are probably common in custody cases,

---

[3]The threshold for recusal for Norwegian judges has developed significantly the last 20 to 25 years. A statement from the Supreme Court judgment in Rt. 2008 p. 1466 is describes the current norm: *[my translation]* "the decisive factor is how it all appears – from the point of view of the accused and the observing member of the general public. If there are, from an objective point of view, sound reasons to question the judge's impartiality, the judge shall not partake in adjudication." It is then stated that "the issue of impartiality based on the judge's prior dealings with the case, go further, and altogether includes the judge [. . .] expressing himself or herself in a manner that is liable to impair the confidence in the ability of the judge to meet the case, the defendant or the evidence with such an open mind as presupposed by our procedural rules – including ECHR article 6 no. 1 and the Courts of Justice Act section 108".

particularly in light of the roles of the experts in these cases. There is no doubt that even such statements have the purpose of affecting the parents' willingness to settle and the terms of such a settlement, and that they may have a fundamental impact on the terms of the settlement. Therefore, they are problematic in a rule of law perspective, because of the lack of some of the fundamental legal safeguards of adjudication.

When arguing that evaluation may lead to an improper pressure to settle, I have been met on several occasions with statements that settlement in custody disputes in many cases is in the best interests of the children. I have been asked whether it is my opinion that the procedural rights of the parties should prevail at the cost of the best interests of the children.

Ultimately, this line of reasoning entails that concerns regarding the lack of procedural safeguards and the rule of law must recede when a judge or expert believes that a settlement should be reached. In my opinion, this is a grave fallacy. Procedural safeguards and the rule of law are first and foremost in place to lay the foundation for reaching the right decision in a case—the decision that the correct application of the law on the facts of the case entails. If parents feel pressured to reaching a settlement that they believe not to be in the best interests of the children, the reason for this may be an unrealistic view of their own parental capabilities or a lack of understanding of the child's needs. However, as long as the main hearing has not taken place, with thorough presentation of evidence, there is no basis to justify settlement pressure in the form of evaluative statements with the assertion that this would be in the best interests of the children. A similar point of view is expressed by Nordhelle (2011):

> In the fervour to resolve custody disputes in a simple and flexible manner, it seems as the rule of law has been lost in some cases – and the major losing party is the children. [My translation].

Summing up, neither judicial settlement efforts at the preparatory stages of the trial nor the mediation process is designed to present evidence and law in a manner that enables a third party to make informed evaluations. This is especially acute in custody and contact cases, which involve complex decisions that affect the future life and welfare of a child.

It has been argued by several authors from different disciplines that the conclusions to be drawn from an expert evaluation must not be overestimated and that other evidence must be presented to lay a sound foundation for the court's decision (Lundeberg 2009; Nordhelle 2010, 2011; Haugli og Nordhelle 2014; Schøitz 2006). This makes a strong point for exercising considerable caution and restraint with evaluative statements and refraining from exerting settlement pressure in mediation in preparatory hearings. In addition to the risk of a settlement entailing a custody and contact arrangement that is not in the best interests of the children, a settlement reached as a result of pressure from the mediator(s) may be problematic and counter-productive for another important reason as well. There is reason to believe that when a parent is dissatisfied with the way a settlement has been reached, the settlement may be less durable than it would have been if the parents perceived the process as sound and just. This is underlined by the Ministry of Children And Equality in the guidelines for the handling of custody and contact cases (Veileder Q-15/2004, see also Nylund 2011; Breivik and Mevik 2012).

It is common knowledge that persons who feel wronged by the legal system can become repeat litigators, because they feel the need to correct the injustice they believe they have suffered. In other words, if a parent has accepted a settlement that is significantly different than he or she envisioned at the outset of the trial, it is crucial for the robustness of the settlement that the process has been good. In a best-case scenario, the process has caused the party to change his or her mind. A more probable scenario is that the party has concluded that the settlement, in spite of his or her position, is a result he or she is willing to live with, based on his or her own and the legal counsel's assessment of the process risks and the strains and costs of a continued legal dispute. In the opposite scenario, the settlement is the result of mediator pressure, without such careful considerations as described above. It can then be said that the party has formally accepted the settlement without really accepting it (Nylund 2011).

There is sound empirical basis for the assertion that satisfaction with the process has significant impact on how a party assesses the outcome (Adrian 2013). Furthermore, it is stated in the preparatory works of The Children Act that the parties should not be pressurized to settle, and that the settlement should be experienced as a result of the parents' own choice (Nylund 2011 with references to Ot. prp. no. 29 2002–2003 and NOU 1998: 17).

If the parties are aware that the mediators may preside over the main hearing or conduct the expert evaluation pursuant to section 61 no. 3 should the case not be settled, this may in itself affect the mediation process negatively. It may cause the parents to act strategically when communicating with the judge and the expert during the mediation process, rather than contributing to a productive mediation process with open communication, in the best interests of the children (Nylund 2011). The risk that parties may act strategically rather than contributing to a constructive mediation process was an important reason for the main rule for court-connected mediation that a judge who has mediated should not preside over the main hearing (The Dispute Act s. 8-7 (2)) (NOU 2001: 32).

In my view, there is no doubt that the level of awareness and critical reflection among the population of judges, experts and lawyers on the role of the mediators in custody disputes must be increased. This requires more extensive mediation training than currently in place (See also Nordhelle 2011; Breivik and Mevik 2012; Haugli and Nordhelle 2014). The judges and experts must also be thorough in their communication to the parties of what judicial settlement efforts entail and of their respective roles in this process.

7 What Is the Point of Judge and Expert Mediators Who Do Not Evaluate?

When confronted with critical views on evaluation in mediation, some argue that it seems pointless to use judges and experts, such as psychologists as mediators, if they are not supposed to evaluate. I will address this issue in the next few paragraphs.

In my opinion, there is no doubt that the expertise of judges and experts is an important factor in mediation and judicial settlement efforts even where a strictly facilitative mediator role is observed. In the role of mediator the ability to listen and ask good questions that capture the issues that are important to the parties and thereby enabling better communication is essential. In order to ask good questions, it is very useful to have sound knowledge and understanding of the legal, psychological as well as practical and financial issues custody and contact arrangements give rise to.

The judge's legal professional expertise and experience can help him or her determine what might be relevant and important to focus on when structuring the process through questions etc., helping the parents to have a sound basis for their negotiations and enabling them to critically evaluate the strength and weaknesses of their own positions and assertions.

The expert has sound knowledge about the important factors for a child's wellbeing and development and also about common feelings and reactions connected to the breakup of relationships and custody disputes. The judge and expert can use their professional knowledge and experience to ask the right questions and fashion the process to the needs of the parties, thereby achieving a better and more reflective dialogue with the parties, and first and foremost *between* the parties.

Furthermore, the expert and the judge may use their expertise to give *general information* that the parties may, in turn, use to assess their own situation, the case and different settlement options. General information in this sense may include descriptions of relevant statutes and other sources of law without expressing points of view regarding how they may or may not be applied to the facts of this particular case. Experts may, in general terms, describe what factors must be taken into account when determining what types of arrangements are workable for children of different ages (Similar Nordhelle 2007). An example, which is adapted from a statement made by an expert in the courtroom at a preparatory hearing, could be:

> When determining which custody and contact arrangements will work for a child, the age of the child must be considered. For smaller children up to the ages of two to three, if is often important that the timespan *between* contact with each of the parents is not too long, but the timespan of each visit does not necessarily have to be very long. For older children, duration and continuity is generally more important. For smaller children, it may in some cases be wise to have mid-week contact without the child sleeping over, to keep the frequency of contact at a sufficiently high level.

It must, however, be underlined that in some cases it may be debatable whether what is said could be considered general information without evaluation. Some psychological and legal issues are debated. Nevertheless, there is undoubtedly some legal and psychological information that can be given by judges and experts without entailing a problematic evaluative mediator role. It is, however, crucial that judges and experts alike are conscious about the nature of the information they share and do not inadvertently present their own opinions under the guise of general information. It is also crucial that they make it absolutely clear for the parties that the information given is of a general nature and that it does not include the application of this information to the particular circumstances of the case at hand.

In the Ministry of Children and Equality's guide for the handling of custody cases, it is clear that the ability to ask good questions and to give general information is considered the most important tasks of the expert in the preparatory hearings (Veileder Q-15/2004).

8 How Do We Achieve Mediation That Provides Good Quality Outcomes Without Evaluation?

8.1 The Power of Feeling Heard, Understood and Empowered

In my opinion the most important asset of mediation compared to adjudication in cases concerning custody and contact is the opportunity to facilitate better communication between the parties and, thereby, de-escalate the conflict. This, in turn, lays the foundation for amicable settlement with arrangements that are more robust than those forced on the parties through adjudication. There is little doubt that reduced conflict and more robust arrangements often will be in the best interests of the children. Prolonged disputes between parents may cause health issues and social problems for the children (see e.g. Rød et al. 2008; Paradis et al. 2009).

In order to utilise this potential of the mediation process, it is essential that the parties feel ownership of the solutions, as opposed to feeling pressured by the mediators, see section 6 above in this article. This means that the mediation process should focus on enabling the parties to reach a mutually acceptable agreement that is in the best interests of the children.

I therefore firmly believe that mediators should prioritise spending time on breaking through the barrier of the parents' positions and enabling them to speak openly about their interests and needs. Especially, there should be a good dialogue concerning the needs of the children. In a good mediation process each of the parents should be enabled to tell his or her side of the story without interruptions from the other parent, and this may be the first opportunity they have to do so.

In the preparatory hearings of custody cases, there is a lot going on besides settlement efforts, and, as a consequence, basic and well-known mediation techniques are perhaps not utilised to their full potential: The mediators can help each of the parents to feel heard and understood by *summing up* what has been said. Such summing up from the neutral may make it easier for each of the parents to hear the message delivered than when presented by the other parent. Mediators may also improve communication by *rephrasing* provocative statements phrased as personal attacks on the other party, to more concrete statements that address the actual problem, and thereby *reframes* the issues to be dealt with in the mediation (See for instance Vindeløv 2007a, b; Moore 2003). An example could be:

> *Father*: "She is incredibly irresponsible!" *Mediator*: "Could you elaborate on that with an example?" *Father:* "A few weeks ago our eight year old son came home from his mother's and told me that he had been to the emergency room after a rough tackling at soccer practice a few days ago! I have to be told these things immediately! It is so typical of her!" *Mediator*: "So you feel that mother does not always give you important information about the children?"

This simple example shows that the mediator can change the focus from a general characteristic of the mother as an irresponsible person to the actual problem: That the mother has not given the father essential information about the health and wellbeing of one of the children. While inflammatory general characteristic hardly sets the foundation for constructive dialogue between the parties, problems with the information exchange between the parents is a concrete issue that can be somewhat easier to address.

Another important approach in custody mediation is for the mediator to show each of the parties' *empathy*. This may show both parents that it is entirely possible to have an understanding of how the other party views and experiences the situation without having to agree with the other party (Vindeløv 2007a, b). Parents who are not able to agree on custody and contact arrangements for their children out of court may feel that they are perceived as problematic people and even bad parents, which may lead to defensive behaviour. Empathy may help.

In custody cases, it is sometimes difficult for parties to separate the feelings of hurt and betrayal from the breakup from the issues at hand, which is a settlement arrangement in the best interests of the children. Some mediators try to steer the parties away from expressing feelings and discussing issues concerning the breakup and might even explicitly instruct the parents to focus on the children rather than their own hurt feelings. However, this may be counterproductive, since parents may not be cognitively capable to negotiate constructively without having been able to vent and be met with empathy—at least from the mediator. On the other hand, there are limits to the resources that can reasonably be used for handling a dispute within a court setting. The parents may need a break from settlement efforts to work on the hurt from the break-up in therapy (Nordhelle 2016). By spending time on the parties' stories and dialogue, important information about facts, feelings, interests and needs come to the surface, and the parties feel heard and understood. This may make the parties more ready to talk constructively and openly about possible solutions than trying to convince them through evaluative statements.

8.2   Scope and Need for Evaluation?

It can be argued that under some circumstances the judge or expert can or should evaluate to some extent in course of the mediation. The mediation concerns the wellbeing of the children, and the children are not parties to the custody dispute.

There may be a need for some evaluation to lower obviously unrealistic expectations or unfounded perceptions of one or both parents, or to prevent them from settling on terms that are clearly contrary to the best interests of the children. The court's responsibility to ensure that both the process and the outcome safeguard the best interests of the children may under certain circumstances entail that the judge or expert expresses some points of view or assessments.

The fundamental issue is, however, that in light of the problematic aspects of an evaluative mediation process, the mediator should, as an overriding main rule, stay within the boundaries of a purely facilitative role. If evaluative techniques are to be used at all, this should be the result of careful consideration and only when the mediator considers that the settlement process cannot proceed in a manner that would be in the best interests of the children without some evaluation.

If evaluation occurs regularly, the process will fail to achieve its potential, and there is a risk that the judicial settlement institute resembles a form of simplified non-binding arbitration (Nylund 2011). This does not serve the best interests of children, because the level of conflict between parents will typically not be reduced significantly and the settlements may be less durable.

Furthermore, evaluation may lead to the parties positioning themselves, rather than communicating openly. Problems, interests and settlement options may remain under the surface, and important factors to determine the best interests of the children may be concealed (Nylund 2011).

If the parties are unable to reach an agreement in mediation without being subjected to considerable evaluation from the judge or expert, the court should abandon the settlement efforts and handle the case through means of adjudication with a main hearing and subsequent judgment. It is crucial that there is a clear line between settlement and judgment, section 6 above in this article.

The court must be conscious of the difficulty for some parties to understand the difference between a settlement and a judgment, and not least between evaluative statements from the expert in the role of mediator/helper/mentor (The Children Act section 61) and as part of an expert evaluation for the purposes of the main hearing (section 61. no 3). This difficulty is quite understandable considering the fact that the judicial settlement efforts take place in a court room, as part of preparatory hearings, with the courtroom scenography and symbolism, and where the expert in many cases has conducted some investigations prior to the meeting, i.e. talked to the children, parents and perhaps also others.

When discussing whether some evaluation is acceptable or not, it must be considered which stage of the process the mediation takes place. At an early stage, it is particularly problematic to evaluate, for two reasons: Any evaluation requires sound knowledge of all relevant aspects of the case. Secondly, there has been considerable criticism regarding the soundness of expert evaluation in general, and in custody cases in particular, highlighting that there is a considerable risk of erroneous conclusions (Nordhelle 2010, 2011; Haugli and Nordhelle 2014; Schiøtz 2006; Lundeberg 2009; Breivik and Mevik 2012).

Furthermore, it is valuable that the parties feel heard and has had ample opportunity to express their own points of view before any evaluation. Evaluation often affects the focus of the dispute resolution process, and the parties may become defensive rather than creative. This may be a missed opportunity for the parties to work out arrangements that they feel ownership to, and which are nonetheless sound, seen from a perspective of the best interests of the children. In a worst case scenario, the evaluation may lead to one or both parties losing faith in the mediators' neutrality and impartiality, thus halting the mediation process.

At a later stage in the settlement efforts, when the parties have had ample opportunity to present information, points of view and suggestions, some evaluation may be justifiable depending on the circumstances, but nevertheless with a considerable caution that the reality of custody cases is complex and requires thorough evidence before any conclusions should be drawn.

Particularly in a preparatory hearing that takes place after the trial of one or more interim custody arrangements, with the expert as a mentor, some evaluation from the expert in particular may be reasonable. The expert has had the opportunity to observe how the arrangements have worked during the interim period. It makes sense for the expert to report on what he or she has observed, including what has worked well and what seems to have been more problematic. Such a report should, however, stay within the boundaries of the expert's terms of reference as a mentor. This role does not include assessing the parents' personality, their abilities and qualities as care-givers or what arrangement is in the best interests of the children.[4]

Regardless of whether one believes the parents should be given evaluative feedback or not, it is a reality that the judge, when facilitating settlement needs feedback from the expert on his or her observations during the interim settlement period. Otherwise, it would be difficult to co-mediate. And the parties must be given the same information as the judge to ensure that the adversarial principle is observed. If the information is not shared with the parties, the judge will have to recuse himself or herself from presiding over the main hearing. However, the problem with information flow is in itself a reason to consider changing the current system where mediation efforts are integrated in preparatory hearings to a system where mediation is a separate process led by mediators (judge and expert) who will not partake in further proceedings. Such a model, with a separate court-connected mediation scheme for custody disputes, is in place in Finland (Salminen 2018). If the expert sums up the experiences from the interim settlement period and evaluates how the settlement has worked, this may constitute such extensive evaluation that the expert has stepped outside the boundaries of the role of mediator and should leave further mediation efforts to the judge. Unless the expert's feedback on the interim settlement is limited to pointing out details of the arrangement that may or may not have worked, the confidence in his neutrality and impartiality as a mediator can reasonably be weakened in the eyes of the parties.

This may or may not in itself infringe the legal requirements for impartiality, but equally important: the loss of trust in the mediator's neutrality may be detrimental to the mediation process, and to the parents' perception of procedural justice. It can be, therefore, argued that after evaluative feedback from the expert, the judge should be

---

[4]The role of the mentor is described in the preparatory works, see Ot.prp. no. 29 (2002–2003) and NOU 1998: 17.

the sole mediator and stay within a purely facilitative role. Any evaluation from the expert should also be documented in writing, to ensure clarity about what has been said, if the case is adjudicated.[5]

9   The Interaction and Cooperation Between the Judge and the Expert in the Mediation Process: Potential Problems

9.1   The Problem at Hand: The Expert Has Ex Parte Communication with Parties, Whereas the Presiding Judge Cannot

As described in (Sect. 3) above, settlement efforts in custody court disputes normally takes place in preparatory hearings, and the judge is assumed by the legislator to preside over the main hearing as a main rule should the case not be settled (Ot. prp. no. 29 2002–2003). The judge must therefore observe the boundaries of judicial impartiality, which means that the adversarial principle must be observed. Consequently, caucuses (separate meetings) between the judge and the parties, and receiving information from a party which cannot be divulged to the other, is not allowed. In The Dispute Act section 8-2, which applies in custody cases, c.f. The Children Act section 59, caucuses and confidential information is explicitly forbidden.

For the expert, these rules do not apply. The Children Act 61 no. 1 gives a wide and flexible description of possible tasks for the expert, and *ex parte* communication can be a part of this. It is stated that the court may ask the expert to talk to parents and children and conduct enquiries to clarify the facts of the case, unless the parents object to this. It is common for the expert to talk to the parents separately before mediation.

The expert's duty of professional secrecy does not prohibit communication with the court (The Children Act section 50). If caucuses are to take place between the parties and the expert, it is, however, essential that any information relevant to the case given to the court by the expert is also given to the other party. Otherwise, the adversarial principle will be breached. Although it could be argued that confidentiality is important in caucuses, the preparatory works leave no doubt that The Children Act section 50 must be interpreted literally in this regard – also including caucuses in mediation (Ot. prp. no. 29 2002–2003; NOU 1998: 17. See Dalseide 2004 and Nylund 2011).

It is therefore essential that the expert informs the parties that all relevant information will be shared with the court and the opposing party. Furthermore, it is crucial that the expert is very thorough in telling the judge when information stems

---

[5]The latter is recommended in the national guidelines for the handling of parental disputes (Norwegian Courts' Administration 2016, pp. 13–14).

from ex parte communication, ensuring that the judge is aware of the need for the information to be presented to the other party.

However, the expert is not obliged to report all information received by a party to the judge. Brainstorming of settlement options and strategic discussions are examples of pieces of information that do not necessarily have to be shared with the judge—and in turn the other party—because it is not relevant as a basis for the adjudication of the dispute. However, if the judge and the expert are to function effectively as co-mediators, having different information is impractical.

How information from *ex parte* communication with parties is presented to the judge varies. Sometimes all information is shared with the judge and sometimes only parts of the information are shared. Some judges are very conscious to ensure that all information they have received and that may be relevant should be divulged to both parties to ensure that the adversarial principle is observed, whereas others take a less strict view of this matter.[6] However, as stated above, the judge must ensure that all information that may be relevant to the case is given to both parties (The Dispute Act section 1-1, c.f. ECHR art. 6 no.1).

9.2   *Problems with the Current Regulation and Practice Regarding Ex Parte Communication in These Cases*

The current system requires considerable vigilance and accuracy on part of the expert and judge. In my view, it seems rather difficult to guarantee that the adversarial principle is sufficiently observed. When the judge and the expert discuss the handling of the case, in general, and mediation strategy, in particular, it is nearly unavoidable that the expert sometimes expresses assessments based on conversations with the parents, and that have not been presented to the parties. Even if the expert does not give specific information to the judge, it may be problematic that the judge hears assessments that are based on information that has not been presented to the parties. Although there will be ample opportunity to present evidence in the main hearing should the case not be settled, there is no guarantee that all factors on which the expert based his oral and informal assessments will be presented then. In fact, expressing assessments may be more problematic than presenting specific facts. It is probably easier to see the need for formal presentation of specific facts than vague assessments.

It can be argued that there is a difference between information and assessments that are relevant to the court's assessment of the facts of the case—in other words, information that may serve as evidence—and information and assessments that is shared with the purpose of planning the mediation process.

---

[6]The information is gathered through informal conversations with judges and experts in different district courts and cannot be viewed as a representative selection. However, the material point in this context is to show that there are different approaches and views of this issue.

An example of the latter may be that a parent has told the expert that he quarrels with his ex-spouse when they have to meet whenever the children move from one home to another. This is useful information for the judge to have when facilitating the mediation process, as it means that the judge should make sure that the parents consider this factor when deciding the logistical arrangements for contact.

Another example may be that the expert has experienced that the father needs more encouragement and more questions to be able to communicate openly about his points of view, interests and needs than the mother does, and that his stern looks and short brusque replies are a facade. This type of information helps the judge as a mediator to achieve a good dialogue with and a correct image of the father. None of these examples imply that the judge receives information that needs to be shared with both parties in open court.

However, the line between such information as shown in the examples and information that is relevant to the court's assessment of the facts of the case in a judgement is not clear. An example could be that the expert tells the judge that she has experienced that mother behaves aggressively and escalates conflict, and is easily provoked by questions, and that the judge should be aware of this when mediating. There is no doubt that such information is highly relevant to the judicial settlement process, but, at the same time, such information characterises the mother in a way that is relevant in a court decision on custody and contact.

Another example could be that the expert says that mother seems more yielding and weak than father. Such information is undoubtedly relevant for facilitating the settlement process. However, such personal traits may also affect the court's perception of the mother as a parent.

As shown, the current system where judicial settlement efforts are integrated in the preparatory stages of the trial has some problematic aspects. In the last few paragraphs of this article, I will discuss the need for statutory amendments and amendments of practice in this field.

10 Amendments of Regulation and Practice?

There is little doubt that there was a need for amendment of the process in custody disputes in 2004 to enable processes that were better tailored to the needs of the families.

Introducing the possibility of interim settlements with an expert mentor was a positive step that is likely to increase the chances of settlement. The parents who come to court have not managed to settle at the family counselling offices, which means that the level of conflict is normally fairly high, and that there is likely to be difficulties with communication and cooperation between the parents (Nylund 2018). The parents may also have well-founded concerns about the possible consequences for the child of certain custody and contact arrangements. The fact that the level of conflict is high does not necessarily mean the reason for a parent's unwillingness to settle is the desire to harm the other party. The option of an interim settlement and the opportunity to seek advice from a mentor, therefore, makes a lot of sense. A reduced level of conflict and an improvement of communication between the parents will be beneficial to the children. It can also be assumed that having tested a certain arrangement for a period of time will be conducive for reaching a settlement on an arrangement that serves the interests and needs of the children well.

As shown above, the regulation and practice in these cases has shortcomings. The fact that the settlement efforts are integrated in the preparatory hearings and that both the judge and the expert have other roles in addition to mediating, may create considerable settlement pressure and blur the line between settlement and adjudication, which is problematic in a rule of law perspective. This is amplified by the common view among experts and judges that evaluation is a necessary part of the settlement efforts. These factors, in turn, may lead to settlements of lesser quality and durability.

In my opinion, the overriding principle stated in The Children Act section 48 that both process and outcome should be in the best interests of the children would be better served by having a separate mediation process led by a judge and expert with no other roles than mediating, similar to the court-connected mediation scheme in Finland (Salminen 2018). This would enable the judge mediator and the expert mediator to communicate openly with one another and also to lead all parts of the mediation process as a team—including caucuses (separate meetings).

The latter can be an important tool in custody cases, where the level of conflict is often high, and where there may be a need to explore issues and ask questions that each of the parents are uncomfortable with in a joint meeting. To ensure that the mediators are able to assess whether there are circumstances that makes a proposed arrangement contrary to the best interests of the children, it is essential that the mediators have all the facts (Nordhelle 2011).

Caucuses also enable mediation in cases where there is considerable difference in negotiating strength between the parties. In my experience, there are some cases where settlement would be in the best interests of the children, in order to end a conflict that has taken its toll on both parents and children, but where joint meetings do not work. One of the parents may not be strong enough emotionally to communicate and negotiate constructively while in the same room as the other.

Some fear that a separate mediation process may lead to delay and increase the strain on the children involved should the case not be settled. However, settlement rates are fairly high in custody disputes,[7] and there is no reason to believe that they would be lower if a separate mediation process is introduced, as long as the positive features of the current process are kept: the combination of a judge and an expert as mediators, and the possibility of interim settlements under the mentorship of an expert.

---

[7]In the period of 2010–2014, 2700 custody cases were handled by Norwegian courts, and 1670 of these were settled, amounting to a settlement percentage of 61.9. See The Ministry of Children and Equality, *Evaluering av Barnesakkyndig kommisjon og vurdering av utvidet ansvarsområde* [Evaluation of the Commission on Child Welfare Experts and Assessment of Expanding Their Field of Responsibility] 14 October 2015 p. 69 (data acquired from the Norwegian Court's Administration). However, the total of 2700 also includes cases where mediation was not attempted and where it would not have been suitable because of the circumstances of the case and/or the personal characteristics of the parties. This means that the settlement percentage in cases where mediation was actually attempted is considerably higher.

Legislative amendment in itself is, however, not enough. It is equally important that judges and experts who act as mediators have sufficient training, ensuring that they have the tools to mediate in a manner that enables settlements in the best interests of the children—with the use of facilitative mediator techniques. In March 2017, an expert committee appointed by the Ministries of Justice and Children and Equality recommended that custody, contact and child protection cases should be assigned to specific district courts of general jurisdiction with designated judges with special further training (NOU 2017: 8). This would, in my opinion, be a wise reform.

References

Adrian L (2013) Processretfærdighed – det er også måden, der tæller. Juristen no. 3

Backer IL (2008) Barneloven. Kommentarutgave, 2nd edn. Universitetsforlaget, Oslo

Bernt C (2011) Meklerrollen ved mekling i domstolene. Fagbokforlaget, Bergen

Bernt C (2014) Sakkyndige i barnelovssaker for domstolene: Roller og rettssikkerhet. Tidsskrift for familierett, arverett og barnevernrettslige spørsmål (FAB), pp 178–230 and pp 296–316

Breivik F, Mevik K (2012) Barnefordeling i domstolen. Når barnets beste blir barnets verste. Oslo Universitetsforlaget, Oslo

Dalseide NT (2004) Saksbehandlingsreglene for tvister om foreldreansvar, barnets faste bosted og samvær etter endringslov 20. juni 2003 – noen utvalgte problemstillinger. Tidsskrift for familierett, arverett og barnevernrettslige spørsmål (FAB), pp 172–216

Haugli T, Nordhelle G (2014) Sikker i sin sak? Om barn, sakkyndighet og rettssikkerhet. Lov og Ret 201(2):89–108

Holgersen G (2008) Barnerett. Høyskoleforlaget, Kristiansand

Kjelland-Mørdre K, Rolland ANH, Steen KS, Gammelgard P, Anker C (2008) Konflikt, Mekling og Rettsmekling. Universitetsforlaget, Oslo

Koch K (2000) Når mor og far møtes i retten – barnefordeling og samvær. NOVA-rapport 13/2000

Koch K (2008) Evaluering av saksbehandlingsreglene for domstolene i barneloven – saker om foreldreansvar, fast bosted og samvær. The Ministry of Children and Equality, Oslo

Kovach K, Love LP (1998) Mapping mediation: the risks of Riskin's grid. Harv Negot Law Rev 3:71–110

Lundeberg I (2009) Sannhetsvitnet. Tidsskrift for rettsvitenskap, pp 611–646

Moore C (2003) The mediation process. practical strategies for resolving conflict, 3rd edn. Jossey-Bass, San Fransisco

Møse E (1999) Commentary to ECHR in Karnov. Gyldendal Akademisk, Oslo

Nordhelle G (2007) Mekling II. Sentrale temaer i konflikthåndtering. Gyldendal akademisk, Oslo

Nordhelle G (2010) Kritisk blikk på sakkyndigrollen i barnefordelingssaker. Tidsskrift for Norsk psykologforening, Temanummer: Mekling, pp 744–747

Nordhelle G (2011) Praktiseringen av sakkyndighetsarbeid i barnefordelingssaker – til barnas beste? Tidsskrift for familierett, arverett og barnevernrettslige spørsmål (FAB), pp 176–196

Nordhelle G (2016) Høykonflikt. Utvidet forståelse og håndtering via mekling. Universitetsforlaget, Oslo

Norwegian Courts' Administration. Domstolene i Norge. Årsrapport 2014

Norwegian Courts' Administration. Domstolene i Norge. Årsrapport 2015

Norwegian Courts' Administration (2016) Nasjonal veileder for behandling av foreldretvister

NOU 1998: 17 Barnefordelingssaker - avgjørelsesorgan, saksbehandlingsregler og delt bostad

NOU 2001: 32 Rett på sak

NOU 2017: 8 Særdomstoler på nye områder? – Vurdering av nye domstolsordninger for foreldretvister, barnevernsaker og utlendingssaker

Nylund A (2011) Barnefordelingssaker på godt og ondt, Tidsskrift for familierett, arverett og barnevernrettslige spørsmål (FAB), pp 302–322

Nylund A (2012) Barnefordelingssaker og saker med høyt konfliktnivå. Tidsskrift for familierett, arverett og barnevernrettslige spørsmål (FAB), pp 215–235

Nylund A (2018) A dispute systems design perspective on norwegian child custody mediation. In: Nylund A, Ervasti K, Adrian L (eds) Nordic mediation research. Springer, Cham, pp 9–26

Ot.prp.no. 29 (2002–2003) Om lov om endringer i barneloven mv. (Nye saksbehandlingsregler i barnefordelingssaker for domstolene mv.)

Paradis AD, Reinherz HZ, Giaconia RM, Beardslee WR, Ward K, Fitzmaurice GM (2009) Long-term impact of family arguments and physical violence on adult functioning at age 30 years: findings from the Simmins. Longitudinal study. J Am Acad Child Adolesc Psychiatry:290–298

Prop. 85 L (2012–2013) Endringer i barnelova (barneperspektivet i foreldretvister)

Rød PA, Ekeland TJ, Thuen F (2008) Barns erfaringer med konfliktfylte samlivsbrudd: Problemforståelse og følelsesmessige reaksjoner, Tidsskrift for Norsk psykologforening, p 555-562

Salminen K (2018) Is mediation in the best interest of a child in the child law perspective? In: Nylund A, Ervasti K, Adrian L (eds) Nordic mediation research. Springer, Cham, pp 209–222

Schøitz A (2006) Den (retts)medisinske sakkyndighet. Rasjonalitetsformer og rolleoppfatninger i medisin og juss. Tidsskrift for Strafferett, pp 20–38

The Ministry of Children and Equality (2015) Evaluering av Barnesakkyndig kommisjon og vurdering av utvidet ansvarsområde

Tomm K (1987) Interventive interviewing: Part II. Reflexive questioning as a means to enable self-healing. Fam Process 26:167–183

Veileder Q-15/2004 (2016) The Norwegian Courts' Administration, Nasjonal veileder for behandling av foreldretvister

Vindeløv V (2007a) Mediation. A non-model. Djøf Publishing, Copenhagen

Vindeløv V (2007b) Retsmægling i Danmark – en diskussion om rammer og indhold. Juristen 89:150–155

Vindeløv V (2013) Konfliktmægling. En refleksiv model, 3rd edn. Jurist- og økonomforbundets forlag, København

Mediation in Light of Modern Identity

Ida Helene Asmussen

Contents

Abstract In this contribution, I unfold how adapting a modern identity concept can transform the understanding of mediation. Since the middle of the twentieth century, a new way of understanding identity has developed within sociology and similar scientific fields. Further, within the last 20 years, it has become increasingly recognised that identity is changing and flexible and thus highly context dependent. In the article, I explore how the new identity concept changes the perception of what is going on in mediation. I go on to exemplify the roles that the parties assume. I also provide some central analytical tools of how to approach research analysis when incorporating this understanding of identity. A qualitative study of victim offender mediation (VOM) illustrates my points, but as the points raised here also address the basic premises of the mediation session, the present contribution is indeed also relevant to other fields of mediation research and practice.

I. H. Asmussen (✉)
Faculty of Law, University of Copenhagen, Copenhagen, Denmark
e-mail: idha@jur.ku.dk

© The Author(s) 2018
A. Nylund et al. (eds.), *Nordic Mediation Research*,
https://doi.org/10.1007/978-3-319-73019-6_8

1 Introduction

Mediation theory and mediation research is, to a large extent, based on the assumption that what is expressed by the parties are reflections of their truths, needs and interests.[1] The present contribution to the debate challenges that assumption by showing how a modern social constructivist view on identity changes the analysis of what is going on in mediation. This view of identity changes the dialogue to a matter of presenting a self that fits into a context rather than a matter of expressing authentic needs and interests. The article exemplifies this position by means of the conclusions of a recent study, where this modern view of identity was purposefully used as a theoretical and methodological framework (Asmussen 2014, 2015, 2017).[2] The study points out a series of participant positions and shows how these positions are structured by our Christian cultural roots. Hereby, the change of identity concept leads to a change of definition of mediation from a session where the parties get a chance to express themselves and solve their conflict to a session where predictable values and logics are reproduced and negotiated.

Before moving into the substance, I will give a short introduction to the study that I refer to throughout the article in order to concretise this issue. Having introduced the study and its empirical context, I will elaborate upon the concept of what I term a modern understanding of identity. In continuation of unfolding the concept, I will give a concrete example from a mediation session that shows how this understanding of identity changes the interpretation of what is going on in mediation. Accordingly, I will reflect on how a different understanding of identity influences research methodology and analysis strategy, describing also how I have integrated this approach in the overall study example. I finally present the results of the study in order to show how research built on a different identity concept substantially changes the results of an observation and interview study of mediation.

2 The Study and Its Design

The research that underpins this article takes its point of departure in a qualitative study of mediation in criminal cases. More specifically, the article is based on a series of observations of mediation sessions in Denmark and on interviews with participants.

After 16 years with victim offender mediations (VOM) as pilot projects in a few Danish police districts, offering VOM is now a nationwide possibility in Denmark implemented by a law effective from January 2010 (Lov om konfliktråd 2009). In

---

[1]There are, of course, mediation models based on constructivist social theory, e.g. narrative mediation (Winslade and Monk 2008).

[2]This chapter is based on and combines three earlier publications Asmussen (2014, 2015, 2017).

Denmark, VOM only works as a supplement to standard prosecution and court proceedings and, as a consequence, there are no limits to the kind of criminal offence that may proceed to VOM. There is, however, a minor exception to the separation of VOM and criminal proceedings: in cases where VOM has been pursued and applied, the judge could let an offender's participation in VOM count as a mitigating circumstance when meeting out the sentence.

I carried out the study in three different police districts in Denmark from June through December 2010, representing both urban and rural areas. I observed 12 VOMs,[3] with a total of 52 participants.[4] After having observed a VOM session, I conducted interviews with those participants who were willing to participate. I recorded 43 semi-structured interviews either in continuation of the observation of a VOM or within a maximum of 20 days. Moreover, I did follow-up-interviews with offenders and victims 10–12 months later. All the data was subsequently analysed in depth by means of qualitative data processing software (HyperResearch).

As supplementary, empirical support, I observed one VOM and five conferences[5] in three different VOM districts in Norway and conducted 40 semi-structured interviews with the relevant participants from March through October 2011. In Norway, VOM and other restorative processes can supplement standard prosecution and criminal proceedings in different ways or be a separate alternative to conventional proceedings depending on, among other things, the age of the offender and the kind of criminal offence in question.

3 Identity as Contextual Performance

Erving Goffman is one of the central thinkers to critically rethink the idea of identity as a set of characteristics that we all 'carry around'. Goffman's basic notion is that the way we behave and interact depends on the norms and expectations of the context. As the context is continuously changing, so is the self-performance. As Goffman puts it, the moment we enter a context where other people are present, an interpretation process begins regarding the expectations of the context and how to fulfil these expectations (Goffman 1959).

The interpretation revolves around questions such as: 'what kind of performance is expected from me?' Or 'how do I help others succeed with the role they prefer to play?' Thus Goffman presumes that there is a kind of unspoken, social contract of

---

[3]Six cases involved violence, one a threat against a person, three burglaries, one theft, and one a neighbour dispute. This distribution of offences matches the general distribution in Danish VOMs, see Hansen (2012).

[4]The number is due to the fact that several victims participated in one of the cases and I observed (and interviewed) everyone who participated, including supporters and mediators.

[5]In Norwegian, conferences are called *stormøter*.

individuals helping each other succeed with their performance. This means that one might, for instance, laugh even though one might not find a joke funny; might express interest without being interested; might yawn without being tired, and so on. These responses would typically be expressed in order to help others save face or in order to present oneself as a laughing, engaged or bored (by what is going on) individual. As a consequence of this viewpoint, Goffman understands expressions like these, and interactions as such, as performing a specific self, according to the context rather than being a specific identity.

One of Goffman's examples is a person falling down stairs saying 'oops'. In a Goffman perspective, this is far from a "natural emotional expression" (Goffman 1981) of a person falling. But rather it is a "symbolic gesture . . . constitutive of the meaning of the sequence as a whole" (Rawls 1992) and a message from the sender to the people who observed the fall. With this expression it is indicated: 'I am not drunk, clumsy or used to falling. The act of falling is actually kind of surprising to myself.' In continuation of that one could ask whether you would say 'oops' if you were falling in a place where nobody is nearby. It is thus shown that expressions, to a large extent, are about conveying a certain self rather than transparent expressions of a person's inside.

With this contextual view on human expressions and interaction in mind, we have to modify the idea of what is expressed in a mediation session as the 'parties' truths'[6] as the situation primarily refers to an idea of authentic and absolute selves, not integrating how the context influences the 'truths'. In more theoretical terms, we have to pay attention to a more socio-constructive way of understanding the participants in mediation. A social constructivist would normally not even use the term 'identity', but might prefer the term 'self-presentation', 'performance' etc.[7] Social constructivism is a large 'umbrella' and part of this umbrella includes the interactionist view of the self as a product of a social and concrete situation—here presented through Goffman. This implies that the interests and needs that are expressed in a mediation session are first and foremost something that is created in the context—by the institution as such and by the mediator and other participants, including the discourses and narratives they draw on from various other sources and contexts.

Analytically speaking, this approach means that you are not trying to find out what this and that person seems to have on his/her mind, what seems to be important to him/her, what seems not to be important, etc. Rather, you ask what positions, narratives, discourses are created in the situation.

---

[6]For example, Vindeløv (2012).

[7]For more about social constructivism and the theoretical basis, see Asmussen (2017).

4 How the View of Identity Changes What Seems To Be Going On

Let me provide an illustrative example (cited in Asmussen 2017) that exemplifies how this new view of identity changes what seems to be going on. The following example is drawn from an observation of a VOM in Denmark. It stems from an exchange between an offender and a series of victims whose houses he had broken into. The exchange is taken from the end of a VOM session:

(1) Heather (victim): "It is very commendable of Ray to participate in this."

(2) Stone (victim): "This has been a positive experience. I hope you get your life together."

(3) Harry (victim): "I am hungry. I can't wait to get home."

(4) Ray (offender): "Thank you for letting me be who I am. I see this meeting as a sign of new times."

(5) Joe (victim), sharply: "All we need now is your apology, Ray."

(6) Ray: "I'm so very sorry."

(7) Heather: "I hope we haven't been too harsh on you."

(8) Joe: "Let's not make things too rosy."

If we approach the dialogue from a hermeneutic or phenomenological view of identity, we would look for the needs and interests that we—with our knowledge about mediation theory—expect the victims to express at the meeting. And we would probably consider Joe's statement (statement 5 above) as a need for an apology. However, if we use an interactionist approach to identity as a contextual performance, we would interpret Joe's statement concerning the apology as not necessarily 'brought to the meeting' but as part of the situation—potentially provoked by the altruistic comments of the other participants. So, from a phenomenological point of view, one might see Joe's request for an apology as an expression of Joe's inner needs whereas the interactionist approach would see Joe's request as an expression that is at least partly a result of the context. In continuation of that perspective one could ask whether Joe would have asked for an apology if the others had expressed anger towards the offender.

It is hard to eliminate the possibility that Joe might *not* have expressed a 'need' for an apology if the others had behaved differently. Thus the example illustrates how the context is shaping 'Joe's self'.

5   How to Integrate the Modern View of Identity
       in Research Methodology

As a consequence of the interactionist way of understanding self and interaction as contextually produced, I did not consider the data 'collected', but rather as a product of a specific situation that I myself, as a researcher, was part of. At the same time, one must of course distinguish between observations and interviews. As Dingwall (1997) reminds us: "[...] observation is the most fundamental discipline for the sociologist. In an interview study, we can pick and choose the messages that we hear and that we elicit. In observation, we have no choice but to listen to what the world is telling us" (Dingwall 1997). Though Dingwall has a different epistemological grounding, his point is useful in the sense that observations to a much larger extent involve 'listening to what the world is telling us'—though this way to put it is, of course, rather radical. The interview, on the other hand, is a situation where the respondents retrospectively construct their experiences of the meeting and these constructions would not be produced without my initiative, as opposed to the VOM meetings that would take place whether I was there or not.[8]

In the interview setting I am a co-producer of new strategies and positions—between me as a researcher and the respondent. The way I approach and formulate my questions is, in other words, limiting the room for manoeuvre available for the respondent: "To put it simply, one can't be a 'self' by oneself, identities must be accomplished in 'shows' that persuade...individuals [to] negotiate how they want to be known in the stories they develop collaboratively with their audiences" in the interview situation (Riessman 2016). This way of understanding my own role as a co-producer of the data, especially in the interview situation, was taken into account in the subsequent analysis by continually including my interaction as part of the interpretation of what was said.

Finally, the observation and interview data was merged with document analysis of visitation guidelines, evaluation reports and legal-system negotiations to add more direct data on the organisational and institutional framing of the VOMs and the participants.

6   Relevant Theory for Integrating Modern Identity
       Concepts with Analysis Strategy

As already stated, the present study takes a social constructivist point-of-view based on Goffman, and hence the focus of the research conducted dwells on what was created in face-to-face interaction. Goffman's role theory was supplemented with other theories sharing the same epistemological approach and analytical framing,

---

[8]Highlighting this point, I am inspired by Mik-Meyer (2004).

e.g. Conversation analysis (CA),[9] positioning theory,[10] discursive psychology[11] and Foucault's notions about truth and power. In the following I will briefly explain how I used these frameworks to underpin the analysis in accordance with the modern identity concept.

Grounded in the basic ethno-methodological premise that context is locally and situationally produced and actors accordingly accountable, I combined Goffman's thinking about 'the social self' with symbolic interactionism.[12] Symbolic interactionism offers a textual and linguistic interpretation of the data and thus CA was useful as a source of inspiration.[13] What was, one might ask, for instance, expressed when the offender continually talked about himself as a 'criminal' in grammatical past form and the victims continually talked about the offender as a 'criminal' in the grammatical present and future forms?

Positioning theory is likewise a useful tool for clarifying some of Goffman's central concepts: Goffman's 'role' thus becomes 'position', and 'positioning' is consequently used to illustrate that the research object is a simultaneous and mutual action, where one speaker is actively positioning himself and by doing that he is also positioning the other(s) and *vice versa*. Finally, the concepts of 'position' and 'positioning' help to illustrate that what is 'at play' is always only a small and temporary part of a person's repertoire—the part that is expressed in a certain context.

In order to broaden the analytical approach and to investigate identity mechanisms in a broader context, discursive psychology proved a fruitful inspirational field by opening up questions such as: 'which discourse is this statement drawn from?' Or one could go even further, and ask, *pace* Foucault, 'which logic/truth telling is structuring the discourses expressed in the mediation sessions?' As I will explain in more detail in the following, I found the VOMs to be structured around a confessional ethos.

---

[9]Conversation Analysis has been inspired by ethno-methodology (Harold Grafinkel) and Goffman's theory of interaction. It was formulated in the late 1960s and early 1970s by Harvey Sacks, Emanuel Schegloff and Gail Jefferson.

[10]Wendy Hollway was the first to use 'positioning' in an analysis of gender and subjectivity from 1984, see Harré and Langenhove (1991). Later, the concept was developed, especially within positioning theory, as formulated, in particular, by Rom Harré, Browyn Davies, Luk Van Langenhove and Fathali Moghaddam.

[11]Discursive Psychology developed in the late 1980s and the most quoted work in this regard is Jonathan Potter and Margaret Wetherell's acknowledged book *Discourse and Social Psychology: Beyond Attitudes and Behavior* (1987).

[12]Inspired by Stax (2005).

[13]The overall principles as turn-taking, minimal responses, inter subjectivity and use of grammatical time forms was used. For a more precise hands-on description of the tools, see Asmussen (2014).

7 Participants' 'Truth' Based on Cultural, Christian Roots

What I found when I analysed the VOM sessions was that perpetrators, in particular, demonstrated the characteristics of the 'ideal sinner': regretting, repenting, showing concern for the victim and assuring the other participants of his/her plans for a non-sinful life. I named this position *the exemplary offender* because the individuals in question seemed to embrace a position that met the expectations of the mediator and the victim. In line with that, the majority of victims positioned themselves as matching the exemplary offender by demonstrating charity and forgiveness by downplaying the crime and focusing on the rehabilitation of the perpetrator. I named this position *the altruistic victim.* Against this background, the positions can be seen as a reflection of a certain moral assessment of the situation, structured by a confessional ethos; including the demand for remorse on the part of the perpetrator and the demand for mercy on the part of the victim. Seen through the modern view of identity, this is not mirroring the victims' feelings and needs, but rather how they understand the situation and how the common cultural background is shaping the idea of how one should approach a situation where someone has committed a 'sin' or has been the victim of others' sinful actions.

The conclusions of the study actualise essential parts of Foucault's thinking. Foucault states that the pastor's imperative for confession did not cease with the reduced influence of the church, but continues to function in modern society through the notion of confession as the means of liberation. Foucault has described how the notions of truth and logic of the past are handed down and reproduced in new forms. From the fourth to the sixth century, the task of the pastor changed from ensuring the salvation of the congregation to ensuring that of the individual (Foucault 2000a). The pastor was hence dependent on the individuals allowing him admittance to their inner life of their own accord, i.e. relating their sins. Against that backdrop, the conception was formed that each individual was obliged to confess their sins to God and a series of related practices evolved, including absolution (Foucault 2000a). Seen in this light, mediation is based on the idea of liberation through articulation and externalisation of an inner truth.

Foucault also pinpoints that secular confession is an ongoing theme in modern lifestyle—a catharsis-like willingness to relate one's inside: "one confesses one's crimes, one's sins, one's thoughts and desires, one's illnesses and troubles; one goes about telling, with the greatest precision, whatever is most difficult to tell. One confesses in public and in private, to one's parents, one's educators, one's doctor, to those one loves; one admits to oneself in pleasure and in pain, things it would be impossible to tell to anyone else, the things people write books about. When it is not spontaneous or dictated by some internal imperative, the confession is wrung from a person by violence or threat ...Western man has become a confessing animal" (Foucault 1978). Foucault describes genealogically how the medieval pastoral governance of the Christian confession produced a logic saying that man should be led by the will of relating the truth about one self, and that this truth-telling is still at play in modern society. Today, though not led by the pastor, but by psychologists, therapists, pedagogues, coaches etc. (Foucault 2000b). This 'pastoral governance', stimulating man to govern himself through confession, is arguably also a mantra in mediation.

A smaller group of participants, described as *the uncompromising victim* and *the resentful offender*,[14] presented resistance against entering into the roles in the Christian-cultural 'script'. These 'outliers' can be viewed in the light of Foucault's words: "There is no power without revolt" (Foucault 1999). For these participants, the mediation session became a struggle to redefine the situation. An example of this is a mediation session where a resentful offender with some luck redefines the session from a situation where he should be the one to regret a situation to where the victim should express fault and regret. The way this is done is by claiming that the victim—by reporting the criminal episode—is responsible for the judgment of the offender. The case highlighted below was about threats towards a caseworker who had decided that a father, for a given period of time, should be denied access to his children. In line with the notion of positioning, the offender (re)positions the caseworker as someone who was supposed to help him and is thereby especially obliged to show loyalty, as illustrated in the following statement taken from the mediation session:

> I only have you Camilla (the caseworker), I haven't got anybody else, and (looking at the mediator) she cannot handle me. (Turning back to Camilla) I have to go back to jail because of you. I was only judged because of you.

8   Striving for Christie's Norm Clarification

In cases like the above, played out by the *resentful offender* and/or the *uncompromising victim*, the parties were quarrelling about who should take the blame and the responsibility, or they gave up on the dialogue entirely because it was hard to find a basic consensus.

Christie (1977) pinpoints that mediation is a possibility of discussions as communities, i.e. *"opportunities for norm-clarification"*. He expands this point through a description of the losses potentially involved in upholding the conventional legal process:

> It is a loss of pedagogical possibilities. It is a loss of opportunities for a continuous discussion of what represents the law of the land. How wrong was the thief, how right was the victim? Lawyers are [. . .] trained into agreement on what is relevant in a case. But that means that it is difficult to stage what we might call a political debate in court. When the victim is small and the offender big—in size or power—how blameworthy then is the crime? [. . .] If the offender is well educated, ought he then suffer more or maybe less, for his sins?.

I do not believe the discussion exemplified above fulfils Christie's hopes for mediation, but at least there was a concrete discussion of morale, guilt, responsibility

---

[14]Moreover, the study includes a description of *the therapeutic victim* and a pattern among young men named *offstage performance*. For more about these positions, see Asmussen (2014, 2015).

and different positions in society. These discussions were not actualised in the majority of sessions I observed because, as described above, the session positions were played out by the *exemplary offender* and the *altruistic victim*, and they agreed on the moral situation and role playing. In other words, if we would encourage discussions of norm-clarification, we have to create awareness of these powerful cultural discourses and narratives that guide us to repetition and reproduction. Whatever we do, we cannot wash the human brain clean of language and history (which would indeed create yet other problems); but that said, being more *observant* of our automatic ways of positioning others and ourselves could be a way forward towards creating more space for fruitful discussion, including the discussions of norm-clarification that Christie called for.

9 We Have to Listen to More than the Parties

Approaching mediation with a modern understanding of identity in mind, it is not enough to carry out research that reveals what is at stake for the parties. The approach will have to be supplemented with research that reveals what is at play in the organisations and institutions surrounding individuals: 'how do the municipal institutions contribute to the actions and expressions of the parties?' 'What narratives, discourses and positions are produced and reproduced in the context?' and so on. Otherwise, we are only uncovering half of what is going on. Being aware of the institutional level and making it visible in the mediation sessions could contribute to the substance of and transparency in mediation practise, just as stakeholders will have to stay open-minded and develop practices in accordance with the mediation models that allow for a modern understanding of identity.[15]

In other words, the modern concept of identity forces us to face Christie's famous words about "giving the conflict back to the parties" (1977)—admittedly a far from simple task. As pinpointed here, what is expressed by the parties in a mediation session is much more than their truths. It remains a challenge to ascertain how to best approach mediation in practise and how to most fruitfully approach mediation research; nevertheless, we scholars would do well to rise to this challenge. In this article, I have hinted that the challenge is surmountable. Working towards making changes to mediation ought to be worthwhile in a wider societal perspective, as adjustments could potentially improve the mediation process and thereby the output for the parties. Finally, viewing mediation through the lens of a modern concept of identity will broaden and extend the body of research in the field in a way that will lead to a more nuanced and comprehensive picture of what is going on in—and not least what is achievable through—mediation now and in future.

---

[15]Narrative mediation could be an example of including the social constructivist view in practice, Winslade (2006).

References

Asmussen IH (2014) Fra Retsstat til Omsorgsstat—om syndsforladelse i konfliktråd. DJØF, Copenhagen

Asmussen IH (2015) Performing absolution narratives in restorative justice. Restor Justice Int J 3 (1):28–48

Asmussen IH (2017) Old Goffman as a new research strategy in restorative justice. In: Aertsen I, Pali B (eds) Critical restorative justice. Hart, Oxford, pp 143–159

Christie N (1977) Conflicts as property. Br J Criminol 17(1):1–15

Dingwall R (1997) Accounts, interviews and observation. In: Miller G, Dingwall R (eds) Context and method in qualitative research. Sage, London, pp 51–65

Foucault M (1978) The history of sexuality, vol 1. Pantheon, New York

Foucault M (1999) Pastoral power and political reason. In: Carette R (ed) Religion and culture – foucault. Routledge, New York, pp 135–152

Foucault M (2000a) Omnes et singulatim: toward a critique of political reason. In: Faubion J (ed) Power. Penguin, Harmondsworth, pp 298–325

Foucault M (2000b) The subject and power. In: Faubion J (ed) Power. Penguin, Harmondsworth, pp 326–348

Goffman E (1959) The presentation of self in everyday life. Anchor Books, New York

Goffman E (1981) Forms of talk. University of Pennsylvania Press, Pennsylvania

Hansen KF (2012) Evaluering af konfliktråd – den landsdækkende ordning. Center for Alternativ Samfundsanalyse (CASA), Copenhagen

Harré R, Langenhove L (1991) Varieties of positioning. J Theory Soc Behav 21(4):393–407

Mik-Meyer N (2004) Dømt til personlig udvikling. Hans Reitzels Forlag, Copenhagen

Potter J, Wetherell M (1987) Discourse and social psychology: beyond attitudes and behavior. SAGE, London

Rawls AW (1992) Order of interaction and intelligibility. In: Trevino AJ (ed) Goffmans legacy. Rowman & Littlefield, Oxford

Riessman CK (2016) Performing identities in illness narrative: masculinity and multiple sclerosis. Qual Res 3(1):5–33

Stax T (2005) Duetter fra anden sal – et interaktionelt perspektiv på samtaler mellem hjemløse og socialarbejdere. Københavns Universitet, Sociologisk Institut, Copenhagen

Vindeløv V (2012) Reflexive mediation with a sustainable perspective. DJØF Publishing, Copenhagen

Winslade J (2006) Mediation with a focus on discursive positioning. Confl Resolut Q 23(4):501–515

Winslade J, Monk G (2008) Practising narrative mediation – loosening the grip of conflict. Jossey-Bass, San Francisco

When Is Restorative Justice? Exploring the Implications of Restorative Processes in Juvenile Offence Cases Based on Interviews and Observations in Northern Ireland, Norway, and Orlando, Florida

Katrine Barnekow Rasmussen

Contents

K. B. Rasmussen (✉)
Faculty of Law, University of Copenhagen, Copenhagen, Denmark
e-mail: katrine.barnekow.rasmussen@jur.ku.dk

© The Author(s) 2018   145
A. Nylund et al. (eds.), *Nordic Mediation Research*,
https://doi.org/10.1007/978-3-319-73019-6_9

Abstract In this article, I examine and discuss the implications of restorative processes in juvenile offence cases in Northern Ireland, Norway, and Orlando, Florida. The investigation focuses on the Northern Irish *Youth Conference* model, the Norwegian *Youth Sanction* and *Youth Follow-up* models, and the *Neighborhood Restorative Justice* and *Teen Court* diversion programs of Orlando, Florida. I use interviews with professionals and observations of restorative processes and meetings related to these as the empirical basis for the investigation. In my discussion of the three models, I focus on issues of neutrality/impartiality, voluntarism, punishment, roles of offended parties and communities, and equality before the law based on the theories of Christie, Zehr, Vindeløv and Braithwaite. While the models generally offer possibilities of addressing the individual circumstances of the young offender in a way that the traditional systems they locally compete with do not, the variation in content is so large that I consider if perhaps a community of practices labelled *restorative justice* exists only at the abstract and not at the practical level.

1 What Makes a Restorative Process?

1.1 Levelling the Field

The headline of this article is a reference to the famous research carried out by American anthropologist Michael Moerman among the Lue people in Northern Thailand. In his 1965 article *Ethnic Identification in a Complex Civilization: Who Are the Lue?* he stresses that in order to answer the questions *who* and *what* are the Lue one must look into *when* Lue-ness occurs—either as a result of self-invoking or an external labelling process (Moerman 1965). Does it take just one of these or both for a Lue to be a Lue? Hence, *when* are the Lue and, as a consequence, (and just as important) when are the Lue *not*. This approach has since been very influential in anthropological research, as it accommodates to the non-static nature of an ethnic group. But it has also turned out to be a fruitful attitude to apply to other research fields as well; research fields that—just like ethnic groups—can give the false allure of a limited entity, whose boundaries everyone can agree to. One such research field could be a (perhaps) quasi-juridical term as—say—*restorative justice*, which is the focus of this article.

The article *Words on Words* by the world famous Norwegian criminologist Nils Christie was published in the first edition of *Restorative justice: An International Journal* in 2013. In it the by then 85-year old Christie stresses the importance of choosing the names carefully when talking about 'the core activities for alternative handling of conflicts; the organisations created for that purpose, the role-players and their activities' (Christie 2013). To Christie, the term restorative justice 'sounds as a bad choice'. He particularly dislikes the *justice* part and its inevitable connotation to the institution of Law. Also, the *restorative* part of the term is criticised for inviting a normative understanding of relations and trust (Christie 2013). Christie advocates shying away from various euphemisms—what he calls a 'heroic terminology'—to stay clear of the abovementioned dangers and states "why not simply say so: we work with conflicts and in organisations for handling conflicts" (Christie 2013).

Christie's article seemingly sparked a wave of reflections within the field of RJ-research/practice, as illustrated in this quote from the foreword to a paper also published in this first edition of *Restorative justice: An International Journal:*

> Like so much else that comes from the pen of Nils Christie, his "Words on Words" that have inspired this special issue, and with which it begins, have, as they so often do, inspired us to engage in a meditative reflection on his words and their implications for our thinking and practice. We have sought, through these reflections on the wisdom of Christie's words, to better understand the security governance practices we have been studying, developing and, sometimes, promoting. (Froestad and Shearing 2013)

One security governance practice field in which restorative justice approaches certainly seem increasingly popular to employ is the field of juvenile offences. However, in my experience as a researcher, the rationales behind and the implications of doing so might vary immensely.

As part of my on-going PhD project,[1] I have interviewed and observed professionals working with restorative approaches to youth crime in four countries—in all of which I have been welcomed with great hospitality and openness. I have observed and/or interviewed young people in these same four countries, as they took part in or reflected upon having participated in a restorative process as a reaction to having broken the law. From these interactions, if nothing else, one thing has become very clear: Both the nature of the usage of restorative processes as a reaction to youth crime and the reasons for doing so are so diverse that it seems almost inappropriate to use the same headline to describe them. So:

When is restorative justice?

- Are you practicing restorative justice if you say you are?
- If others (whom?) say so?
- Both?

These are questions that I will not claim to answer in this article. However, evoking the teachings of Moerman, I will try to explore the boundaries of *restorative justice* as used in juvenile cases through examples from the four countries I have included in my research.

I chose these destinations because they each represent years of experience running programs and/or projects where juvenile offences (of varying seriousness) can be diverted to a restorative process.

In the case of the United States, the practices might vary immensely from state-to-state, as well as between judicial districts within a state. I do not have any basis to claim nor suspect that the particular programs I observed are (or are not)

---

[1]The project title is *Ethnic bias in restorative processes? – An examination of access and outcome for ethnic minority young male offenders.*

representative of restorative diversion programs for juvenile offences in the United States. This is why I have chosen to refer to the destination of this research visit by city and state—Orlando, Florida—rather than by country as the other models.

So far I have conducted three research trips to Norway, one to Northern Ireland, and one to the United States during my PhD period. As a consequence, my reflections on the Norwegian use of restorative justice in juvenile cases will take up more space in this article than those concerning the programs in Northern Ireland and Orlando, Florida.

The article will finish with a discussion of how the different usages of restorative approaches to juvenile offences in the four countries can contribute to understanding and recognising the tokens of restorative justice. The models are discussed and compared focusing on a series of key-issues within this research field: *neutrality/ impartiality, voluntarism, punishment, roles of offended parties and communities,* and *equality before law.*

In Denmark, a restorative process cannot substitute a court process in juvenile cases or otherwise. At the discretion of the police sometimes minor cases estimated too small to press charges are referred to konfliktråd—the Danish Victim Offender Mediation Service, but there are no official legislation/guidelines to support this approach. Even so, in the final discussion I have included perspectives from interviews with Danish police officers affiliated with the mediation program on the usage of restorative approaches in juvenile cases.[2]

1.2 Methodological Overview

The basis for this article is not a classical comparative study, even if programs from the three countries are, to some extent, compared. I have employed an eclectic strategy of data collection and analysis. As described below, I present different kinds of data for each program. I do this in order to illuminate which elements of that particular program I find interesting in relation to a discussion of how differently juvenile offender programs operating under a restorative justice label are designed and executed.

The data collection for this article consists of the following:

- *Semi-structured interviews* primarily with professionals working with restorative justice approaches to juvenile cases and, secondarily, with civil parties who had been part of such a process. The interviews have been conducted one-on-one or in groups. Most of them have been recorded, but in some cases I have taken notes

---

[2]In Denmark, konfliktråd is organised under the police, and the all-dominant approach is victim offender mediation (VOM) with one offender and one offended party present. In accordance with this, the official English translation on the Danish konfliktråd webpage is victim offender mediation program. In comparison, the Norwegian konfliktråd is a separate entity under the ministry of justice and offers more inclusive types of mediation as a standard, which the translation Norwegian Mediation Service reflects.

during and after the interview instead. My informants have been anonymised.[3] The interview base for this article is the following: *Norway:* seven interviews, and *Orlando, Florida:* six interviews with a total of eight informants.[4]

- *Observations* of restorative processes with juvenile offenders and their network, as well as other interactions, related to these processes. During and after the observations I have taken notes. I have not recorded any of the observed meetings. In all cases the young people and their parents/network, as well as the present professionals, have accepted my presence after having been presented with my profession and reasons for observing. The observation base is the following: *Norway:* seven interactions, and *Orlando, Florida* seven interactions
- *Presentations* made by professionals/management working with the selected programs
- *Data from studies, reports, evaluations* focusing on usage of restorative justice approaches in juvenile cases (see references)
- *Articles* expressing opinions on various types of restorative justice approaches in juvenile cases (see references)

The samples in the study are limited, and this, of course, entails that the findings presented in this article should not be assumed to paint a full picture of how the three programs operate and to what effect. However, in all three cases the respective program leaders were my gatekeepers in terms of access to interviews and observations. Hence, I expect that I have been introduced to employees and cases which, from the perspective of the program managements, are representative of how the programs work (or how the managements think they should work).

1.3 Theoretical Framework

I will refer to the following works:

- The Little Book of Restorative justice by Howard Zehr[5]
- Conflict as Property, Words on Words, and Widening the Net by Nils Christie

---

[3]With the exception of the Norwegian national coordinator, who has been cited extensively and who has approved these citations.

[4]In addition to this, I have conducted 14 interviews with a total of 20 informants in Denmark in relation to the project. More interviews and observations are scheduled.

[5]In *The Little Book of Restorative justice* a.o. Zehr (2015) introduces a division between the paradigms of Criminal Justice, where offenders "get what they deserve" and restorative justice, where the focus is on "victims needs and offenders responsibility to repair harm". In his latest work, Zehr has moved away from this dichotomy, stating that restorative justice is not necessarily the opposite of retribution. Yet the dichotomy of restorative/retributive seems to remain a pillar of understanding within the field of restorative justice.

- Reflexive Mediation by Vibeke Vindeløv[6]
- Crime, Shame and Reintegration by John Braithwaite[7]

There are different views on the genealogy of the term restorative justice in relation to, for instance, restorative processes/practices and to mediation in terms of what is the subset of what?[8] I will not dive deep into that discussion in this article, but I prefer to reserve the term restorative justice for processes that relate to a criminal offense. And since only such processes are the focus of this paper, I have chosen restorative justice as the headline. I see the terms restorative practices/ processes as a theoretical and methodological continuum, which can include various types of proactive and reactive restorative activities in, for instance, schools and communities, as well as restorative justice approaches to criminal offences at the 'pointy' end of the continuum. I suggest restorative processes/practices and mediation be seen as two entities that share an intersection.[9]

1.4 Reflections on the Researcher's Position

My point of entry into the field of mediation/restorative justice research was that I had worked first as a teacher at a boarding school for teenagers where many of the students were socially and psychologically challenged and later with vulnerable youth and crime prevention in a municipality—both jobs for several years. In 2012, I became a trained youth mediator and experienced how the curriculum—including its introduction to the concept of restorative justice—in so many ways seemed to match the approach I had taken to working with young people and the inevitable conflicts they run into. An approach, which was often challenged by colleagues and others promoting a more 'hard liner', '0-tolerance' attitude to the young people. I liked how this approach legitimised the importance of the parties' (including young peoples) voices, while also promoting their sense of responsibility.

Through my work in the municipality and later through a job in the Danish probation service I have come into contact with many young people who have

---

[6]The reflexive mediation model was developed in the late 1990s, early 2000s by the influential Danish Law professor, mediation researcher, and practitioner Vibeke Vindeløv. Here some of the key concepts are that the mediator must act impartial and respect the autonomy and dignity of the parties (Vindeløv 2012, 1st edition in 2008).

[7]In *Crime, Shame and Reintegration* (1989), Braithwaite focuses on the potential of shame in restorative processes to reintegrate the offender into the community and adjust his/her behaviour away from an anti-social path.

[8]I have participated in two international conferences with a restorative focus: one by the European Forum for Restorative justice, in Leuven, in 2015 and one by the International Institute for Restorative Practices, in Dublin 2017. At both conferences the genealogy of the various terms was a topic for vivid discussions amongst researchers and practitioners both during key notes and in smaller sessions. On this basis I conclude that there is no consensus within the field on this matter. My suggestion as to the genealogy is thus to be seen as one of many perceptions.

[9]More on this point in the discussion.

committed one or more offences and have been in—sometimes repetitive—contact with social services as well as the justice system. In my experience, it seems like there is a lot of room for improvement in the way these young people are met by such systems.

I suspect that restorative approaches have a potential to fix some of the serious potholes in the way we meet young offenders. But—as I hope this article reflects—I am not without concerns on the matter. Hereof the spectrum and quality of practices is a large one. My positive expectations, as well as my concerns, have been motivators for me to add research to my restorative practice.

2 Discovering the Balanced Model of Northern Ireland

2.1 *Successful First Moving in Conflict Heart Land*

In the spring of 2014—a year before officially commencing my PhD project but well into planning it—I went on a study trip to Belfast with a group of Danish crime prevention workers. Here, I got to meet various actors taking part in the restorative justice youth conferences: the facilitators responsible for the youth conferences and the processes before and after, the university personnel training the facilitators, the prosecution services, a judge, the police and a young, former offender and his father.[10]

The Northern Irish youth conferences are based on *The balanced model*, which "gives equal attention to the rights, needs and interests of the person, who has been harmed by the offence, the young person responsible for the harm and the community" (Zinsstag and Chapman 2012). The process of the youth conference is as follows:

- *Pre-conference preparatory work.* Focus is on the need of the parties, what they expect from/after the conference, and how/if they will contribute[11]
- *Youth conference.* The facilitator "facilitates the parties to meet. To tell their stories, to express their emotions, to enter a dialogue with each other, to arrive at a shared understanding and generate a plan [the Action Plan] to repair the harm and to prevent further offending" (Zinsstag and Chapman 2012)
- *Post-conference, completion of Action Plan.* The facilitator and other Youth Justice Agency staff work with the young offender to ensure and promote completion of the plan

---

[10]I also met with several civil institutions performing restorative services. This included an organisation under the Irish Republican Army whose positive experiences with restorative approaches during the final years of the violent Northern Ireland conflict helped spur the current usage of restorative justice youth conferences in juvenile cases. Our hosts were the Faculty of Law at the University of Ulster and Tim Chapman and Hugh Campbell—both internationally renowned for their knowledge and contribution within the research and practice fields of restorative justice.

[11]The participation of the victim in the process is voluntary. If the victim wishes to contribute without personal attendance there are several options, such as videoconference, recorded/written statements and participation behind a one-way mirror.

In terms of resources emphasis is on the pre- and post-conference work. After the conference, the action plan is ratified by a youth court judge to ensure proportionality between the offence committed and the contents of the plan.

No doubt, Northern Ireland has been first mover in Europe when it comes to restorative responses to juvenile offending. Youth conferences have been available by law nationwide in Northern Ireland since 2006 for all juvenile offenders who have admitted in materiality to their offence and wish to have their case handled within this system instead of the traditional judicial system. Evaluations of the 2008 cohort showed that young people are substantially less likely to reoffend (Lyness and Tate 2011).

Further to this, between 2006 and 2009 the offended party participation rate in conferences was 74% (Youth Justice Agency 2009–2010). In restorative justice theory, offended party participation is generally seen as implicit to the process. But as the examples in this article will show, in reality, restorative approaches to youth offending—for various reasons—often take place without the presence of an offended party. In this context, 74% is a very high offended party participation rate.

Offended party satisfaction rates were measured at 90% in 2006 (Campbell et al. 2006) and 84% in 2009 (Youth Justice Agency 2009–2010), which are high numbers compared to offended party satisfaction rates in traditional judicial processes at large. From a political perspective offended party satisfaction is arguably a key factor when substituting traditional responses to a criminal offence with a restorative approach. References to the fluffy concept of 'sense of justice' is often central in resistance towards embarking on restorative approaches to crime. In such a debate, arguments as 'rehabilitation', 'low recidivism', and 'cost-effectiveness' seem to diminish in the presence of 'offended party satisfaction'. It simply seems illogical that vague notions of a 'sense of justice' should triumph over the feelings of the actual offended parties involved.

All-in-all the numbers seemed to be in favour of the Northern Ireland restorative approach to juvenile offences to the extent that it made very much sense for us as Danish crime prevention workers to take a closer look at matters. This is how the study trip to Belfast came into play.

2.2 Empathic Disciplining

The trip to Belfast was my first meeting with restorative justice as an alternative reaction to juvenile criminal offences. We were too many to observe an actual youth conference, but a role-play was employed to show the typical course of a youth conference. From my mediation training in Denmark I was used to this approach, and I volunteered to participate in the role-play. I was the selected to play the young offender. After having red my instructions and received oral guidelines, the role-play began.

One of the most experienced and highly esteemed youth conference facilitators was leading the séance. She had already told us passionately about her work and came across as a very warm, empathetic facilitator.

Yet during the role-play conference I was somewhat surprised by the approach the facilitator took towards me as 'offender'. My mediation training in Denmark had perhaps foremost been based on Vindeløv's previously outlined reflexive mediation model, according to which the mediator must act impartial and respect the autonomy and dignity of the parties. But during this role-play youth conference, the facilitator—in my experience—took a very corrective approach to me as 'offender', asking me several times to sit up straight, look up, speak up ... in ways that—to me—connoted a more authoritative, disciplinary approach. Even if it was just a role-play, this approach did not give me the feeling of being treated as an equal by an impartial mediator. And I was not the only one in the visiting group of practitioners to notice this deviation from what we would perceive as appropriate mediator practice. This experience became a central part of our group reflection after the role-play had ended.

On the other hand, during our trip we had also met a young former offender and his father (as previously mentioned) who had been part of one of the same facilitator's cases. The boy who had committed the offence came from a very vulnerable family background. His father had been in prison for political violence during the boy's adolescent years. He had lived with his mother in a very challenged area. He had had problems with alcohol, substance abuse, and criminal behaviour from a young age. The boy who had committed the offense described how he had experienced both compassion and to be taken seriously from the facilitator, and that the restorative process had sparked reflections to the extent that he had changed his life afterwards. It had been a year since the youth conference when we met him, and he was no longer drinking, using drugs, or committing criminal offences. The father, who was now out of prison, had been incarcerated when the youth conference had been held, but he was part of the conference via skype. This had had a very emotional effect on both father and son, who had both been in tears during the conference. Hearing them tell their stories was, indeed, very moving to us as visitors as well.

As such, my impressions of the Northern Irish youth conferences were dualistic and posed a dilemma, which gave food for thought. On the one hand, it was an eye-opening reminder that, of course, the mind-set behind practicing restorative approaches was not as dogmatic and universally agreed upon as the commonly used theoretical references in this field—with their restorative/retributive dichotomy—might lead us to believe. On the other hand, I was convinced that the Northern Irish youth conference approach—even if its practice had some contradictions with the behind-lying theoretical framework of restorative justice as I had interpreted it — had a lot more to offer than the approach of the traditional Danish justice system as I had experienced it working with young offenders.[12] And when describing the *raison d'être* of the youth conferences the attitude of the professionals involved towards the young offenders was, without exception, empathic and resource-based.

[12]Before my entry into the field of mediation/restorative justice research I have worked for 2.5 years as a teacher at a boarding school for teenagers where many of the students were socially and psychologically challenged and later 5 years with vulnerable youth and crime prevention in a municipality. Through my work in the municipality and later through a job in the probation service, I have worked with many young people who have committed one or more offences and have been in—sometimes repetitive—contact with the social as well as the justice system.

The visit to Northern Ireland certainly made me curious to experience other approaches to responding to juvenile offences within a restorative framework. The first country on my list was Norway due to its similarity to Denmark. Yet Norway has had a much more longstanding experience with restorative approaches to conflict.

3 The New Norwegian Youth Sanctions: The Balance Act Boundaries of Restoring and Volunteering

3.1 Professionalising the Restorative Field

In Norway, two new Norwegian restorative youth sanctions were adopted on 1 July 2014. In these the traditional restorative approach of including those who are directly affected by a harm[13] is extended to include a range of professionals, too. In the context of the elaborate Nordic welfare models, it can indeed seem tempting to include the actors of the social system as well when using restorative justice as an alternative or supplement to the traditional judicial system for juveniles. Especially so for someone like me, who—as a professional working with vulnerable youth— time and time again has witnessed the effects of the often confusing and eclectic myriad of social and legal systems and precautions that are set into motion once a minor has committed a criminal offence.

The new restorative sanctions were anchored in the well-known and acclaimed *konfliktråd* institution (Norwegian National Mediation Service). The service was founded by law in 1991 and has, since 2004, been administrated under the ministry of justice. It is a free and voluntary conflict handling/mediation service offered in all Norwegian municipalities. Both civil and penal cases can be treated (National Mediation Service Act (konfliktrådsloven section 1). Konfliktråd is a popular service. Currently, approximately 7500 cases are handled each year, distributed approximately equally between civil and penal cases.[14] The service's mediators are volunteer 'impartial' laymen who are trained and paid for their service. Often two mediators cooperate on each case. The mediator(s) have one or more conversations with all parties before the mediation. This includes guardians if any parties are minors (Konfliktrådet 2017d). According to the service's webpage, the course of the mediation is as follows: "During the meeting everyone gets the opportunity to tell about their experiences, reactions, and emotions regarding what has happened, and

---

[13]Generally the offending and offended party and their private networks and—if relevant and possible—representatives from the immediate affected community/neighbourhood as, for instance, in the Northern Irish model.

[14]In comparison, the Danish parallel Victim Offender Mediation Service (konfliktråd) handle approximately 650 cases a year (Konfliktrådet 2017a). The two countries have a similar population size.

what they would like to happen in the future. It is the parties and not the mediator, who suggest what should be part of a possible agreement" (Konfliktrådet 2017c). The contents of the meetings are confidential. In penal cases and civil cases referred by the police, a copy of the agreement is sent to the police after the mediation. If no agreement is reached, the police is informed about this (Konfliktrådet 2017b).

The two new forms of restorative youth sanctions are as follows:

- *Ungdomsstraff* (youth sanction), which is for more serious and/or repeated offences. It is an alternative, restorative sanction for criminal offences that would have otherwise meant spending time in jail. The court decides whether this sanction is suitable for the individual offender/offence.
- *Ungdomsoppfølging* (youth follow-up) is an alternative, restorative sanction for less serious offences than in the case of youth sanction. The prosecutor or the court can decide on this option if a professional team concludes that the life situation and behaviour of the young offender indicates that he or she will benefit from close professional/private follow-up.

The sanctions were a result of years of successful pilot studies and represent a merger between restorative justice conferencing and coordinated efforts of the social system. They both entail a restorative meeting and a youth plan (see below). But as the seriousness of the offences committed vary for the two forms of sanctions, they differ in terms of the length of the follow-up period and of the sanctions possibly imposed if the young offender does not stay committed to the contents of the plan.

- Both types of sanctions are coordinated by a *youth coordinator*. The youth coordinators are based at the Mediation Service, but are professionals as opposed to the mediators, who are laymen. The process of the sanctions is (ideally) as follows:
- *Coordination group meeting:* Youth coordinator (YC) coordinates an initial meeting with professional parties relevant for the case (school, police, social workers etc) to discuss whether a youth sanction/youth follow-up is profitable for the young person.
- *Information meeting*: YC contacts the young offender and his/her guardians to inform about the process, asks if they are interested in such process, and, if so, makes sure the process is voluntarily engaged in.
- *Preparation meeting:* YC and mediator/s meet seperately with the young person and their private network *to prepare for the restorative meeting.*
- *Restorative meeting* with offended party and relevant networks of both parties takes place, facilitated by one or two laymen mediators from the Mediation Service. YC participates.
- *Youth plan meeting* with the young offender and his/her relevant private and professional network, during which the youth plan is developed, agreed to, and signed by all parties. The Youth plan includes various initiatives targeted at ensuring that reoffending will not take place, for instance, curfews, full school attendance, tutoring, sports, anger replacement therapy, drug testing, community

service etc. The plan includes obligations for both the young offender and the private/public networks, and all parties can be held accountable for neglect. The meeting is coordinated by YC and held immediately after the restorative meeting.

- *Monthly follow-up meetings* coordinated by YC throughout the duration of the sanction with the young offender and his private and professional network. The youth plan is revisited; are all parties keeping to the agreements? If not, YC takes the lead in bringing the parties back on track or, if necessary (due to repetitive/serious neglects), sending the case back to the court/police for alternative sentencing/sanctioning.

The new sanctions were passed by a unanimous parliament, and it was decided to base them in the konfliktråd organisation, which had no previous experience with handling juvenile sanctions. This decision was made to emphasise the restorative element, as well as to ensure a different approach than that of the established sanction organisations.[15]

Yet in the article *Widening the Net*, published 2 years after the aforementioned Christie-article, Christie strongly opposes the affiliation between konfliktråd and the two new forms of juvenile sanctions (Christie 2015). Christie was a strong advocate for the necessity of laymen mediators in the Norwegian Mediation Service. With the new Norwegian juvenile sanctions, Christie (2015) argues the service would have penal powers, which will lead to the service losing its civilising strength. Christie warns against the new professional army of 'child savers' and their extensive power to influence the life of the young offenders. With the circle of professionals including social workers, teachers, police officers, and probation workers acting as both quasi legislators, quasi police, and quasi judges the separation of powers are *de facto* put out of play (Christie 2015). Furthermore, similar to concerns of my own after the trip to Belfast, Christie points out, that the volunteer participation of the young offender is very questionable in this construction and thus the very core foundation of the Mediation Service is at stake, Christie (2015) warns.[16]

In the three following sections I will discuss these three concerns of Christie: voluntariness (Sect. 3.2), mixing the punitive and the restorative (Sect. 3.3), and the professionalisation of at least part of the mediation service (Sect. 3.4).

3.2 A Voluntary Process?

The formal answer to Christie's latter critique could be that the consent of both the young person and the guardian must be given before applying to enter either youth sanction and youth follow up, and it can be withdrawn at any time during the

---

[15]For instance, kriminalomsorgen/friomsorgen (probation services).

[16]Christie used the more accurate English translation 'conflict boards' for konfliktråd in his texts. Yet according to the konfliktråd webpage, the official English translation is Norwegian Mediation Service, so this is the translation which is used in this article.

process.[17] So far I have conducted two study trips to Norway focusing on the konfliktråd organisation and its undertaking of these sanctions. During my first trip—in the fall of 2015—the sanctions were still quite new and my interactions were with the management, the responsible coordinators as well as other professional actors involved. In March 2017, further to interviewing several professional actors, I observed various stages of the sanctions involving the young offenders and their private network and interviewed some of these parties as well. Based on these interactions, it is my impression that the management as well as the coordinators of the sanctions are very focused on informing both the young offenders and their guardians of the voluntary nature of the sanctions—as well as the consequences of withdrawing their consent—throughout the process. This element is stressed as very important in both my interviews and in the written and oral information to the young person and his/her guardian(s).

An initial independent evaluation was carried out one year after the sanctions were initiated. In the evaluation report the issue of voluntariness was treated thoroughly, demonstrating that this was taken very seriously by both youth coordinators and mediators. The explanations of young offenders in the report showed that, in general, the young offenders and their guardians had been informed about the process of the sanctions before choosing participate. Yet the young offenders' experiences of this information varied from having been thoroughly informed to signing in panic to avoid jail or signing while under influence of drugs; hence, having no good recollection of the information. The guardians, too, have a mixed evaluation of the information they were given prior to giving their consent, ranging from feeling thoroughly informed to feeling very under-informed. The findings in this evaluation has led to new more elaborate procedures on consent (Eide et al. 2016). During my observations in March 2017 I saw the new consent documents in action. In the consent meetings I observed, they were thoroughly read and explained (and if necessary interpreted) to both the young offender and the present guardian. After explaining each point the offender and guardian were asked if there was anything unclear. Follow-up questions were asked by the YC to make sure the content was understood. It seemed to be a very thorough and highly emphasised process.

But even if the offender and guardian understand the contents, does this make the participation volunteer? What if the young offender does not *really* want to participate in mediation, but he or she *would* prefer it over going to jail, for instance? These seemed to be relevant concerns in relation to the Northern Irish and the Norwegian models alike. In the article *Angreb på mæglingens DNA—ansatser til en diskussion om tvungen mægling* (Attack on the DNA of Mediation—Approaching a Discussion on Forced Mediation), Adrian and Vindeløv make the following point on voluntariness and mediation (my translation):

---

[17]Besides consent from both the young offender and his/her guardian the prerequisites for being granted either of these alternative sanctions are as follows: the young person admits to the crime committed and that he/she is willing to accept responsibility for it—a.o. by agreeing to meet the victim in a Mediation Service meeting.

The point is however not that voluntariness should be seen as a choice between two goods, but might as well be seen as a choice between two evils. The choice is nevertheless there. The difficulty of accepting this as a choice is probably rather the difficulty of accepting that you are in a tough situation where you have to take responsibility for choosing what should happen. Whether you like it or not, you have a problem that is not removed by disregarding responsibility for the choice (Adrian and Vindeløv 2014).

Thus, following the argument of Adrian and Vindeløv, for young offenders who have to choose whether or not to accept one of the new Norwegian sanctions, the possibly bad range of alternative choices does not change the fact that there *is* a choice—and hence voluntariness.

But if the alternative—in the case of youth sanction—is for the young offender to go to jail, wouldn't one be willing to accept almost any alternative? And maybe even play along with accepting guilt and meeting the offended party without *really* feeling remorse, thus wasting time and resources of all involved and risking re-traumatization of the offended party.

Certainly to some critics the notion that the offender might gain anything other than a clearer conscience from participation in a RJ-process is unacceptable, or even unethical—not so only in Norway but internationally. But if this further gain includes initiatives/actions that might make the offender substantially less likely to reoffend than the traditional sanction in question, where would this leave the ethics?

3.3 Conflict Re-theft vs the Noble Cause of Fighting Recidivism

So what is the inside assessment of the Mediation Service so far regarding mixing a restorative and punitive approach?

The two Norwegian youth sanctions of 2014 are based on four pilot projects running from 2006–2008. Each project included around 50 young offenders otherwise facing unconditional jail sentences. The results showed a staggeringly low recidivism rate at around 10%, compared to an approximate 80% reoffending rate for juveniles who had been incarcerated for an offence during the same period (Kvello and Wendelborg 2009). Even before these results there was political agreement in Norway that sending young offenders to jail was, in principle, not acceptable, and here was a seemingly very viable solution to what could otherwise be done in the case of serious youth offences.

Yet even as early as in the 1970s Christie argued against using the allure of a possible fall in recidivism as the reasoning behind facilitation meetings between offender and offended party, even if he suspects such a fall to be likely. Christie's notions on conflict are claimed to have laid ground for the Norwegian Konfliktråd, earning him the informal title as their father. Hence, the critique coming from him 40 years later regarding the Mediation Service's harbouring of the new youth sanctions hit hard.

It seems obvious, that there *is* a discrepancy between the layman principles and the striving towards a minimal relation of the Mediation Service and the judicial system, on the one hand, and the professionalism and the (arguably necessary) focus on legal equality of the juvenile sanctions of 2014, on the other. And so even if the service was already organised under the Department of Justice before the new sanctions came along.

The national coordinator for the Norwegian Mediation Service, Lasse Rolén, was also responsible for one of the successful pilot projects, which arguably brought about the new sanction.[18] He has the following reflections on the placement in Konfliktråd and on Christie's critique: In terms of the placement in the Mediation Service, according to Lasse Rolén, this decision was made because the legislators wanted something different from the existing juvenile sanctions, and they wanted restorative justice to be at the core of this new invention. Rolén was approached to design a front running pilot project. He describes the mandate this way:

> From the beginning, when the government gave us this mandate, the purpose was to create something new within the criminal procedure. And I remember, we were at a meeting in the government quarters – the bombed house over there[19] – and asked 'will we not be given any guidelines?' And they said 'no, because we want you to create something new based on the principles of restorative justice and processes, the consideration of the best interests of the child, and individual plans for the course of the sanction. And you must coordinate the existing resources.' That was the mandate. And that is what we did and what we have been doing since the beginning. So the model we developed and are working with is based on these principles. But we are nowhere near full success yet, because we are still in the start-up phase.

After the pilot projects had proven very successful, the legislators wanted a national arrangement. The arguments for placing this in the Mediation Service were (1) an emphasis on the restorative aspect was desired, (2) as part of the punitive system, the new sanctions would have to be based in a state-based structure, and (3) there was a desire for the new sanctions to be substantially different than the existing ones and thus there was no wish to place them in an existing punitive structure. Furthermore, one of the pilot projects had been anchored in the Stavanger konfliktråd seemingly without disadvantages to either the project or the local service. And so the decision was made.

Lasse Rolén, on the one hand, thinks that placing the sanctions in the Mediation Service can help ensure a more restorative focus in accordance with the original mandate. On the other hand, he does acknowledge Christies warnings, sharing concerns that a classical, sanctioning approach is sneaking up on the work with the young offenders:

K: "So your notion is that you might have been pulled a little too far towards that which already existed?"

---

[18]Lasse Rolén has now retired. He was acting national coordinator when the interview took place in March 2017.

[19]The government quarters were bombed in the Oslo terrorist attacks, 22 July 2011.

L: "That which existed, yes. And it is often like that when you are inventing something new, it is difficult to hold on to that era of pioneering. Then you can quickly relapse to the prehistoric times. [...] You are not successful in maintaining the pioneer era for a sufficiently long time."

[...]

K: "So could one at the end of the day worry that Christie was right and that this (the new juvenile sanctions) has been some kind of fifth column action, which could destroy the Mediation Services from within?"

L: "Yes... Well, Nils Christie told me just before he died – I was at the institute giving a lecture – and he said ... he thanked me for a very exciting lecture. He thought it was interesting. But he said 'you know I am worried'. I said 'yes, and in some ways your worries are real. But it will be up to us to take care of those founding principles, so that your worries will not come through – to put it like that.' A development is taking place. I cannot tell the future. I am merely launching some thoughts as to how we should base ourselves on the founding principles. It has developed a little off track – I can't tell in which direction – but as of now we are not able to stick fully to the principles upon which this was supposed to be based."

Hence, in Rolén's opinion, it is too soon to say whether placing the new sanctions in the Mediation Service will turn out to be the right decision. But he also stresses that he is very focused on keeping the restorative approach at the very core of both the new sanctions and the Mediation Service as a whole.

3.4   The Conscientious Chain of Caring Professionals

And what are the experiences regarding re-professionalising a field that had been consciously and carefully de-professionalised with success only a few decades back? Youth coordinator '1' shared these reflections on whether or not the role of the professional youth coordinator is true to the restorative foundation of the Mediation Service:

K: "O.K. So traditionally Konfliktråd were built on a foundation of laymen principles and Christie's idea of giving back the conflicts to the people."

1: "Mm. To those who own them."

K: "[...] and the professionals should stay out of it. How do you feel that your role as youth coordinator fits into the Mediation Service in this perspective? Do you feel there might be a conflict between those two positions?"

1: "Yes. Very much so. I can sense that. Because the traditional Mediation Service is mainly about restoring and facilitating a meeting between people. But with us youth coordinators and the new sanctions the Mediation Service has become punishment executors and this can lead to conflicts of interest. Everything the Service deals with is based on consent. And this is also the case for youth sanction and youth follow-up. But it is a consent with some cracks in the rear-view mirror.

Which could be a prison sentence. And then the young person has to choose between prison or youth sanction. And if they choose youth sanction they will have signed to that it is based on consent. But I have to put in actions, which require a lot from the young person. So I am thinking, it might not be a full consent all the way. But it is in order to avoid something which is worse. So that can in a way lead to a conflict of interest in the Mediation Service.

"Also the restorative process might not take up a huge amount of space in a long course of a youth sanction. There is the restorative meeting between the young person and the offended in the beginning. And when that is done the youth plan takes over. And it is not necessarily so that something from that meeting makes its way into the youth plan (see footnote 21). And then – in a way – the restorative part is over.

"But then again you can interpret in a different way too. And if you think about the whole course of the sanction the young person is restoring something towards him/herself towards the community. Towards parents. Then you can interpret it that way. So if you are focused on the restorative angle throughout the sanction, it depends on how you interpret it. And how you define restoration."

Youth coordinator '2' had the following perspective on the double role of the Mediation Service and restorative theory meeting the reality of being a youth coordinator:

2: "I find it very rewarding (being a youth coordinator). Because I can see how it works for some young people. It has opened a possibility for the young person to be heard. I feel that if you are a good youth coordinator and you are doing a thorough preparatory job with those, who will be in the follow-up team,[20] and you are good at establishing positive relations with the young person, which leads to him or her really getting involved in the follow-up, the impacts can be great. That is how I feel based on what I see. [. . .]

"But [. . .] it is like this . . . in theory all of this sounds very good, but in practice there are challenges, which I in a way see every day. One is that I am very focused on the sanctions in the Mediation Service should be an alternative to the existing sanctions. Probation service etc. Now I am afraid we might become too similar to them."

K: "O.K."

2: "That we are somehow too controlling and sanctioning."

K: "Yes. And you fear that this will take up to much focus?"

2: "Yes. I am afraid of that. And it makes me want to be a voice, which blows the whistle if the Mediation Service in a way lose its grip and integrity. As an

---

[20]A follow-up team consists of the young offender, the youth coordinator, the young person's professional and private network. The team meets once a month throughout the sanction period with the youth coordinator as facilitator. The professional network includes e.g. children's services, a teacher (if in school), probation services, and a police officer, and more professional participants are mandatory in case of youth sanction compared to youth follow-up.

organisation that should focus on a restorative process and relations between the Mediation Service and the young person."

As the quotations above suggest, my visits to the Norwegian Mediation Service so far leave the clear impression that—while also stressing the importance of the future wellbeing of the offended party—the people working with the two forms of juvenile sanctions based here care deeply about the future wellbeing of the young offenders with whom they come into contact. And that this is their main reason for choosing this profession. In the following example, youth coordinator '1' tells about his reasons for applying for the job:

1: "[The job is] very versatile. And I like working with the vulnerable – those who have the harshest conditions. It ended up that way when I taught in high school – that I was asked to work with those young people, who many of my colleagues thought were difficult and challenging. But at the end of the day I thought that when you back track a little and see why they are like they are, then I had no problem saying 'I think they deserve another chance'. There is something there. But many of my colleagues would not take on that job, because it was hard work, they were externalising, it was heavy. But I liked being in it and understanding why it is like it is. Why they are like they are. Then it is much easier to change the path forward – to help them on this path."

Hence, the focus of the youth coordinators is—in my experience from interviews and observations—resource-based in both words and in action. I have not once experienced punishment of the offenders articulated as a rationale for their work. The common notion amongst them seems to be that a 'chain' of caring professional as well as private help is provided around the young offender with the youth plan as the guide.[21] A chain that can be removed at the young person's (or his/her guardian's) will. That a less friendly alternative will then take over is something that they are aware of and live with, but not something they necessarily condone or think they can be held responsible for.

---

[21]The youth plan is almost equivalent to the Northern Irish action plan. Just as in Northern Ireland, the young person must keep to the plan, and if this is not the case, the young person risks going back to court and complete the alternative, court-ordered sentence instead. Yet in Norway there is a big emphasis on the responsibility of the professional parties, too—not just on that of the young person. It is designed and agreed upon in a separate meeting in the follow-up team (including the young offender). The meeting normally takes place immediately after the restorative meeting, but without the offended party and his/her network. The plan contains various case dependent actions that the young person and the professional/private network are mutually obliged to carry out, e.g. drug testing, anger management, physical training/sports, community work, scheduled homework etc.

3.5 And (Restorative) Justice for All?

Another point to consider in terms of equality before the law is that in Norway—as opposed to in Northern Ireland—the access to youth Sanction and youth follow-up is a matter of estimate. As described above, the young offender cannot participate without his or her own consent as well as that of his/her guardian. Yet it is, depending on *inter alia* the seriousness of the charge and the life situation of the offender, up to a judge, the prosecution and/or a coordination group of professionals (including e.g. (case dependent) children's services, school, police and youth coordinator) to decide whether the young person could benefit from such a sanction *and* whether such sanction is an appropriate/proportionate response to the offense. The former would typically involve questioning whether, for instance, the quite heavy artillery of a youth follow-up might be over the top compared to a—disregarding the offence—relatively positive and stabile life situation of the offender. The latter can, for instance, mean that in very serious cases it can be seen as violating to the public sense of justice for the offender to receive youth sanction instead of a jail sentence. However, such conclusion is extremely rare, since the general tendency in Norway—as mentioned—is to avoid the incarceration of minors, but is has happened in a few cases.

In this way the elastic heart of the Norwegian sanctions of 2014 perhaps seems more in congruence with the—ideally—individual approach of restorative justice than with the principal of equality before the law. But where there is room for judgment calls social research has continuously showed us there is also room for (more or less both traceable and conscious) discrimination. Professional does not equal neutral, so how do we ensure that the decision made is in the best interests of the young offender, as well as the local community and perhaps society as a whole (whatever the latter might mean)?

The same elasticity also goes for estimating when a youth plan—the core of the two 2014 types of sanctions—has been diverted from to such a degree, that the young person has not lived up to it and the case needs to be sent back to the judge/prosecution in order to put something else in play. This could, for instance, in the case of youth sanction, mean jail time for the young offender. Within the legislation it is up for the youth coordinator to decide when enough is enough, but in reality the decision is made with other professional members of the young person's follow-up team and/or coordination group (for instance, police, children's services, probation services, prosecution, teacher etc.) as well as the local management of the Mediation Service where the case is based.

As illustrated in the quotations above, holding this (co-)power to decide when to stop trying to 'restore' is not something the professionals working with the sanctions at the Mediation Service seem to enjoy. Yet the rationale seems to be 'rather us than someone else' as the perception within the Service—as outside critique also has suggested—is that the people working here will stretch very wide to keep a (consenting) young person 'on-board'. This dilemma, of course, contains universal relevance wherever ideology meets practice.

Just as in Northern Ireland, the principal of equality before the law also suggests that an offended party not wanting to participate in a restorative meeting should not hinder an offender's access to the Norwegian sanctions of 2014. Hence, if necessary, restorative meetings are held without the presence of an offended party, leaving it up to the Mediation Service mediator to bring the offended party's perspective into the meeting in order to spark the young offender's reflections upon his/her actions.[22] Contrary to the intention, it has proven difficult for the Mediation Service to ensure a high rate of offended party participation for the restorative meetings. In my interviews several youth coordinators estimated offended party participation to be as low as around 50%. This estimate was confirmed by the management as a number that had also come up in a recent internal evaluation.

3.6 The Show Must Go On: When Offended Parties Decline the Invitations

This is obviously an undesired state of events that has given rise to self-reflection in the Mediation Service. How can this be and how can it be changed? As to the first, experience points to the amount of time passing between the offence and the meeting as the key problem: Before a restorative sanction is set in motion, typically a long period of investigation, casework and preparation will have passed, perhaps causing the offended party to have lost interest in the offence. Arguably especially so for less serious cases, which make up the majority of the juvenile cases handled by the Mediation Service—including *ungdomsoppfølging* cases. As to the second question—how to fix this—several suggestions are in the pipeline. For instance, it is being suggested that the Mediation Service—if possible—should have more lenient options to arrange the restorative meetings while the investigation, case work etc. is still going on.

Also, there are suggestions to 'upgrade' the process of the offended party as well so that he or she is not left with a (couple of) pre-meeting(s) and the restorative meeting itself, but can—at his or her own will—be entitled to some sort of follow-up period as well. This suggestion has been made in order to avoid a feeling of re-traumatisation by the offended party, based on the difference in attention he or she gets compared to that of the young offender in the present design of the new sanctions.

---

[22]In Norway, the restorative meeting is facilitated by a layman Mediation Service mediator. The youth coordinator is present. After the restorative meeting with/regarding the victim is over, the victim (and participants related to him/her), if present, and the Mediation Service mediator leave the room. The youth coordinator takes over the facilitation of the second part with the purpose of agreeing to a youth plan. The participants in the second part are the offender, his/her guardian and maybe other personal relations, and the professionals team including the youth coordinator—all of which are present for the first part of the meeting as well.

Even if this approach might be tempting, several of the Norwegian National Mediation Service personnel stressed the importance of not 'luring' the offended party into participating for the sake of the offender—in order to help him/her not to reoffend. The offended party should participate for his/her own sake; otherwise, the risk of re-traumatisation is big. Especially if the young offender does not behave the way the offended party expects him/her to in the meeting afterwards.

But judging from the current state—if offended party participation is as low as 50%—might this be the final reason to call out the Norwegian sanctions of 2014 as cases of *not restorative justice'ness*? This would certainly seem to satisfy Christie and other critics. I asked several employees at the Mediation Service about this perspective. The following quotation is from an interview with youth coordinator '2':

K: "So what did you know about restorative processes before you started?"

2: "Only theoretical knowledge. I had read about the history of konfliktråd [. . .] but I had never seen how it worked in practice."

K: "No"

2: "So, in practice, it is different from what you read about it. [. . .] I am thinking, if you say, you are working at the Mediation Service, people will assume I am working with restorative meetings. What I see as a challenge in [the sanctions] is that there is often no restorative meeting with an offended party. [. . .] And that is a big problem. For the offended party that he or she doesn't get to meet those persons who have caused them harm. But it is also a big problem that the young person does not get to meet those who has been put through whatever they have done. Because I feel it has such a positive effect on them to see that. What I really like about this job are the times when you hear the story of the offended – it has such a great effect." [. . .]

K: "But is what you are doing 'restorative processes' then?"

2: "Well, yes, because I don't think restorative processes is about what we know as the restorative meeting between the offender and the offended party. I think that restorative processes can also be seen in relations to school, teachers, parents etc. In a way, I think that all this relations work that we do and get into the plans is, in a way, based on the thoughts behind restorative processes. [. . .] So, yes, I feel like I am working restoratively. That is what is in the back of my mind when I am working with a youth plan [. . .] that is what I want to come forward. The purpose of the youth plan is that their trust in people and institutions they somehow have to relate to will increase."

The other employees I interviewed had similar perceptions on the matter of offended party participation. They all agreed that it was an important focus to bring up the number of offended party participants. But they also suggest that the restorative process in these juvenile cases can and should not be diminished to the meeting between offended party and offender. As previously demonstrated, in their view it is just as much a matter of restoring the young person's relations with family, society etc. as well as restoring his/her options of and believe in a future without crime/unconstructive behaviour. And this view is arguably compliable with interpretations of restorative practice increasingly gaining terrain within pedagogical practice in, for instance, schools and youth work.

4 Orlando, Florida: An Alternative 'Community' Approach

4.1 Diverting Young Offenders Restoratively

While the Norwegian youth coordinators seem inclined to have a resource based, non-penal approach to the youth sanctions they coordinate, my impression from visiting two restorative justice juvenile programs in the Florida was somewhat different.

In November 2016 I made a research trip to the Ninth Judicial Circuit Court of Florida to study two diversion programs for first time juvenile offenders only.[23] The newest—and to me most relevant—of the two programs was the *neighborhood restorative justice (NRJ) program*. This was also the program that brought the Ninth Judicial Circuit Court of Florida to my attention with the following website description:

> The Ninth Judicial Circuit Court of Florida is broadening its reach into its localized communities in an attempt to aid neighbourhoods in repairing the harm that is caused by crime. The Neighborhood Restorative Justice Program will empower the victims and the communities in a process of restoration. Through the non-adversarial methods of negotiation, conferencing, mediation, and reparation, a restorative solution to the harm of crime will be discovered. Crime is a violation of the entire community. The damage that is caused by crime affects victims, offenders, their family and the community as a whole. Restorative justice attempts to solve the damage of crime by actively involving all concerned parties. (Ninth Judicial Circuit Court of Florida 2017a)

Note that this program uses the terminology 'victim', which is largely in accordance with Zehr's terminology. In Northern Ireland and Norway the primarily used terminology is 'offended party'.

The other program juvenile diversion program of the Ninth Judicial Circuit Court was the longer running *teen court* program. Even if this program did not have *restorative* as part of the title, the understanding of the professionals working with this program was that it was based on a restorative framework. The teen court program is described as follows on the Ninth Judicial Circuit Court of Florida website (Ninth Judicial Circuit Court of Florida 2017b:

> Teen Court is a voluntary diversion program from Juvenile Court or school suspension and provides the following:

---

[23]Offenders under the age of 18 years. There is no lower age limit. The youngest participant in the NRJ program so far was 8 years old. His was facing charges for battering/disobeying his mother and was omitted to the program at the mother's request

A forum for defendants to explain their involvement in the offense

A structured environment in which the words and actions of defendants who admit their wrongful acts are evaluated and judged by a jury of their peers

The opportunity for defendants to accept responsibility for their actions by fulfilling the jury's sentence of community service hours and future jury duty assignments, both of which are designed to be constructive and rehabilitative.

The two programs have the same target group in the district regarding age of the offender and nature (seriousness) of the offence. Whether a young person is offered one or the other depends on the zip code in which they live. The teen court program has been running since 1994 and is the most widespread of the two, covering the whole district except the few zip code areas running the Neighborhood Restorative Justice Program. The NRJ program has been running since 2000 and is available as a diversion option only in the areas of *Apopka* and *Eatonville*.

4.2   A Very Alternative Restorative Experience

In the case of the NRJ Program, I had the opportunity to observe two juvenile accountability conferences and interview the professionals and neighbourhood board involved. Both conferences took place an evening—one after the other—at a very remote firefighter training facility in a rural community—one of the two that had been selected for the program.

The professionals present were:

- *a youth coordinator* from the court (one of two), who had the responsibility of bringing the case to the board, and
- *a school resource officer* (a police officer with part of his schedule assigned to be present at a local high school), who follows up on compliance to the agreed sanctions.

The neighborhood board were three volunteer women of Caucasian descent. I would estimate them all to be between 50 and 70 years and to have an upper middleclass background. All of the women had been involved in the program for a number of years and at least one of them had served on the board since the beginning in 2000. The women had no relations to the young offenders in either of the two cases, nor had they have any relation to/knowledge of the offences prior to coming to serve on the board on the evening of the two conferences.

The contents of the sanctions plan was very standardised, as a norm entailing:

- Letter apologizing to victim (i.e. arresting police officer and the school respectively)
- Letter apologizing to parent
- Letter saying good bye to marihuana (if applicable)

- Assignment explaining worst case scenario during the offence and what one would do to avoid a similar situation in the future, and
- A number of civil service hours decided by the board before the conference at an institution/organisation of own choice
- Curfews (details were agreed upon in the conference)
- Random drug testing

Other options were boot camps, drug treatment, anger management classes etc. The contents of the plan have to be carried out within a certain time frame, around 6 months depending on the offence. The young person meets with the board again approximately half way through the sentence and towards the end of it.

In both cases the offenders were of Hispanic descent and came from poor single parent families. In the first case it was a 15-year-old boy[24] and in the last case it was siblings, a 13-year-old girl and a 11-year-old boy.[25] After the young offenders had explained their version of the offences, the women on the board took over. As I experienced it, their attitude was very disciplinary. The main focus was on how the children should respect the police officer and other authorities no matter what.

The boy in the first case performed better in terms of dressing for the occasion, speaking clearly and behaving very respectfully during the conference, so towards the end of his session, both the women on the board, the police officer and the court coordinator took a more friendly approach to him, increasingly focusing on his possibilities in the future. A specific concern of mine during this conference was that the mother clearly did not understand English very well, yet the contents of the conference was only very sporadically interpreted to her by the coordinator. But, all in all, the experience did not seem to have been negative for neither the boy nor his mother.

As for the two siblings the charge was more serious. And it only added to the seriousness of the case that both siblings tested positive for marihuana at the mandatory—previously announced—drug test upon arrival at the conference location. Yet even if I do agree that this case was serious because of their age, considering that same aspect—their age—I found the approach of the boards, the police officer and the coordinator to be very overwhelming.

In an attempt to scare to kids from smoking marihuana again the women on the board and the police officer interchangeably warned how the goal of the two older co-offenders and the mother of the co-offenders was most likely to get the siblings addicted to marihuana, to have them sell drugs for them, and very possibly also to

---

[24]He was a high school student who had been charged with resisting arrest. His explanation, which was not contested by the coordinator from the court, nor the police officer, was the following: He had left the stadium during a break in a football match to meet a friend outside. Standing in a group of Hispanic youth they were approach by the police, who told them to leave the area. The boy objected, as he had a ticket and wanted to go back in for the next part of the game. He did not get to show the ticket, but was arrested instead and charged with disobeying an officer and resisting arrest.

[25]The two siblings had broken into a school with two older boys and played with a fire extinguisher. A 'silent alarm'—recording what went on the building without letting the perpetrators know it—tipped off the police. All four of them were arrested at gunpoint by police/dog patrols.

smoke them both unconscious in order to be able to 'rape them again and again' before 'trafficking them off to another country'—stressing that 'this happens to boys too'.[26] Through most of the session both the mother and the two siblings were in tears. The siblings seemed very ashamed and were very much out of their comfort zone. When asked they only spoke in very short sentences. This was commented negatively on and perceived as provocative by the women on the board. When asked how she felt, the mother said that she was concerned, distressed, disappointed, and ashamed—all of which her appearance seemed to confirm.

In my experience, the focus of the conferences was one of 'telling off'—by the women on the board, by the coordinator from the court, and (partly) from the police officer. It did not seem like there was a lot of interest in or room for the perspective of the children in these conferences.

On a more positive remark, towards the end there was a lot of encouragement as to how the children could work towards a better future for themselves. Especially in the first case where the boy's dreams of becoming a firefighter really seemed to be positively boosted by the support of especially the board and the police officer.

Also there was a clear emphasis on empowering the parent. This empowerment did, however, seem to act as a double edged sword for the siblings in the last case. As mentioned, the mother was very concerned, disappointed and angry—with good reason. She asked for stricter sentences than intended by the board; for instance, promoting her son's participation in a boot camp for which he was too young.[27] And when the police officer asked for permission to 'go through their phones' she granted it with pleasure. This to me was concerning, as I felt that this approach clearly exceeded the limits of what would have been a likely outcome of a court case.[28]

4.3   Empathic Hard-Liners: We Scare Because We Care

After the conferences I spoke with the board about the two cases. They were all very optimistic about the first case. And in the second case they talked about how they felt compassion for the mother and her difficult situation. The conversation was very empathic and the mood was relaxed and very different from the quite a lot tougher atmosphere during the conferences. I was asked about my perception of the conferences and told them how the approach was quite different and a lot harsher compared to the restorative processes I had experienced elsewhere. But it did seem to me that

---

[26]From my field notes it is not clear who said what between the police officer and the women on the board. But both the officer and at least two of the women were part of the story telling, in which the parties seemed to continue to top each other in order to stress the seriousness.

[27]The solution was that the boot camp would be added to his action plan to be completed towards the end of his sentence time when he would have turned 12 years old and have sufficient age.

[28]Being no expert in American juvenile cases this is solely based on my perception, but I do not actually know what court precedence is regarding privacy laws in cases like this.

this approach was overall probably a positive alternative to what young offenders might otherwise experience from the justice system.

I also asked about the absence of the offended parties, and the answer was that they were not part of these processes and that the board was somehow representing the victim's perspective. This answer was surprising to me as—judging from the previously outlined webpage description of the program, which stresses that the program *'will empower the victims'*—I would have assumed that offended parties play a central role in the program. But they all agreed that it would be an interesting perspective to work at including offended parties in some cases. I raised the question as to how they felt about the processes' potential to include more serious offences, explaining how even murder may be included in Norway and rape in both Northern Ireland and Norway. They all seemed very surprised by this possibility and agreed that this wide approach was probably not a possibility in the United States. But they did think it could be a possibility to test including some cases that were somewhat more serious that the current ones, because they all agreed, that the offenders had a much better chance of succeeding after this program than after having been through the traditional justice system. As discussed later, this view was substantially backed up by internal reoffending statistics. The women on the board explained how this was the big motivator for them to volunteer for the program. They stressed how great it was to meet young offenders again towards the end of the sentence and see how they made great efforts to change their ways.

Later I spoke with the police officer alone for a while. He too was passionate about being part of the conferences, as he thought they allowed for a much more efficient way of dealing with juvenile offences. Throughout the sentence period he acts as a mentor for the young offenders. He explained how he would 'break them down until they cry and then build them up'. Again a very different approach to 'restoring' than what I had previously been exposed to. Yet without a doubt this approach was founded on a wish to help the young person get back on track rather than an urge to punish.

The following evening I observed five seperate cases in teen court divided in two different court room settings. Here, the setting was different. It simulated a real court case, where only the judge was an actual judge and all other parts, prosecutor, defender, court clerks etc. where played by teenagers who had volunteered for the program, which would give them credits for college, amongst other things. The jury was a mix of volunteers and young offenders who had previously had a case before the teen court, and whose service on the jury for a decided number of evenings was part of their 'sentence'. But the general attitude towards the offender and the contents of the sanctions were similar. And here too—in spite of the attempt to simulate a real court case—no offended parties were present.

One mother tried to object to her daughter having to apologise to her, since she did not feel the daughter had anything to apologise for. The judge explained to her that she was forced to listen to her daughter's apology if the daughter should stay in the program. The following apology from mother to daughter did—needless to say—not ring very genuine heartfelt, nor did the acceptance by the mother.

During my stay I interviewed the leader of the NRJ program, who was overall happy with its performance. And seemingly with very good reason: She shared internal reoffending statistics from the program, which had been consistent around 6% for all the years. An internal study from April 2016 based on the 2014 cases showed a combined recidivism rate of 7.65% after one year for the two programs. These results, she told, were substantially better than those of the traditional approaches to similar juvenile offences. This had led to more serious cases like burglary being tested in the program as well.[29] She stressed how the principle of both programs is early intervention, applying the least restrictive options through a more holistic approach than the normal—and more expensive—procedures of the court.

I also interviewed the two youth coordinators[30] in this program and the manager of the teen court program individually. All of them—including the NRJ program leader—definitely stressed the aim to help the young people and how they were rooting for them to make it to a crime-free future. But the two NRJ coordinators and the teen court manager also emphasised how these programs were an option to hit young offenders with harder sanctions than they would have received in a court. There was also a lot of emphasis on 'outsmarting' the young people, not falling for their tricks, etc. as if the base assumption seemed to be that young offenders were not to be trusted.

This line of argumentation was in strong contrast to my experiences interviewing RJ professionals in Norway and Northern Ireland. It is unclear to me how much of this emphasis on punishment was motivated by countering arguments that the staff seemingly often runs into on these programs being too soft on offenders, and how much was based on their personal sensations on this matter. Arguably one is likely to influence the other, and in the United States the rhetoric concerning—also juvenile—crime is without a question much harsher than in Northern Ireland or the Nordic countries. Yet the Florida Department of Juvenile Justice has a whole 'myths vs facts' section on their webpage dedicated to clarify common misperceptions on juvenile offending. This includes a series of referrals to research stating that establish the inefficiency of counter productivity of various hard liner tactics in preventing and handling youth offending (Florida Department of Juvenile Justice 2017). This list interestingly includes boot camps and 'scare them straight-tactics,' which makes it odd that these factors appeared so prevalent in restorative programs in the same state.

A final point regarding the Florida programs concerns the reason for joining them: For the offenders, the main attraction of the diversion programs is that nothing will go on your record. This is the key argument used to get juvenile offenders to submit to a process that possibly entails substantially more elements of punishment/disciplining than a sentence for the same first-time offence in the court system

---

[29]With the large rates of private gun ownership and 'stand your ground' laws in the United States, invading a private home by committing a burglary is not only considered a serious crime but also a very risky one. In terms of the reoffending rates for juvenile offences handled in the traditional system, I asked for a referral but I have not been able to locate the numbers.

[30]One of them was the coordinator from the conferences the night before.

would. Yet if the young person has been arrested in relation to the offense, the arrest remains on record even if the offence itself does not. And the currency of 'nothing-on-record' might be devaluating fast as colleges, employers and others are catching on to these new forms of state disciplining and are now starting to ask in application forms, whether the applicant has ever participated in a diversion program. And as the program workers stress, it is not recommended that you lie.[31] It will be interesting to see how this development affects future participant motivation for these types of programs.

5 Discussion: When Is Restorative Justice?

As a Danish researcher and practitioner I do envy those countries who have applied restorative processes as alternative sanctions. Yet I think the variety in the practices I observed in Northern Ireland, Norway and Orlando, Florida points to several themes of consideration when using restorative approaches in juvenile cases:

5.1 Neutrality/Impartiality

Based on my observations and of those of other researchers before me, it can be argued whether or not a term like 'neutral' or 'impartial' is applicable at all in the context of restorative processes.

Besides the easy, Foucaultian argument that impartiality and neutrality are, of course, impossible, positivist constructs, perhaps the idea of the neutral, impartial mediator simply has no place in a setting where a prerequisite for attending is that the parties are in overall agreement who is the offender and who is the offended? Zehr argues for this view. Yet, if I attempt to put myself in the shoes of a young offender, I must admit that I prefer the Norwegian take on the facilitators role—certainly to the very normative approach I experienced from the facilitator in Florida, but also to how I perceive the facilitators role in Northern Ireland, based on the conference role play. The Norwegian approach was—if not impartial—certainly less judgmental, which seemed to leave more room for the young offender to take responsibility for the situation him/herself.

---

[31]It is possible to pay for your records to be sealed. This can be done only once and at a cost of $75. If done the records will be invisible to most employers except central government, the military, and jobs requiring a security clearance.

5.2 Voluntarism

Are the parties in a restorative meeting really as voluntary as they ideally should be? Research has continuously demonstrated how social/structural pressure to attend exists with other types of mediation/restorative processes, too.[32] Yet it seems to be a very present point of concern for juvenile offenders for whom the alternative to participating is often very clear and most likely less agreeable. And should they choose to attend, the participants are indeed under social pressure to take on certain roles of, for example, showing remorse (offender) and accepting apologies if given (offended).

A choice is a choice—even if it is a bad one, as Vindeløv and Adrian argue. In this sense all of the programs discussed in this article *are* voluntary, but as demonstrated several of the professionals involved are concerned as to how it affects the restorative process if the young offender considers participation to be not a positive opportunity, but rather the least bad of a range of bad possible choices.

But this dilemma should hardly come as a surprise when even according to the founding theories of the 1970s and 1980s, i.e. Zehr, Braithwaite, and to a large extent also Christie, the re-integrative shame and moderate social control/pressure etc. are a core elements when addressing offenses in a restorative manner. And both my observations and those of so many other previous researchers have demonstrated how especially young offenders can respond to the questionable voluntarism of their participation simply by saying very little—an act of silent resistance to the exercise of power they experience. This was, for instance, the case for the two siblings in Florida.

Can this dilemma fully be avoided? Should it? I suggest that part of the answer to this question is to ask ourselves whether we offer young offenders other, better alternatives? If this is not the case at present—which I am inclined to think—based on my observations and those of others, there might be some consolation to be found in how the training and approach of the facilitator/coordinator/mediator can seemingly make a large difference as to how comfortable and participatory the young offenders appear during the restorative meeting. In this regard, again, the Norwegian model seems to come out on top.

5.3 Punishment as Rationale

Is punishment non-compliable with restorative processes? The older (wiser?) Zehr argues no. And the argumentation of the Florida professionals—that the restorative approach allows for juveniles committing minor offences to experience harder consequences than the traditional system—seems to suggest they support this view. This type of argumentation has not been visible in my data from Norway or

---

[32]For instance, mediation in custody cases.

Northern Ireland. But as mentioned in the introduction, the majority of the data for my project is collected in Denmark, and in some of my interviews with employees in the Danish police working with the Danish konfliktråd, I have come across similar arguments. Perhaps this coincidence is related to the political climate in both countries—United States and Denmark—currently focusing a lot on 'tough on crime' rhetoric. Though, of course, arguably much more so in the United States than in Denmark, but I have met with members of the Danish parliament justice counsel discussing RJ potential on several occasions, and here a suitable (hard) punishment has definitely been a frequent concern.

Furthermore, both Danish justice counsel politicians and the leadership of the national VOM program have argued for initially testing the use of restorative approaches as an alternative to traditional ones only in cases of minor offences—just as it is the case in the Florida models. Even if this approach contradicts the research in the field, which seems almost unanimously to confirm that the more serious the case, the more efficient the use of restorative processes (Strang et al. 2013). Perhaps in such a political climate the idea of restorative approaches seems too inconceivable if the offense is too serious and if the potential to include a tough sanction is not underlined by the advocators? Yet the ideals of practice of the Danish konfliktråd seem to lean towards those of the Norwegian ditto, having a much less judgmental and punitive outset than what I observed to be the case in Florida.

5.4 The Offended Party

When a restorative process becomes a right (as in Northern Ireland) or a potentially granted juridical sanction (as in Norway) for the offender it makes sense that it is no longer up to the other, offended party to decide whether the process can take place. Yet it is also obvious that it would go against restorative justice theories if the offended parties were forced to participate. This creates space for the dilemma of restorative meetings taking place without offended parties.

In both Norway and Northern Ireland the clear ideal is including the offended parties in the restorative meetings. Yet, especially in Norway, the Mediation Service is realising that with an offended party participation rate at approximately 50% in the restorative meetings connected to the new sanctions, something has to be done if the ideal is also to be the norm. Suggestions have been made to include offended parties much earlier in the process and to offer the offended parties more elaborate processes as well. Yet the Mediation Service personnel point to the importance of not over-nudging offended parties into participation, as this raises ethical questions as well as increases the risk of re-traumatisation. And they argue that restoration should be seen in a broader perspective than just a meeting between offender and offended party.

Of course in the Florida model, the absence of an offended party was part of the structure, with the NRJ community board taking on the perspective of both offender and community.

5.5 The Role of Community

As described, restorative justice theory often entails a triangular approach to an offence with the corners made up by *offender*, *offended party*, and *community*. In the practices I have observed, especially the involvement of the 'community' seems to pose a challenge. What is the community? How can/should it be involved? In my observations there are different takes on this matter: In Northern Irish conferences, the 'community' is involved if relevant. In the restorative meetings of the Norwegian sanctions it seems to be the public 'network' of the young offender—for instance, a teacher and/or a local police officer—who largely stand in for the role of 'community'. In the Florida conferences, the role of 'community' was played by a board of civil volunteers from the area who had no connection to either offender, offended party or offence.

To me the diverse interpretations of 'community' in the three models suggest that the triangular model of the restorative theories might be just that—theoretic—but often difficult to put into a meaningful large scale practice. And as I see it, with no offended party present, and with the estranged 'community' board—having no direct relations to the offender of offence—the restorative/conflict theories of Zehr, Braithwaite, Christie, and Vindeløv seem extra hard to recognise in the Florida programs.

5.6 Equality Before the Law vs Individual Concerns

Who decides who gets to access a restorative process? And on which basis? These are central concerns in my PhD study. In all of the observed models, the offender has to admit to the offence and wish to take part in the restorative process. Apart from this the approaches of the three observed countries are very different: The Florida model is only accessible to juvenile first-time offenders who have committed less serious offences, and it is up to the prosecutor to offer diversion of the case to the programs. Further to this, the zip-code of the offender decides which model might be available. In Northern Ireland it is the young person who gets to decide whether he or she wants a restorative process, and only a few case types—murder and particularly violent rapes—are excepted, because there are mandatory sentences for these offences in the law even for juvenile offenders. In Norway, in principle all case types are open to restorative processes, but it is up to a judge or a team of professionals (depending on the seriousness of the offence) to decide whether a restorative process is an appropriate choice for the specific offender having committed the specific offence(s).

The Norwegian model *is* more elaborate, invasive—and also more expensive—than the Northern Irish one (and, of course, also than the Florida program). This seems to place a perhaps self-imposed obligation on the responsible parties not to overuse the new restorative toolbox. As a consequence—and somewhat in line with

Christie's concern—there is seemingly a growing awareness of not 'over treating' young offenders by involving them in one of the new types of sanctions if they may not need the close follow up.[33] This could especially be seen as the case for less serious offences committed by young people in otherwise positive life circumstances. But at the other end of the spectrum in the more serious cases, individual concerns to the offender's life situation can be decisive in whether a youth sanction is found appropriate. So, in principle, two young offenders having committed similar offences—or even an offence together—can be found fit and unfit, respectively, for youth sanction or youth follow-up depending on their personal situations.

In this regard the Norwegian model has received some criticism for going against the principle of equality before law. But in this case it is actually an old argument by Nils Christie, which can come to the defence of the new sanctions: No actions are the same. The law is making actions equal/comparable by deducing them. This approach is a prerequisite for talking about legal certainty in the shape of equality before law and predictability. But at the core of restorative approaches stand individual considerations and concerns to individual offended parties, offenders, and offences (Christie 1977). In this view, restorative approaches to juvenile legal offences face an inherent paradox of trying to force two opposites to coexist.

5.7 Mediation and/or Restorative Justice: Laymen vs Professionals

Do professional restorative facilitators in juvenile cases indicate a favouritism of (unwanted) disciplining by the state over (wanted) civil social control? Are we re-stealing the conflict as Christie suggests? Again I think these questions call for a consideration of the present alternatives for young offenders.

In a revised 2015 edition of *The little book of restorative justice* Zehr includes a list of what he thinks restorative justice *is not*. *Mediation* is on this list. This is, of course interesting in the context of the book on mediation research that you are reading right now. According to Zehr, mediation and restorative justice are related, in that they will both normally aim to include an encounter. But they differ because mediation connotes that "parties are assumed to be on a level playing field", and this assumption can be inappropriate or offensive in the case of restorative justice. Also, according to Zehr, in the case of restorative, an important component is that "a wrongdoer must admit to some level of responsibility for the offence". This leads him to conclude that "the 'neutral' language of mediation may be misleading and even offensive in many cases".

So why is this article even in a book on mediation research?

---

[33]Opting out of offering a restorative sanction does not mean that the young offender cannot participate in a restorative meeting at the Mediation Service. This possibility will often be promoted and was already used widespread before the new sanctions of July 2014.

As I suggested in the introduction, restorative processes/practices and mediation can be seen as two entities that share an intersection. And as the examples from my field studies in this article have shown, in the Nordic countries—with Norway as the first-moving flagship—some of the core ideals of mediation seem to be intertwined with the principles for performing restorative justice, which again seems to cause dilemmas for both theorists and practitioners.

One of these principles is that of de-professionalising the conflict and giving it back to the people who own it. This is the core principle in the conflict theory of Christie, as first put forward in an inauguration speech at the Center for Criminological Studies, University of Sheffield and later published in the article *Conflict as Property* (Christie 1977). The Norwegian Mediation Service adhere to the principle of layman mediators in accordance with Christie's beliefs.

But today, in accordance with Zehr's revised opinion, within the Norwegian Mediation Service there are suggestions that the term 'mediation' is sometimes inappropriate. Disregarding whether the case is part of the new juvenile sanctions or handled classically in konfliktråd, Senior Advisor at the Norwegian Mediation Service Kjersti Lillioe-Olsen suggests that in criminal cases the term *meeting* is often more suitable. This perhaps supports Christie's euphemism free '*we work with conflicts*' introduced in the beginning of the article. But just as Christie dislikes 'restorative justice' because it connotes the institution of law, maybe the term 'conflict' can also seem simplistic and offensive to for instance a victim of sexual assault.

5.8 So, When Is It Restorative Justice?

And should that even be the name? Like Christie, I am not enthused by the term either. I agree that especially the 'justice' part is problematic. And not only for connoting the institution of law, but because it is a confusing word with both subjective and objective aspirations, which makes promises that neither the justice system, nor restorative alternatives can be guaranteed to fulfil. Furthermore, I think the examples from the three countries presented in this article show that the contents of models for addressing juvenile offences claiming to *be* restorative justice can vary to the extent that it hardly makes sense to file them under the same headline.

So, if we do allow, accept, or even promote self-labelling within the field of restorative justice it might result in a community of practices existing only at the abstract level, but whose common traits are hardly recognisable at the practical level. But perhaps this is a natural consequence when half of this semantic entity—namely 'justice'—seemingly has very differing individual, local, and national connotations throughout the globe. How could 'restorative justice' then be universal? And if we were to insist on more universally applicable standards for restorative justice, then who gets to be the RJ police?

Yet, when seemingly not only apples and pears, but all sorts of fruits and vegetables are currently mixed into the same bowl, I will argue it does call for further strengthening the existing debate on the relevance, terminology and borders of restorative justice as a research field.

But the difference in contents and in the roles and reflections of the involved 'child-savers' set aside, they appear to have one thing in common: Overall they offer possibilities of addressing the individual circumstances of the young offender in a way that the traditional systems they locally compete with do not. In this sense they can all be seen as restorative compared to the locally availably alternative. And for all three programs this seems to have the effect of less juvenile reoffending, which ultimately ought to be a good thing.

References

Adrian L, Vindeløv V (2014) Angreb på mæglingens DNA – ansatser til en diskussion om tvungen mægling. In: Blume P, Henrichsen C (eds) Forvaltning Og Retssikkerhed: Festskrift Til Steen Rønsholdt. DJØF forlag, Copenhagen, pp 13–31

Braithwaite J (1989) Crime, shame and reintegration. Cambridge University Press, Cambridge

Campbell C, Devlin R, O'Mahony D, Doak J, Jackson J, Corrigan T, Mcevoy K (2006) Evaluation of the Northern Ireland Youth Conference Service. NIO research and statistical series: Report No. 12. Statistics and Research Branch of the Northern Ireland Office, Belfast

Christie N (1977) Conflicts as property. Br J Criminol 17:1–15

Christie N (2013) Words on words. Restorative justice. Int J 1(1):15–19

Christie N (2015) Widening the net. Restorative justice. Int J 3(1):109–113

Eide AK, Andrews T, Strømsvik CL, Gustavsen A (2016) Stemmer "kartet" med "terrenget"? Underveisrapport fra en følgeevaluering av ungdomsstraff og ungdomsoppfølging. Norlandsforskning A/S, Bodø

Florida Department of Juvenile Justice (2017) Myths vs. Facts. http://www.djj.state.fl.us/research/fast-facts/myths-vs-facts

Froestad J, Shearing C (2013) Meditative reflections on Nils Christie's 'Words on words', through an African lens. Restorative justice. Int J 1(1):31–46

Konfliktrådet (2017a) Konfliktråd i tal. http://konfliktraad.dk/konfliktraad-i-tal.aspx

Konfliktrådet (2017b) Hva skjer etter et meklingsmøte. http://konfliktraadet.no/hva-skjer-etter-et-meklingsmoete.311345.no.html

Konfliktrådet (2017c) Hva skjer under et meklingsmøte. http://konfliktraadet.no/hva-skjer-under-et-meklingsmoete.311344.no.html

Konfliktrådet (2017d) Ofte stilte spørsmål. http://konfliktraadet.no/ofte-stilte-spoersmaal.5391477-313363.html

Kvello Ø, Wendelborg C (2009) Prossessevaluering av det treårige prosjektet: Oppfølgingsteam for unge lovbrytere i Kristiansand, Oslo, Stavanger og Trondheim. NTNU Samfundsforskning AS, Trondheim

Lyness D, Tate S (2011) Northern Ireland Youth Re-Offending: results from the 2007 Cohort Statistical Bulletin 2/2011 Belfast. Statistics & Research Branch, Youth Justice Agency, Belfast

Moerman M (1965) Ethnic identification in a complex civilization: who are the Lue? Am Anthropol 67(5):1215–1230

Ninth Judicial Circuit Court of Florida (2017a) Neighborhood Restrorative Justice. http://www.ninthcircuit.org/about/programs/neighborhood-restorative-justice

Ninth Judicial Circuit Court of Florida (2017b) Teen Court. http://www.ninthcircuit.org/about/divisions/juvenile-court/teen-court

Strang H, Sherman LW, Mayo-Wilson E, Woods D, Ariel B (2013) Restorative justice conferencing (RJC) using face-to-face meetings of offenders and victims: effects on offender recidivism and victim satisfaction. A systematic review. Campbell Systematic Reviews, Oslo

Vindeløv V (2012) Reflexive mediation. DJØF Forlag, Copenhagen

Youth Justice Agency (2009–2010) Annual report and accounts: report on the work of the Youth Justice Agency of Northern Ireland 2009–2010. Stationary Office, London

Zehr H (2015) The little book of restorative justice. In: The big book of restorative justice. Good Books, New York, pp 1–108

Zinsstag E, Chapman T (2012) Conferencing in Northern Ireland: implementing restorative justice at the core of the criminal justice system. In: Zinsstag E, Vanfraechem I (eds) Conferencing and restorative justice: international practices and perspectives. Oxford University Press, Oxford, pp 173–203

Part III
Children's Rights and Mediation

The Involvement of Children in the Process of Mandatory Family Mediation

Renee Thørnblad and Astrid Strandbu

Contents

R. Thørnblad (✉)
RKBU North, Faculty of Health, University of Tromsø – The Arctic University of Norway,
Tromsø, Norway
e-mail: renee.thornblad@uit.no

A. Strandbu
Department of Education, University of Tromsø – The Arctic University of Norway, Tromsø,
Norway
e-mail: astrid.strandbu@uit.no

© The Author(s) 2018
A. Nylund et al. (eds.), *Nordic Mediation Research*,
https://doi.org/10.1007/978-3-319-73019-6_10

Abstract Mediation is mandatory for all separated divorcing/separating spouses and co-habiting partners in Norway with children under the age of 16. A mediation model called "Children in Mediation" (*Barn i mekling*, known as BIM) systematically includes children in the mediation process. In the article, we address two key issues based on statements from children to their parents as well as questionnaires completed by mediators and children in 250 mediations. Our first focus is on how the children's actorship is expressed in the mediation context. We show that when given the opportunity, children largely choose to speak up, and we present some examples of their statements. We thematise the contradictory considerations of participation and children's right to protection and assert that children's potential vulnerability cannot, in general, justify preventing them from participation. Our second focus is on children's experiences of their own participation and their general views on the inclusion of children in mandatory mediation and relationship breakdowns. In this analysis, we include how the level of conflict and problem accumulation in the family impacts the children's decision-making about whether to participate or not. In the absolute majority of cases, children have positive experiences of their participation and encourage other children to participate. These assessments were made regardless of the level of conflict and degree of problem accumulation in the family.

1 Introduction and Presentation of the Question

In Norway, it is mandatory for all spouses and co-habiting partners with children in common under the age of 16 to attend a one-hour-long mediation in the case of relationship breakdown.[1] Further mediation is offered up to a maximum of seven hours as and when required. The purpose of mediation is to help parents arrive at good custody arrangements, including parental responsibility, support maintenance, living arrangements, and time with the children. Mediation is also mandatory before any instigating court procedures on child custody and visitation. These two different types of mediation are called mandatory mediation in conjunction with separation and mandatory pre-action mediation, respectively. In Western societies, children are increasingly regarded as actors who should be given the opportunity to be heard. This also applies in mediation situations. This is in line with the UN Convention on the Rights of the Child and Norway's national legislation, which both state that children have the right to express their own opinions in cases that are important to them. Separation and divorce are regarded as one of the important contexts in which children must be heard.[2] How this is to be done in practical terms is a topic for discussion both in the field of mediation and in policy development. Children depend on adults looking after and taking care of them, and the right to be heard

---

[1] Marriage Act section 26 and Children Act section 51 fourth subsection.
[2] According to UN General Comment No. 12, 2009, points 50 and 52.

must be balanced against their need for and right to protection. There are many objections to involving children. One is that it is *unnecessary*, since most parents agree on care arrangements. Another objection involves fear that children shall be made to feel responsible for decisions, and that they will be involved in conflicts between parents or find themselves in a conflict of loyalties. Other objections are that children may feel manipulated by their parents and under pressure to make certain statements, or tell lies (see e.g. Bondevik and Meren 1997; Langballe 2007; Schoffer 2005). Such objections may be characterised as concern that the involvement of children in mediation may be a further *burden* on children who already find themselves in a difficult, high-conflict or stressful life situation. It is particularly the latter that is being addressed here. Our aim is to make the wishes of children visible, as well as their experiences, assessments and preferences on the inclusion of children in the mediation process.[3] The questions we are trying to answer in the article can be summed up as follows:

- Do children want to participate in the mediation process?
- How do the children view their own participation in the mediation process?
- Do children involved in different divorce processes want to participate in the mediation process?
- What are the important "messages" communicated by children to their parents by participating in the mediation process?
- Which general recommendations about participation do children who have participated in the mediation process give to other children?
- Are the children's experiences and assessments of their own participation related to the conflict level, mediation type or level of problem accumulation in the family?

2 Frameworks for and Practice of Children's Participation in Family Mediation

The general principle of mediation is that it takes as its starting point only the subjects of the mediation (in our case mothers and fathers), and the norm is not to involve children in the practice of mediation. General Comment no. 12 of the UN Committee on the Rights of the Child, however, states that children have a right to be heard in mediation on family breakdown. Sandberg (2010) refers to the statement of the Child Committee, and points out that the general principle of mediation cannot be the norm in cases where the mediation also deals with another person (in this case the child), and the agreement which is reached impacts on child and parents in equal measure. One question yet to be resolved is *who* should hear the child. Sandberg

---

[3]This contribution builds on and refers to parts of two publications from the study *Hearing children in mediation* at RKBU Nord, at University of Tromsø: Strandbu and Thørnblad (2015) and Strandbu et al. (2016). The Wøyen Foundation has given financial support to the study.

points out that it can be difficult for parents to distinguish between their own interests and those of the child in decision-making about where to live and custody arrangements, and therefore recommends that the child is heard by someone other than the parents.

The right of children to be heard in mediation has traditionally, at least in Norway, been interpreted as the responsibility of the parents, and common practice has been for parents to attend mediation without their children. Section 2 of the Regulations concerning mediation pursuant to the Norwegian Children Act and Marriage Act states that the mediator *may* speak directly to the child in connection with a mediation, but is not obliged to do so. However, the mediator *must* inform the parents of the right of the child to state an opinion and of the parental duty to talk to the child about the separation and the approaching change in the family circumstances. An evaluation of the mediation service in Norway showed that mediators only rarely gave parents such information. In 38% of the mediations the mediator had not informed the parents of the children's right to speak, and in 41% of the mediations the mediator had not informed the parents of their duty to hear the children (Ådnanes et al. 2011). International studies show that children are often not informed or heard when decisions are made in connection with separation.[4] This has also been the situation in Norway, where mediators talking directly to children has been the exception rather than the rule. Mediation has to a large degree been *about* the child and what is the child's best interests, but without the child itself stating an opinion. In their study, Ekeland and Myklebust (1997) found that a mediator talked to the child in 2% of mediations. Fourteen years later, Ådnanes et al. (2011) found that children were heard in 4% of mediations. In the past few years there has been an increase in this number in Norway, and a mediator talked to the child in 8.4% of the mediation processes in 2015 (Bufdir 2016). This increase is to a large degree linked to the spread of the mediation model "Children in Mediation" (BIM).[5] In international literature, the various models for hearing children in mandatory mediation are divided into *Child-focused mediation,* where the mediator attempts to "bring the child into the room" *indirectly* by focusing on the child in conversation with the parents, and *Child-inclusive mediation*, which implies that the child is in various ways *directly* included in the mediation process (McIntosh et al. 2007). The BIM-model must be regarded as child-inclusive mediation. In the BIM-model, children are systematically included in the mediation process from the beginning.[6] The mediator initially has a brief, informative conversation with both children and parents present where the procedures and intentions of the meetings are described.

---

[4]See for example Mantle and Critchley (2004).

[5]The Norwegian name of the mediation model *Barn i mekling*, abbreviated to BIM, has here been translated into *Children in Mediation*. The BIM-model was developed by mediator Gjertrud Jonasen at the Family Counselling Office at Grenland, Norway.

[6]All parents were given the opportunity to invite the children to participate in the BIM-mediation process. Children participating do this in accordance with the parents' initiative and the children's consent.

The parents subsequently leave the room, and the mediator continues the conversation with the child on its own. This conversation, which lasts for approximately 20–25 min, is known as the *children's conversation*. Where there are several children in a family they all take part at the same time, as long as they and their parents are happy with that. The purpose of the children's conversation is threefold: helping the children to *understand* what is happening in the process of change which the family is going through; *preventing subsequent difficulties* by giving the children the opportunity to "express their own reactions and feelings in connection with the separation"; and the main aim, which is linked to Article 12 of the UN Child Convention and the child's *democratic right to participation*. The child must be given the opportunity to "have their opinions taken into account [. . .] and to say what they think should happen".[7]

The three different aims are reflected in the following three questions that structure the children's conversation: (1) What is happening/has happened? (2) How are you feeling? (3) Is there anything you would like to say to your parents? What the child wishes to communicate to the parents is called *the children's message*. The mediator formulates the children's message in writing as closely as possible to the child's own wording. When the child conversation is over, mediation is carried out between the parents without the child being present. The mediation starts with the mediator communicating the children's message to the parents. When the mediation is over, the child is brought in for a new *inclusive conversation* between the child, the parents and the mediator. In this concluding conversation the child learns what the parents have decided. If the parents fail to reach agreement, the children are informed of this and that the parents will continue with mediation for several sessions. The children do not participate in the subsequent mediation. However, children and parents are invited to come back for an evaluation and any adjustment of the plan after 6 months. The structure of the evaluation conversation is the same as described above.

The BIM-model has triggered several discussions about the role of children in mandatory mediation. Should children always be invited to join their parents in mediation or are there situations where children ought not to attend? If so, who should decide—the mediator, the parents or the child itself? Other questions are about *when* the mediator should talk to the child, how children should be informed of the purpose of mediation and their right to be heard, and what being heard in connection with mediation actually implies.

A review of international research shows that children are rarely heard in cases where the parents agree (Ask and Kjeldsen 2015). Mediators assume that parents in such cases make decisions that are in line with what is in the best interests of the child, and that a conversation with the child is therefore unnecessary. Children are also rarely heard in very conflicted mediations. This is because of difficulties in obtaining consent to children taking part from parents in conflict, but also because of a desire on the part of the mediator to shield the child from potential risk, pressure and

---

[7]Description of the BIM-model, Bufetat Region Sør (2016).

conflict of loyalty: *"Most mediators agree that it is important to shield the children, and that there should always be an assessment as to whether inclusion would involve a risk to the child, both in relation to the degree of conflict between the parents and the child's level of development"* (Ask and Kjeldsen 2015). Knowledge reviews show, however, that there is no research base for the claim that inclusion of children in the mediation process poses a risk to children's development and well-being (Ask and Kjeldsen 2015; Rapport RBUP 2017). Children's participation in mediation processes is not common—research thematising the involvement of children in such processes from a child's perspective or showing the consequences of their participation is therefore very limited.

3   Clarification of Concepts and Analytical Starting Point

Our starting point is the understanding of children in childhood sociology, i.e. that children are regarded as actors who participate in their own representations (James et al. 1999). As family members, children are both influenced by and influence co-operation, communication and relationships in the family. This is also the case when families break up. In BIM-mediation, children have the opportunity to influence the agenda, and participate as more than just informants who are being "heard" on the issues that are of interest to parents or mediators. Children are involved in the process of family change, and are actors who, as well as being influenced by their parents' break-up, can influence the establishment of new family practices afterwards. This ontological starting point has epistemological implications. Research that starts with a view of children as actors emphasises that *a child perspective* is not only a *perspective on children* – but *children's own perspective*. A consequence of this is that children are important participants in this study.

The concept of *participation* is defined in various ways in the literature. We lean towards Hodgkin and Newell (2007) who define participation as being included in the decision-making process through discussion. The participation of children, which is the main aim of the BIM-model, does *not* imply participation in the actual mediation between the parents, but *to be included in the mediation process* as follows: (1) joint conversation between parents, child and mediator before the child conversation; (2) separate child conversation between child and mediator before mediation, and formulation of the children's message; (3) joint conversations between parents, child and mediator after mediation; (4) participation in the evaluation of the co-operation agreement 6 months later; and (5) children themselves may contact the mediator.

There are differing understandings in the literature of the concepts of *conflict, conflict level and high conflict*. Ekeland (2004) identifies conflict with factors like unequal distribution of power and emotional engagement, dependency, and differing needs and interests. Conflict *level* can be defined and evaluated through factors like the subject matter of the conflict, the problem accumulation in the family and psychological aspects (Ottosen 2016). In their research review Helland and Borren

(2015) estimate the proportion of high conflict cases to be "between 12 per cent and 25 per cent of couples in mediation or after a break-up in Norway, depending on criteria and population". Ottosen's (2016) analysis of the development in family law conflicts in Denmark describes approx. 20% of divorcing parents as having considerable conflicts. *"Of those, around half appear to have serious conflicts. These so-called high-conflict couples are as far as can be judged a relatively constant number"*.

The Norwegian Directorate for Children, Youth and Family Affairs (Bufdir) employs the term "high conflict" about arrangement for contact or custody of children/parental disputes that end up in court and about mediation where *" the conflict between the parents is acute, in deadlock and/or the children's care situation is at risk as a result of the parental conflict."*[8] Gulbrandsen's (2015) study of the interaction during mediation between parties where both felt there was high conflict, elaborates on the term "high conflict": The parties had enduring, contrary views on important issues, a strong distrust of each other, high emotional pressure and defensiveness, absence of any positive response, irreconcilable presentation of the case, repeated negative exchanges, interruption of constructive clarification, and both seeking support for their views from others involved in the case. In our study we asked the mediators to assess the conflict level between the parents without an explicit definition of the concept. There is still reason to believe that the mediators based their understanding on the elements described above.

4 Method and Data Collection

The data collection followed the trial of the BIM-model during the period 2012–2014, where 21 mediators at 4 family counselling offices in 2 regions participated.[9] The family counselling offices were recruited to the study at different times in 2014. Quantitative and qualitative data were collected through questionnaires and interviews. The results that are presented in this contribution are based on analyses of the text material from "the children's message" in 250 mediation cases during the period 2012–2014 and quantitative and qualitative data collected through questionnaires from children and mediators in 217 mediation cases in 2013–2014.[10]

The questionnaires were completed by the mediators after the final joint conversation between children, parents and mediator, while the children completed their form immediately after the children's conversation.[11]

---

[8]Norwegian Directorate for Children, Youth and Family Affairs (Bufdir) 2016.

[9]In total there are 42 family counselling offices in Norway.

[10]The data material from 2012 consisted of only "the children's message".

[11]Four cases where the child had completed part of the questionnaire, but where there was no mediator questionnaire, have been excluded. Three questionnaires completed by children were also excluded because of missing ID-number.

The mediator questionnaire had information about the type of mediation (separation mediation or child legislation mediation), the mediator's subjective assessment of the conflict situation between the parents and whether the case had other worrisome conditions. The categories under "Other worrisome conditions" were "issues around drugs/alcohol", "violence issues", "psychiatry", "failure of care" and/or "referred to children's services". The more categories that had been ticked by the mediator, the more troubled we can assume the family is. Conflict between parents can be evaluated and measured by the use of various parameters and informant perspectives—both the parents' own, the children's and the mediators' perspectives (Nilsen et al. 2012). In our study, the mediators assessed the conflict between parents immediately after the first hour of mediation, by marking a visual, analogue scale from "no conflict" (0%) to "very high conflict level" (100%). Research by Guldbrandsen and Tjersland (2013) show that mediators are accurate in their assessment of conflict level between parents at the start of a mediation process.

The children's questionnaire had six questions. In five of the questions the children were asked to put a mark along a visual, analogue scale from "sad face" ☹, via "neutral" (-) to "smiley face" ☺. Qualitative data material was collected through the sixth, open question, where the children were asked to formulate their own opinion after the conversation with the mediator, and their own assessment of the involvement of children in mediation. Of 356 children in 217 mediations, 345 children (97%) answered one or more of the questions in the questionnaire. Of these, 138 children (40%) also answered the open question in their own words. The children's formulations that are presented in this text material have been analysed quantitatively and qualitatively.

One question that is often raised is whether children are credible informants in research. The hierarchical power relationship between children and adults is a factor that might contribute to a form of respondent bias. This means that the respondent expresses agreement with the researcher's point of view or gives what the respondent assumes is the wanted answer. The design of this study enables children to respond freely to the questions posed. Neither parents, mediators nor researchers were present while they completed the questionnaires. It is worth noting that the children in our study scored the scales differently and expressed differing views in the open question, something which strengthens the impression of truthful answers.

4.1 Selection: Children, Type of Mediation, Conflict Level and Degree of Problem Accumulation

During the trial of the BIM-model there was no selection of cases that were "suitable" or "not suitable" for this type of mediation. All the parents who requested mediation were given a verbal and/or written offer of mediation according to the BIM-model. Our material has been collected from all the 217 mediations that were carried out in accordance with the BIM-model and consent was given to taking part in research. There was an even distribution of boys (49.4%) and girls (50.6%) in the age range 4–20, most of them were between 7 and 15 years old. The average age was 10.8 years. There were more 12-year-olds than any others in the selection (13.5%). Of 217 mediations, 70% were separation mediations (95 marriage breakdowns and 55 breakdowns of co-habiting partners). The remaining 35% (65 cases) were mandatory pre-action mediation, where one of the parents had taken the other to court. In 2 of the 217 cases the type of mediation was not given.

The 217 mediations in the selection represent cases with mediator-assessed differing conflict levels between the parents. The average conflict level, as reported by the mediators, was 37%, with a standard deviation of 34.6. In 17% of 217 cases, the conflict level was above 80% of the maximum, while the conflict level in 49% of the mediations was under 20%. Median conflict level in pre-action mediation was considerably higher (69% of the maximum) than in mediation in conjunction with separation (24%). A credible explanation of this difference is that these parents had previously been through mediation and failed to reach agreement (Fig. 1).

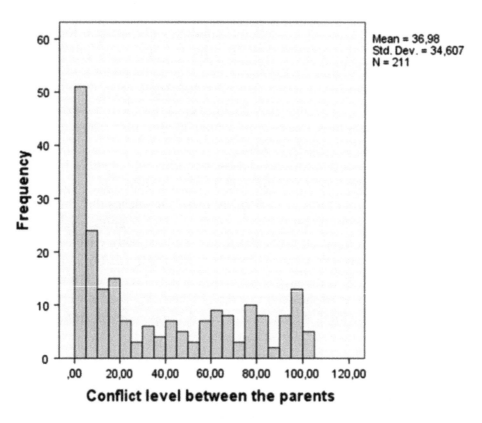

Fig. 1 Histogram of conflict level between the parents

4.1.1 Problem Accumulation in the Family

According to the mediators, several families in the selection faced challenges beyond those posed by the relationship breakdown. In 43 mediations (20%), one or several "other worrisome conditions" were ticked by the mediators. In 25 cases one such concern was ticked, in 12 cases two were ticked, in 3 cases three were ticked and 3 cases there were four. The degree of problem accumulation in the family is assumed to be proportionally increased by the increase in the number of ticks for "other worrisome conditions". The issue most frequently ticked by the mediators was "referred to child protection services" (12% of the 217 mediations). This implied that the family already was in contact with the child protection services, or that a message of concern was sent to the children's protection services after mediation was finished (Table 1).

The degree of problem accumulation is higher in mandatory pre-action mediation compared with mandatory mediation in conjunction with separation. In pre-action mediation it is far more common to have one or several worrisome conditions in the case than in mediation in conjunction with separation. In 27 of 65 pre-action mediation cases (41.5%) there was at least one issue of concern, while the equivalent figures in cases concerning mediation in conjunction with separation were 16 of 150 cases (10.7%).

There is also a correlation between conflict level and problem accumulation, i.e. where there is a high level of problem accumulation there is also a high conflict level. In cases where the mediator had not ticked any worrisome conditions, the conflict level was 31% of the maximum. Where there was one issue of concern, the conflict level was 57%. Two worrisome conditions meant a conflict level of 66%. In the cases with the highest problem accumulation, the conflict level was 72% with three ticked worrisome conditions, and 82% with four ticked. Collectively there is a

Table 1 Information about cases

Variable	Number of cases	Percent
Type of mediation		
Mandatory mediation in conjunction with separation	150	69.8
Mandatory pre-action mediation	65	30.2
Number of worrisome conditions[a]		
0	174	80.2
1	25	11.5
2	12	5.5
3	3	1.4
4	3	1.4
	Median	Standard deviation
Mediator-assessed conflict level[b]	37.0	34.6

[a]Mediation between co-habiting partners and mediation between married partners shown together
[b]Number of issues in the case (max. 5). Drugs and alcohol, violence, psychiatry, failure of care or referred to children's services scale from 1 to 100

significant correlation between the number of worrisome conditions and the mediator-assessed conflict level (F = 8.4; p < 0.0005).

4.2   Analysis of Quantitative and Qualitative Data

Combining different qualitative and quantitative methods involves a methodologically pragmatic position since the researcher is dealing with both constructivist and positivist research traditions. This provides answers to research questions that require different research methods. Such a method combination can be described as a "convergent-parallel approach", where qualitative and quantitative data are collected in parallel, but analysed separately but at the same time (Edmonds and Kennedy 2013). In this way, the results of the analysis based on qualitative and quantitative data can complement, nuance or "correct" each other.

The free text ("Use this space to write anything else you would like to say about participating in mediation") in the children's questionnaire was analysed both qualitatively and quantitatively. We used topic-centred qualitative analysis to take a closer look at whether some topics particularly characterise, or are repeated in, the children's free text (Thagaard 2013). During the first read-through we differentiated between the children's expressions of positive, nuanced or negative experiences, and a last category where the statements from the child are not linked to mediation. Variations in the children's statements are then systematised in terms of mediation, degree of conflict between the parents, and the degree of problem accumulation in the family.

The text material containing the so-called "children's message" is analysed qualitatively, with a focus on how children execute or perform their actorship and where they position themselves in the mediation context. The categories we present were derived from the variations, common features and patterns we interpreted from the texts. Categories can be described as demarcations of topics derived from analysis, or as "containers", where one can place observations (Aase and Fossaskåret 2007). The content analysis is not theoretically unbiased, but in the sense that the material, i.e. the children's message to their parents, is not read or systematised based on pre-constructed categories. The patterns in the material are organised on the basis of our interpretation of the children's life situation at the actual time when mediation took place, and where in the families' process of change the children focused their attention. The result is formulated in four analytical categories: "breakdown", "preservation and improvement", "reorientation" and "security". As with other categorisation, the categories are not fully adequate or exhaustive, but their purpose is to render visible vital features of the children's situation, their opinions and assessments.

Descriptive analysis showed the conflict level, degree of psychosocial strain and types of mediation in the selection. The same goes for the children's experiences, wishes and opinions connected to their inclusion in the mediation process. SPSS version 22 was used for this analysis. Significance was assessed at level 0.05. In some families more than one child completed the questionnaire, and dependency between the children's answers might therefore occur. The children completed the questionnaires in the same room, and without anyone checking whether they talked to each other. The children's individual answers may therefore be influenced by what their siblings wrote. Multiple level analysis was used in order to manage data dependency (Strabac 2012).

4.3 Representativeness and Relevance

Whether our results have any validity beyond this selection depends e.g. on the representativeness of the selection. That is to say to what degree the selection reflects the total population who go through mediation. All the parents who were offered BIM-mediation and consented to participate in research are included in the material. The selection is thus not chosen strategically, but based on self-selection. In 2014, the year of the majority of our cases, the selection consisted of 12% of all mediation at the four offices. Recruitment through self-selection could possibly skew the selection, in particular, with regard to the legal base, and the level of conflict and problem accumulation. However, this does not appear to be the case in our material. Mandatory pre-action mediation constituted 30% of the data material; the national average was 34% in 2014 (Bufdir. 2015). There are big differences in conflict levels and risk factors in the 217 cases. In 17% of the cases the conflict level is shown as between 80–100%. In 20% of the cases the mediator had ticked one or several "worrisome conditions", and 12% of the cases had been referred to the children's services. The size and composition of the selection (legal basis for mediation, age and gender of the children, conflict level, risk factors and geographical distribution) make it probable that the results yield knowledge that is valid and has relevance beyond the selection that took part in the study.

5   Results from Quantitative and Qualitative Qnalysis

First, we present the extent of children's participation and show a few examples of children's messages to their parents' mediation session. We then present a descriptive analysis of children's satisfaction with the mediation process. Subsequently, a multiple level analysis is used to further investigate any connection between children's experiences, opinions and wishes to be included in the mediation process, and the mediator's assessment of the degree of conflict between parents, type of mediation and number of worrisome conditions in the family. Finally, results from a qualitative analysis of children's formulations about their own experience of mediation are presented.

5.1   Children's Participation and Their Message to Parents

One important result in our study is that children who are given the opportunity, actually *want* to participate in the mediation process. Of all the 250 mediations there were only three where the child/children did not want to make a statement to their parents. Originally, children between the ages of 7–16 were invited to attend when their parents were having mediation. The fact that also older and younger siblings (aged 4–20) wanted to participate confirms this wish.

Children's statements to the mediator contained a broad range of messages to parents. The messages ranged between "breakdown", "preservation and improvement", "reorientation" and "safety", which became our analysis categories. In the *"breakdown"* category, statements relate to *being in* a process of change from one family with a mother, a father and children, to new family constellations. The next category, *"preservation and improvement"*, refers to the children's wish for the parents to be reunited, or for family customs and traditions to continue after the divorce. The main issue here is the child's wishes in relation to arrangements, co-operation, and preservation of, and maybe improvement in, relationships in the divorced family. In the *"reorientation"* category, children may be well into establishing new relationships with their parents' new partners, and they talk about new family constellations. In the fourth category, called *"security"*, it is not the actual breakdown which is most prominent, but rather issues with varying degrees of seriousness related to the child's care situation, and that may be intensified as a result of the breakdown. Each of the four analysis categories will be discussed in more detail with examples of the children's message to their parents.

5.1.1   Breakdown

The children's messages express a variety of emotions related to the family breakdown. For most of them, the breakdown of the relationship between their parents is a great burden, and they show a huge range of emotions. Many state that they are uncertain, surprised and confused. It is hard to understand that their parents are getting divorced, and some find it strange that the parents have not told them before. The relationship breakdown between their parents has come like a bolt out of the blue for many of the children, something which they are unhappy about and wish to communicate back to their parents. Some children express anger, but the most prominent feeling in this category is sadness. They spend a lot of time thinking about what has happened, and many say they sometimes cry. Many ask the mediator to tell their parents that they need more attention and to be comforted. Others communicate a wish for their parents not to constantly ask how they are, because it makes them cry.

Many of the children say it is good to be able to talk to someone other than the parents. It also emerges that the children worry a lot, both for themselves and for one or both of the parents. Several wonder how the parents are. One pair of siblings expressed it as: "The older one of us wants the parent who does not have the children with them to be all right when the children are with the other parent. Doesn't want them (the parents) to be sad even if they live in separate houses. Wants them to do things that make the children happy." We interpret this to mean that it can be a burden for the children to think about their parents missing them. Another example of this is from a 10-year-old girl who says she feels a little bit guilty when she spends time with just one of them, but she has a solution: "I want you to live together – be with you at the same time." When the children talk about their parents missing them, many see it in terms of what is fair. The children often understand fairness in terms of children sharing their time equally between the parents: "I want to be fair – spend just the same time with both" (13-year-old girl). One pair of siblings say: "We are fine. We can stay one week with each of them, that makes it fair for both mum and dad. And then there is no need for dad to miss us." The material shows clearly that the children feel particularly sorry for and/or are worried about their father. One of the children says the following: "I think about dad a lot – that he's going to be all right. That he needs to know that I love him."

Some of the children are worried about the future and say they miss their parents, that they are not used to spending long periods away from one of them. Some fear that the parent they see least of is going to disappear altogether. A large number of the children talk about having emotional problems as a result of the divorce. Others point to the practical consequences of the relationship breakdown. For many it is important that the parents live near each other, and also near the school. They do not want to change schools, and it is important to keep their friends after the separation. Some experience a conflict between the wish to spend time with the parents and the consequences this has for life outside the family: "I like being with dad, but I don't have any friends there." Some say it's okay to have a 50/50 arrangement, while others point out that their parents wish for such an arrangement is a problem for them: "It is hard to share ourselves equally between parents. Everyday life is very busy, don't want 50/50."

The minority, who state that life is all right, that their parents' divorce is almost a good thing, relate this to, among other things, increased access to material things. The relationship breakdown can provide room for negotiation or an opportunity to make wishes come true. There are several examples of children asking the mediator to tell their parents that they would like a pet. One pair of siblings ask the mediator to tell the parents that they would like a dog. Two 10-year-old girls would first like a budgie, then a dog at their mum's and tropical fish at their dad's. We do not know whether these are wishes the children have previously conveyed or whether they have arisen in relation to the family break-up. It could be that the children have registered sympathy and willingness to listen in the situation, something which might make it possible for wishes, which would previously not have been granted, to come true for the children.

5.1.2 Preservation and Improvement

Many children focus attention on preserving and improving relationships in the family. Hope of reconciliation is prominent. Many say they love both mum and dad, and that they wish their parents would fall in love with each other again. Even more convey a wish for family relationships and traditions to carry on as before even if the parents have separated. One pair of siblings say the following: "We want the houses to be as similar as possible (rules, arrangements). We want mum and dad to spend more time together, not be alone all the time. We want to have a nice time in cafes, and go on holiday together. We don't want to move to another town. Staying two weeks (with each of them) is OK." Holidays, traditions, anniversaries and festivals (like Christmas and Easter) are recurring topics in the children's message. Two sisters, 9 and 6 years of age, ask the mediator to write the following to their parents: "We want everybody to be together for part of the summer holiday. We want everybody to be together the day before Christmas Eve and Christmas Eve every year. We want us to still do things together, for example, go to the cinema, go swimming or go to cafes." A nine-year-old boy says: "I would like to be with both of them on New Year's Eve, on birthdays and, for example, on beach holidays abroad".

A large number of the children's statements deal with arguments between the parents. The children want more co-operation and friendliness. A 10-year-old girl puts it like this: "You are stupid to get divorced. You have to stop arguing and going on at each other, because it makes me sad. I still get a tummy ache when I think about it." Many ask the mediators to tell their parents to stop arguing. One pair of siblings aged 16 and 14 say: "We do not want you to argue and shout at each other." One of the siblings says explicitly that they do not want to be the *subject* of the arguments. It is a problem that the parents make derogatory comments about each other: "We do not want to listen to arguments and discussions. Do not want to know what the other parent is doing wrong. It makes it hard to be with that person." For children who want the divorced family to still spend time together, arguments become threatening and destructive. Some ask the mediator to tell their parents that they are glad there are now fewer arguments.

5.1.3 Reorientation

Reorientation concerns the effort made by the children in order to adjust to a new family situation. Many convey a feeling of insecurity in view of the forthcoming changes. Some have practical questions about where their toys and things will be, whether there will be room for all the siblings in mum's small, new flat and where they will celebrate their birthdays. If the parents have a new partner, the children's reorientation may also include their relationship with new family members and the children's position in new family constellations. Some convey that they are not ready for their parents to have new partners: "Dad should not get a girlfriend quite yet, first we need to get used to them not living together" (11-year-old girl and 7-year-old boy). For others, life has moulded into a new shape. Their parents' new partners have been introduced and have become part of everyday life. A 7-year-old girl puts it like this: "I'm fine. Mum has a new boyfriend and dad has a new girlfriend. They're nice. I want to live a little with mum and a little with dad." Two siblings aged 15 and 11 also say things are fine. At the same time they have clear views on both the parents' new partners and, not least, on the process: "The holiday with A (dad's new partner) was too soon, although it went well. A needs to stop hugging us quite so much, she's a little too "mummy-ish". She's a nice lady. She just needs a few adjustments. It'll be fine once we get to know her a little better. K (mum's new partner) is quite OK, and very funny." Even if several of the children say that being introduced to new family members was fine, they still emphasise that they enjoy celebrating their birthday with mum and dad, that contact with siblings is important and that they want to do things with the whole original family together.

5.1.4 Security

This category describes statements that cause concern about the children's security and care. Recurrent topics of concern are aggression/violence, big conflicts and parents' alcohol and drug use. One 13-year-old boy asks the mediator to convey the following message to his parents: "I do not want dad to be drunk when I am at his house." The statement from two siblings aged 13 and 15 was: "Dad should not drink alcohol when we are there. We want to continue to spend time with dad as long as he doesn't drink." Another pair of siblings say they are willing to try the arrangement whereby they spend one week with each parent, but then dad has to stop drinking and he has to learn how to deal with the medication for the child's condition. Some children describe very concretely what does not work, and also suggest possible solutions. Two youths ask the mediator to tell the parents the following: "We want to have a nice childhood until we are 18. We want to live with our uncle for an indefinite period. If not with our uncle, then our choice would be with dad. To mum: Stop lying. Get rid of your druggie friends and prioritise your family. Quit making us feel guilty. Stop slagging dad off. We want to have contact with our parents, especially with dad. Mum can visit us at dad's, but she mustn't say bad things about our father." Others are clear about what they want, but it is not always that obvious *why* they want it. One 11-year-old girl wants the mediator to tell her parents that she is really quite OK with mum, and she does not want to stay the night with dad: "I only want to meet him during the day, and not at his house." Another child says: "I want to live with mum. I don't trust my dad. I do not want to have any contact with dad AT THE MOMENT."

These children direct the attention directly and indirectly to parents who do not sufficiently look after their children's needs/provide sufficient care for their children. In the worst scenario, this describes parents from whom the children need protection. In rare cases this is about poor care from both parents, however, several cases concern worry or insecurity when the children are with one of the parents. As far as the children's message in the "security" category is concerned, it may look as if the problem is not the divorce *per se*. Statements describe other conditions rather than the actual relationship breakdown, but the breakdown may reinforce something that is already problematic. If one of the parents has represented security and stability and compensated for the other parent's failing care, the child may experience the family breakdown as risky. The child will in the future have to live with a parent who fails in their responsibility to look after the child's needs, without the presence of the safe carer.

5.2   Children's Experiences, Opinion and Preferences About Their Inclusion in the Mediation Process

Three of the questions in the child questionnaire concern children's experience of the child conversation: "Were you able to say what you wanted to the mediator? Did the mediator understand what you meant? Did you enjoy talking to the mediator?" In the vast majority of cases the children expressed very positive experiences from the child conversation. Most of them found that they to a great extent were able to say what they wanted to say. On the visual, analogue scale from sad face (0%) to smiley face (100%), half the children put a mark against 100%. Seventy per cent of the children put the mark between 90 and 100%. Median score is 93% of the maximum when it comes to how children experience being able to say what they want to the mediator. For the question about whether the mediator understood what the child meant, the average of the marks given by the children was 92%. The average of the children's marks for whether they liked talking to the mediator was 86% of the maximum.

The children's opinion was also sought on the inclusion of children in mediation in general: "Do you think that children and young people should be able to take part in mediation?" The children were very positive towards this. The average level of the children's marks was 88% of the maximum positive. The fifth and last question where the children were asked to mark a long, visual, analogue scale was: "Did you want to take part in the mediation when your parents suggested it?" The average of the children's markings in this case was 64%.

In the study we were interested in possible variations when children's experiences were compared with different features of the situation the child and the family were in. Figure 2 illustrates the correlation between the children's experience of being able to say what they wanted to the mediator, and the degree of conflict between the parents. The X-axis in the figure shows the mediator's assessment of the conflict level, with "no conflict" on the far left and "very high conflict" on the far right. The Y-axis shows children's experience of being able to say what they wanted to the mediator, where 0% is a sad face and 100% is a smiley face. As the figure shows, the children experienced to a very great extent that they were able to say what they wanted to the mediator, also in cases where the mediator had assessed a high degree of conflict between the parents. For each percentage point of conflict level increase,

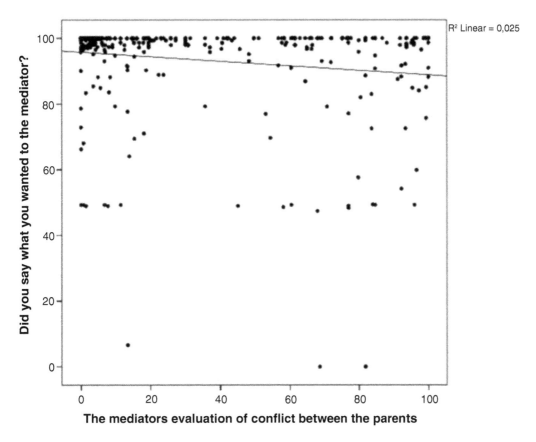

Fig. 2 Children's experience of talking freely with the mediator—and conflict level in the family

there is a decrease of 0.07% in the children's experience of speaking freely. The horizontal line in Fig. 2 gives a graphic presentation of this.[12]

Table 2 below show the results of bivariate multilevel analysis where the correlation between the children's assessments and each of the three predictors—*type of mediation, conflict level and worrisome conditions*—are assessed one by one. There is significant correlation between conflict level and the question "Were you able to say what you wanted to the mediator?" (t = −2.90; p < 0.05). There is a negative correlation between these two variables, which means that an increase in conflict level gives a lower score on the experience variable, although the correlation is very small. There was no other significant correlation between the variables, and the effects were generally quite small. In other words, the conflict level in the family only affected the children's experience of being able to say what they wanted in conversation with the mediator to a small degree.

Through multivariate analysis where all the predictors (type of mediation, conflict level and worrisome conditions) are assessed simultaneously, we were able to estimate the unique contribution of each variable to explain the children's

---

[12]The line in Fig. 2 is based on a linear regression analysis, while the significance of the relationship between conflict level and the children's experience of being able to say what they want to the mediator has been assessed by multilevel analysis.

Table 2 Bivariate multilevel analysis

	Type of mediation	Conflict level	# Worrisome conditions
	Diff[a]	r[b]	r[b]
	t	t	t
Were you able to say what you wanted to the mediator?	1.71	−0.16	−0.07
	0.91	−2.90*	−1.27
Did you enjoy talking to the mediator?	−1.24	−0.11	−0.02
	−0.41	−1.91	−0.23
Did the mediator understand what you meant?	−1.98	0.02	−0.02
	−0.95	0.29	−0.30
Did you want to do this when your parents suggested it?	−4.21	−0.04	0.05
	−0.92	−0.47	0.96
Do you think other children and young people should take part in mediation?	2.86	−0.11	−0.06
	0.87	−1.35	−0.84

*$P < 0.05$
[a]Estimated difference between mandatory mediation in conjunction with separation and pre-action mediation
[b]The Pearson correlation

Table 3 Multivariable analysis

	Type of mediation	Conflict level	# Worrisome conditions
	T	T	T
Were you able to say what you wanted to the mediator?	−0.83	−2.64*	−0.11
Did you enjoy talking to the mediator?	−1.63	−2.54*	0.56
Did the mediator understand what you meant?	−0.83	−0.10	−0.34
Did you want to do this when your parents suggested it?	−1.51	−1.61	1.15
Do you think other children and young people should take part in mediation?	0.003	−0.91	−0.26

*$P < 0.05$

experiences, opinions and wishes in terms of their involvement in the mediation process. The results of the multivariable analysis are shown in Table 3 below. Here there is also a significant correlation between conflict level and "Were you able to say what you wanted to the mediator?" ($t = −2.64$; $p < 0.05$), adjusted for the number of worrisome conditions and type of mediation. There is also a significant correlation between conflict level and "Did you enjoy talking to the mediator?" ($t = −2.54$; $p < 0.05$), adjusted for the number of worrisome conditions and type of mediation. In both cases there is a small negative correlation: an increase in conflict level gives a slightly lower score for children's experiences.

It is natural to expect a certain positive correlation between "Were you able to say what you wanted to the mediator?" and "Did you enjoy talking to the mediator?"

(The Pearson correlation between the two variables is r = 0.39 in this case). It is therefore not surprising that the results are similar in these two cases.

When summarised, these results show that in total, the conflict level, type of mediation and number of worrisome conditions have a relatively small effect. In order to illustrate the strongest correlation between conflict level and "Were you able to say what you wanted to the mediator?" in the multivariate analysis, the experience variable is estimated to decrease by 0.08 percentage points for each percentage point increase in conflict level. This illustrates the following point: as long as the children felt they were able to say what they wanted to the mediator, it would it would be very difficult to find strong effects from any of the predictors. Regardless of conflict level, type of mediation or degree of problem accumulation, most of the children had positive experiences of their participation as actors in mediation.

6 Nuances in the Children's Experiences from Qualitative Analysis

The vast majority (75.4%) of the 138 children who answered the free text question, expressed positive experiences and attitudes to the inclusion of children in the mediation process. 15.2% of the children did not provide any information that could be linked to having taken part in mediation, while 9.4% gave critical and/or negative contributions. This minority said it was boring, unnecessary or difficult. One of the children wrote that mediation ought to take into consideration "that there are delicate situations with parents; they can become difficult if both are present". Half of those who wrote critical and/or negative comments said that they had been given too little information and/or had felt compelled to attend. One of them wrote: "At first I didn't really know what mediation was, so then I was a little unsure." One child felt there was too little time for the child conversation.

The majority, who expressed positive experiences, used concepts like "important", "fantastic", "fun", "good", "okay", "great fun", "pleasant", "smart", "great", "fine", "really cool", and "really good". Several relate their positive experiences to the characteristics of the mediator, and described the mediator as "pleasant", "kind", "easy to talk to", "she understood", "it felt safe", and "she said lots of good things". Several of the children explicitly emphasise that it was positive to be able to talk to someone "neutral". Three of the children wrote: "It was lovely to talk to someone other than mum and dad." "I thought it was good to be able to talk properly to someone who really understood me." "Generally it can be easier to 'talk straight' to someone who is 'detached'." The children emphasised that it felt good to be able to tell someone outside the family what was happening and what they were thinking and feeling. The children often used emoticons to express that it felt good to "ease the burden" and tell someone other than their parents what they thought and felt: "I have no more words left. Managed to say everything☺." "It was good to be able to speak openly about what I wanted. It was a great help☺ Nothing else☺." "I think it was quite good to be able to say it rather than keep it inside!" "I enjoyed taking part in mediation, because now I will get over things I find difficult or things I don't like." One child involved in a mediation where the mediator had ticked three worrisome conditions in the family, wrote the following: "Looking forward to explaining how I am in 6 months' time."

Several of the children explain their positive experiences in terms of having been able to state their opinion, participate in the discussion, and some felt that they were able to participate in decision-making: "I think it's good that we are allowed to take part in mediation because we are the ones who have to listen to all the discussions, and therefore it's important that we are able to say what we feel." "It's a good place to be able to talk about what we think and feel about parents getting divorced. And even if it is the parents who decide in the end, it is a good feeling to be able to say what we feel and participate in the decision." "I would like to have it a bit more often, because then we can change something if it doesn't work." "I thought it was really good to have the opportunity to say what I wanted, and I hope this is something which will continue."

6.1   The Children Generalise: "All Children Should Be Allowed to Take Part"

Several of the children make statements on behalf of *children as a group* in the free text. The children generalise the value of accompanying their parents to mediation, when they e.g. write: "This is something absolutely all children should be allowed to take part in before their parents' divorce. It might help both the children and the parents." Another writes that it was a good way to get children to "speak openly and fully", but thinks that it is "more meaningful for children who are really troubled by the divorce". One of the children gives some advice to other children: "It was really nerve-wracking to be here and talk. But, you see, it is the best thing to do right now. To others who are coming here I would just like to say that there is no need to worry. Because it was actually really nice to be able to talk about it."

6.2   Children's Experiences in Relation to Conflict Level, Degree of Problem Accumulation and Type of Mediation

Of the 138 statements from children in the free text box, 29 (just over 21%) were from children in cases where the mediator had ticked other worrisome conditions.[13] In 72% of these statements (21 of 29), the children pointed to positive experiences

---

[13]As previously mentioned, the mediator had ticked "other worrisome conditions" in 43 of the 217 cases (20%).

with participating in mediation, compared with 74% (81 of 109 statements) in cases where there were no worrisome conditions. It is worth noting that all the seven children in whose cases the mediator had ticked three or four worrisome conditions in the family, made positive statements about taking part in mediation (Table 4).

In the analysis of the children's free text we have also taken a closer look at statements from children in cases where the conflict level has been graded as below 20% or above 80% of the maximum, and statements from children in mandatory mediation in conjunction with separation and mandatory pre-action mediation respectively. The results of this analysis is presented in Tables 5 and 6.

As is shown, the children are positive to involvement in mediation, including in cases with a high conflict level (83% positive statements). Nearly 10% of the children in the cases with a high conflict level came up with negative and/or critical statements. When we compare statements in different types of mandatory mediation, we see that there are 80% positive statements in mandatory mediation in conjunction with separation, and 67% positive statements in mandatory pre-action mediation.

Table 4 Children's statements in the free text compared with degree of problem accumulation

Number of worrisome conditions	Number of children		Positive statements		Negative and/or critical statements	No information about the mediation
0	109		81 (74 per cent)		8 (7 per cent)	18
1	16		12		3	1
2	6	29 children	2	21 (72 per cent)	2	2
3	5		5		0	0
4	2		2		0	0
	138		104 (75.4 per cent)		13 (9.4 per cent)	21 (15.2 per cent)

Table 5 The children's experiences compared with degree of conflict between the parents

Conflict level	Number of children	Positive statements	Negative and/or critical statements	No information about mediation
Below 20%	73	55 (75%)	3 (4%)	15 (21%)
Above 80%	23	19 (83%)	2 (9%)	2 (9%)

Table 6 Children's experiences compared with type of mediation

Type of mediation	Number of children	Positive statements	Negative and/or critical statements	No information about mediation
Mandatory mediation in conjunction with separation	95	76 (80%)	7 (7%)	12 (13%)
Mandatory pre-action mediation	43	29 (67%)	5 (12%)	9 (21%)

7 Summary and Concluding Discussion

- Children chose to participate when they were given the opportunity to do so.
- The children experienced to a large degree that they were able to say what they wanted to the mediator, including in cases where the mediator had assessed a high conflict level between the parents.
- Children recommend other children to take part in the mediation process. The children's experiences and assessments of their own participation is only to a very small degree associated with the conflict level, type of mediation and degree of problem accumulation in the family.
- There are marked contrasts in what children convey in their "messages" to parents. This ranges from, for example, a wish that the parents are reunited, to requests for fewer arguments and less alcohol, or wishes of a material kind. Starting from what they regard as important in both their own and the family's situation, they contribute to the agenda of the mediation. It also gives some children the opportunity to tell an outsider about insecure family circumstances.

Our study shows that children who are given the opportunity to speak in their parents' mediation process will make use of the opportunity. This is in keeping with research results from the courts, which show that the vast majority of children take the opportunity to be heard in parental conflicts (Skjørten 2014). We have investigated whether the conflict level, type of mediation and degree of problem accumulation in the family are significant for the children's experiences of being included in the mediation process, and we found that this is of very little consequence for the children's assessments after participation. Whether the conflict level is high or low, whether we are talking about mandatory mediation in conjunction with separation or mandatory pre-action mediation, and whether there is a high or low degree of problem accumulation, has very little impact on how satisfied children are with being able to participate themselves, or on their recommendations to other children about participation. In the main, analysis of the qualitative data expands and confirms the following results. The majority of children are positive to children's participation. A small minority wrote in their free text responses that they thought it was boring, unnecessary and difficult, that they felt there wasn't enough time, that they felt pressurised, had been given too little information and/or were uncertain beforehand. None of the children said that they felt insecure or threatened by having their own conversation with a mediator. Children who accompany their parents to mediation are in differing phases of the changing family circumstances. Some have just been told, without any pre-warning, that their parents are getting divorced, while others have been living in a situation governed by conflict between the parents for a while. The children's life situation also varies, and children have different competencies and predispositions in terms of being able to handle the situation that has arisen in the family. Through the children's message we have seen that children face very different challenges in connection with the divorce. For some children their care situation is under serious threat as a result of the parents no longer living together.

The position of children in the family and in society in the Western world has undergone radical change throughout history. Today, children are to a much greater degree regarded as entitled to give an opinion—and with a right to speak up in cases that concern them. Children's rights to both participation *and* protection, however, is still a challenge that creates uncertainty in differing sectors about which practices are best able to promote "the best interests of the child". In the mediation model, from which our data are collected, the consideration for children's participation and protection is handled by clarifying the division between the roles and responsibilities of parents and children. This is concretised by definition and demarcation of conversation topic, and the points in the mediation process when children participate. Children do not participate in decision-making and are, for example, never asked where they want to live. We do see, however, how the dominant discourses in our society are coming through into some of the children's statements concerning "fairness" in custody arrangements. In line with norms and policies of equally shared parenting, many children put forward opinions where a 50–50 division of living with each parent is regarded as the most "natural" and fairest solution.

The view of children in difficult life situations is often coloured by a one-sided opinion of "the vulnerable child", or the child as "victim" of the parents' divorce. In line with other age groups, children can be vulnerable and exposed, with additional need for protection, but children are also socially active beings who can influence both their own situation and their environment (James et al. 1999). Moving on from the rights given to children in the Child Convention and the mediation regulations that are established in Norway, the question is no longer *whether* children should participate, but *how* participation can be carried out "in the best interests of the child".

Children's participation makes them visible as subjects with their own thoughts, feelings and opinions about the divorce process that they are part of. Not all children may feel the need to talk to a mediator, but even children in families where the parents agree may need it, as several of our informants stated. As previously shown by Haugen (2007), children's experiences of a divorce and the establishment of new family constellations may deviate from those of their parents. It is difficult to predict which of the children have no need to have a conversation with an outsider and who may have the greatest need. Children in families with a high conflict level, and, in particular, children with a high degree of problem accumulation, may be the children with the greatest need for, and benefit from, their own conversation with a mediator. At the same time, as mentioned, it is often in such situations that children are not heard in a mediation process (Ask and Kjeldsen 2015). According to Langballe (2011), it is not damaging for children to talk about sensitive subjects; however, it may be unfortunate if the child is not taken seriously or believed or protected or if the child does not see any purpose in talking about sensitive topics to the adult. If information about unacceptable home conditions for children becomes available it is therefore necessary for the mediation authority to provide an adequate response, such as, for example, offering to help individual children and families or taking measures through collaborating agencies.

The purpose of universal arrangements such as mandatory mediation is to reach the whole population of divorced parents. When children are included, it means that the mediation authorities come into contact with a wide range of children—including those who previously have had no contact with the children's services and who are in need of help. The handling of children and families with serious problem accumulation and conflict involves co-operation between family counselling and child protection services, the courts and other relevant authorities.

Increased participation by children in the mandatory mediation process clarifies the children's position as actors/co-creators in the changing family circumstances. Through children's actual participation in the mediation process, their position is "magnified", and it is reasonable to assume that their indirect and direct influence in decision-making processes will increase and become clearer in the future. The position of children as participants might thus challenge and destabilise traditional hierarchies between children and adults. As active participants, children will in the future probably have expectations that challenge both mediation and parents in the changing family circumstances caused by relationship breakdowns.

References

Aase TH, Fossåskaret E (2007) Skapte virkeligheter: kvalitativt orientert metode. Universitetsforlaget, Oslo

Ådnanes M, Haugen GMD, Jensberg H, Rantalaiho M, Husum TL (2011) Evaluering av mekling etter ekteskapslov og barnelov. Er meklingsordningen tilstrekkelig innrettet mot de vanskelige sakene, opplever foreldrene mekling som nyttig, og er barnets beste en rettesnor for avtalen? SINTEF, Trondheim

Ask H, Kjeldsen A (2015) Samtaler med barn. Rapport 2015:4. Folkehelseinstituttet, Oslo

Bondevik M, Mehren IS (1997) Terapeuters møte med barn og foreldre i konfliktfylte situasjoner. Hovedoppgave i psykologi. Universitetet i Oslo, Oslo

Bufdir (2015) Årsrapport 2014. 05/2015

Bufdir (2016) Årsrapport 2015. 04/2016

Bufetat Region Sør (2016) Beskrivelsen av Barn i mekling- modellen (BIM)

Edmonds A, Kennedy T (2013) An applied reference guide to research designs. Quantitative, qualitative, and mixed methods. Sage, Washington

Ekeland T-J (2004) Konflikt og konfliktforståelse: for helse og sosialarbeidere. Gyldendal akademisk, Oslo

Ekeland T-J, Myklebust V (1997) Brukarperspektiv på foreldremekling ved samlivsbrot. Tidsskrift for norsk psykologforening 34(9):767–778

Guldbrandsen W (2015) Obligatorisk mekling med foreldre i store konflikter: Vurdering av utfall, konfliktdrivende tema og hva som bidrar til at dialogene mellom dem kan fortsette. Doktorgradsavhanding. Psykologisk institutt. Samfunnsvitenskapelig fakultet. Univeristetet i Oslo, Oslo

Gulbrandsen W, Tjersland OA (2013) Hvordan virker obligatorisk foreldremekling ved store konflikter? Tidsskrift for velferdsforskning 16(1):17–30

Haugen GM (2007) Divorce and post-divorce family practice: the perspective of children and young people. Ph.D.-avhandling. NTNU, Trondheim

Helland MS, Borren I (2015) Foreldrekonflikt; identifisering av konfliktnivåer, sentrale kjennetegn og risikofaktorer hos høykonfliktpar. Folkehelseinstituttet, Oslo

Hodkin R, Newell P (2007) Implementation handbook for the convention on the rights of the child. Atar Roto Press, Geneva

James A, Jenks C, Prout A (1999) Theorising childhood. Polity Press, Cambridge

Langballe Å (2007) Forholdet mellom frie og spontane beretninger fra barn i dommeravhør, og påliteligheten i barns utsagn. Tidsskrift for Norsk Psykologforening 44:868–877

Langballe Å (2011) Den dialogiske barnesamtalen – Hvordan snakke med barn om sensitive temaer. Nasjonalt kunnskapssenter om vold og traumatisk stress. http://www.nkvts.no/biblioteket/Publikasjoner/Den -dialogiske-barnesamtalen-hvordansnakke.pdf

Mantle G, Critchley A (2004) Social work and child-centered family court mediation. Br J Soc Work 34(8):1161–1172. https://doi.org/10.1093/bjsw/bch134

McIntosh J, Wells YD, Smyth BM, Long CM (2007) Child-focused and child inclusive divorce mediation: comparative outcomes from a prospective study of postseparation adjustment. Family Court Rev 46(1):105–124

Nilsen W, Skipstein A, Gustavson K (2012) Foreldrekonflikt, samlivsbrudd og mekling: Konsekvenser for barn og unge. Rapport 2012:2. Folkehelseinstituttet, Oslo

Ottosen MH (2016) Analyse om udviklingen i familieretlige konflikter. Notat. SFI Det Nationale Forskningscenter for velfærd, København

RBUP Rapport (2017) Barn i mekling, En systematisk oversikt om effekter av å involvere barn i meklingssamtaler

Sandberg K (2010) Barns rett til medbestemmelse – et juridisk perspektiv. In: Kjørholt AT (ed) Barn som samfunnsborgere – til barnets beste? Universitetsforlaget, Oslo

Scoffer MJ (2005) Bringing children to the mediation table: defining a child's best interests in divorce mediation. Family Court Rev 43(2):323–338. https://doi.org/10.1111/j.1744-1617.2005.00032.x

Skjørten K (2014) Foreldretvister og økt vektlegging av barns synspunkt. Tidsskrift for familierett, arverett og barnevernrettslige spørsmål 12(2):79–81

Strabac Z (2012) Flernivåanalyse. In: Eikemo TA, Clausen TA (eds) Kvantitativ analyse med SPSS. En praktisk innføring i kvantitative analyseteknikker. Tapir Akademisk Forlag, Trondheim

Strandbu A, Thørnblad R (2015) Hva står på spill? – Barns deltakelse og budskap i mekling. Fokus på familien: Tidsskrift for familiebehandling 43(3):271–291

Strandbu A, Thørnblad R, Handegård BH (2016) Involvering av barn i foreldremekling. Tidsskrift for familierett, arverett og barnevernrettslige spørsmål 14(4):360–386

Thagaard T (2013) Systematikk og innlevelse. En innføring i kvalitativ metode. Fagbokforlaget, Bergen

Mediation and the Best Interests of the Child from the Child Law Perspective

Kirsikka Salminen

Contents

Abstract What is the best interests of the child in family mediation and is mediation in the best interests of the child? In this article, I use child law and the United Nations Convention on the Rights of the Child combined with mediation theory to discuss these questions. Both mediation and the best interests of the child are open for multiple interpretations. Using facilitative and evaluative mediation theory and the legal concept 'the best interests of the child', I explore and compare the understandings of these concepts as they apply to family mediation. This includes a discussion of the advantages and disadvantages of facilitative as well as evaluative mediation orientations in terms of protecting the best interests of the child. Finnish court-connected family mediation is a combination of both mediation orientations, and the mediator is obliged to secure the best interests of the child. From a theoretical point of view, this seems to be a challenging combination.

K. Salminen (✉)
Faculty of Law, University of Helsinki, Helsinki, Finland
e-mail: kirsikka.salminen@helsinki.fi

© The Author(s) 2018
A. Nylund et al. (eds.), *Nordic Mediation Research*,
https://doi.org/10.1007/978-3-319-73019-6_11

1 Introduction

During the past decades society at large has increasingly recognised the subjective legal rights of children. Also, the modern child law perspective has been born (see more on this concept below). Simultaneously, various applications and use of mediation as an alternative to court litigation in child custody disputes has increased. In Finland, court-connected family mediation is one application of mediation. Finnish court-connected family mediation is based on two mediation approaches: it is primarily facilitative with some evaluative elements included. The best interests of the child is according to national legislation and the United Nations Convention on the Rights of the Child (UNCRC), the primary consideration in actions concerning children, such as court-connected family mediation in child custody disputes. The best interests of the child is, however, a complex term that can be approached from various disciplines. The child law perspective is one way to view the requirements set for mediation by the best interests of the child.[1]

This article focuses on two mediation approaches: facilitative and evaluative mediation and explores how do these orientations (approaches) support the best interests of the child from a child law perspective. My aim is not to present one mediation model as favourable over the other or to discuss the purposes mediation is developed for but rather to shed the light of child law perspective on these two mediation approaches.

In this article, the facilitative and evaluative mediation, as well as the best interests of the child, are anchored to certain definitions that are compared with each other. The aim is also to problematise and open for discussion the operation of the best interests of the child and its elements in mediation. The context in this article is Finnish, but the idea of mediation models and the child law perspective are international. This article is partly based on a larger research project that is focused on Finnish court-connected family mediation and, thus, the Finnish context is shortly presented here, too.

This article combines legal doctrine, especially the child law perspective, with conflict and mediation theories through comparing these systems with each other. Legal rights discussion focuses on legal rights and promotes legal security. The mediation discussion focuses on conflicts, communication, interests, needs and agreements.

---

[1]The author is conducting doctorate research on this topic in Finland with law and mediation theory based approach and qualitative empirical data. This article is loosely based on the theoretical and non-empirical sections of the yet unpublished dissertation.

2 Court-Connected Family Mediation in Finland

In Finland, a country about 5.5 million inhabitants, every year about 30,000 children go through their parents separation. About 90% of all divorcing or separating families solve child custody and contact issues without court proceedings. In about every tenth separated family the conflict escalates (about the numbers, OM 25/2013). In the Nordic countries, about 10% of all child custody disputes are brought to court (Ervasti and Nylund 2014). In Finland, the court proceedings are either litigation, where the outcome is either a judgment or agreement, or court-connected mediation. In 2014, about 800 cases went to court-connected family mediation (Salminen and Ervasti 2015).

In Finland, the parents have the right to agree on child custody and contact right but best interests standard limits their choices. This need for evaluation by the authorities brings a certain tension to mediation, since party self-determination[2] is typically seen as the core element of mediation (Welsh 2004; Bush and Folger 2005; Shienvold 2004; Roberts 2008; Ervasti and Nylund 2014; Nylund 2016). Also, the neutral, objective and non-authoritative role of mediator is seen as incompatible with need to secure the best interests of the child (Ervasti and Nylund 2014).

In Finland, the court-connected family mediation is a public service offered by the courts and voluntary for the parties to participate. Also, out-of-court mediation is available for families in Finland (Haavisto 2018). Court-connected family mediation is thus only one of many mediation models and practices in Finland. In this article, the focus is limited to this one specific mediation.

Court-connected mediation is an alternative to litigation in the court to resolve disputes and make arrangements (HE 114/2004 vp). The process is regulated in the Act on mediation in civil matters and confirmation of settlements in general courts (Mediation Act 394/2011, laki riita-asioiden sovittelusta ja sovinnon vahvistamisesta yleisissä tuomioistuimissa). The Act on Child Custody and Right of Access (The Child Custody Act 361/1983, laki lapsen huollosta ja tapaamisoikeudesta) regulates the legal substance of child custody and contact right.

Finnish court-connected family mediation is built on facilitative and evaluative mediation orientations (HE 114/2004 vp, Ervasti 2011).[3] In the Mediation Act, the objective of mediation is an amicable resolution of the matter (section 3). The mediator shall assist the parties in their efforts to reach agreement and an amicable resolution. On the request or with the consent of the parties, the mediator may make a proposal for an amicable resolution. The proposal may be based on what the mediator deems appropriate in view of what the parties have brought forward in the mediation (section 7). Finnish court-connected family mediation has thus a problem solving perspective to mediation (Ervasti and Nylund 2014). It also

---

[2]Self-determination has many aspects. One central element is the party's informed consent that builds on sufficient amount of information in order to promote understanding and free and well-grounded decision making, see Nolan-Haley (1999).

[3]For the concepts of facilitative and evaluative mediation, see Riskin (1996).

includes elements of legal decision making, since the agreement between the parties can be made legally enforceable by the mediator (sections 8 and 9). The mediator has to evaluate, to some extent, the outcome so that the agreement is not breaching the law or a third party's rights, which is a prerequisite stated in the Mediation Act section 8. To what extend mediators evaluate the agreements is unclear.

The best interests of the child gives family mediation a special goal. In the Finnish court-connected family mediation the mediator is obliged by law to secure that the process and the resolution are in the best interests of the child (the Mediation Act section 10 with reference to the Child Custody Act, especially section 10). According to the preparatory work and the reports of the Ministry of Justice in Finland, mediation safeguards the best interests of a child when the conflict in the child's growth environment is diminished and there is an alternative to a full-scale court trial (HE 114/2004, OM 25/2013, see also Auvinen 2006; Aaltonen 2000, 2015). Internationally and in Finland, too, the negative effects of the parent's continuous conflict on children are recognised (McIntosh et al. 2008; Parkinson 2011; Skjørten 2005; Mueller-Johnson 2005; Johnston et al. 2009; Rejmer 2003; Karttunen 2010; Sinkkonen 2011). Due to their internal conflict, new family structures or, for example, lack of sufficient information, the parents may be ignorant to the needs, interest and rights of their child.

In Finnish court-connected family mediation the mediator is a district court judge. The judge-mediator is assisted by an expert mediator. The expert mediator in child-custody disputes is a social worker, psychiatrist or psychologist specialised in divorcing families and child development psychology. Legal, as well as social and psychological experts, are thus present in mediation.

In theory, Finnish court-connected family mediation can be classified as child-informed, child-focused and child-inclusive mediation, since the law focuses on the best interests of the child and makes child participation possible (see Taylor 2002; Ervasti and Nylund 2014; Parkinson 2011; McIntosh 2000; McIntosh et al. 2008; Saposnek 2004, in Finland also Aaltonen 2015). In practice, child participation in Finnish court-connected family mediation is not typical (the child participates in about 2% of mediations, according to OM 25/2013.) The child is not a party of the custody-proceedings in national legislation. In mediation, the child is not represented in the process other than through his or her parents (or other person having the custody).

3   Child Law and the Best Interests of the Child

Child law is interested in what are the legal rights of the child and how do they appear in various fields of society, systems, processes and life (Freeman 2012a). Child law has been called as an umbrella perspective that can cover all the other fields of law (Bendiksen and Haugli 2014). The more traditional understanding of child law focuses on the child's family relations and objective perspectives on the best interests of the child. During the past few decades, the perspective has turned to the subjective legal rights of children within family and society (Hakalehto-Wainio

2013). The focus in modern child law is protecting the child's legal rights instead of only protecting the child (Freeman 2012b; Hakalehto-Wainio 2013; Nieminen 1992; Parkinson and Cashmore 2008; Pajulammi 2014; Gottberg 2006).

Today's children have subjective legal rights. The United Nations Convention on the Rights of the Child (UNCRC) is in Finland on top of the legal hierarchy of child's rights (Kangas 2013; Hakalehto-Wainio 2013; Toivonen 2017). Many of the child's rights are also confirmed in the national legislations of the Nordic countries and also in EU legislation. Today the child law perspective is one important element in Finnish court-connected family mediation since Finland, like most of the counties in the world, are bound to the UNCRC's mandate to fulfil the legal rights that belong to children. The rights-based child law perspective thus sets special requirements for family mediation.

According to the UNCRC article 3, in all actions concerning children, the best interests of the child shall be a primary consideration. According to the Committee on the Rights of the Child (CRC), the best interests of a child assessment should be carried out with full respect for the rights contained in the UNCRC and its optional protocols. In addition, the best interests of a child should be evaluated on a case-by-case basis and adjusted to the needs of the specific child in question, since children are not a homogenous group (CRC General Comment 14; CRC General Comment 12). Standard information about children's wellbeing, experiences and participation may not always be the key to reach the best interests of a child in individual cases.

The expression "primary consideration" in article 3 of the UNCRC means that the best interests of the child is not on the same level as all other considerations. The strong position of the best interests of the child is justified, since children are legally in special situation (CRC General Comment 14). Children are under guardianship of adults and have limited ability to act legally. Children are thus dependent on adults' behaviour. Through paying attention to the legal rights of the child, we pay attention to and respect the child as an individual human being with human rights.

According to the CRC "the full application of the concept of the child's best interests requires the development of a rights-based approach, engaging all actors, to secure the holistic physical, psychological, moral and spiritual integrity of the child and promote his or her human dignity" (CRC General Comment 14). In Finland, Toivonen has stated that the child's rights are legally binding and the ignorance leads to breach of the child's human rights (Toivonen 2017).

From the child law perspective, the best interests assessment should follow two steps. The first step is to within the specific factual context find out what are the relevant elements, give them concrete content and assign a weight to each in relation to one another. The second step is to follow a procedure that ensures legal guarantees and proper application of the right. The assessment is individual, the decision maker carries it out and it requires the participation of the child (CRC General Comment 14). Concrete examples of the best interests assessment in mediation are given later in the text.

The best interests of the child should be viewed individually and on a case-by-case basis. Even though all the rights should have independent value, the elements of the best interests assessment may be in conflict with each other and in certain circumstances. Not all elements are relevant in every case, and different elements can be used in different ways in different cases. In weighing the various elements the purpose of the assessment should be bared in mind: to ensure the full and effective enjoyment of the rights recognised in the UNCRC and the holistic development of the child (CRC General Comment 14).

According to the CRC, the decision maker is obliged to secure the fulfilment of the best interests of the child. Further, it is stated that the obligation to have the best interests of a child as a primary consideration applies to mediation, too (CRC General Comment 12; CRC General Comment 14). From the perspective of the mediation theories one can, however, ask who has the obligation to fulfil the best interests of the child, since the parties' self-determination is a central element of mediation and the mediator should not have an authority to decide the case. Facilitative and evaluative mediation have somewhat differing approaches to this question, and the approaches are presented later in the text.

The child law perspective has been incorporated into family mediation. The best interests of the child and the child's legal right to participate have been recognised and child-informative, child-focused, and child-inclusive mediation have been developed (see McIntosh 2000; McIntosh et al. 2008; Roberts 2008; Parkinson 2011). The following chapters focus on how the traditional facilitative and evaluative mediation orientations can reflect the rights-based best interests assessment.

4 Facilitative Mediation Approach to the Best Interests of the Child

Approaches to and ways to define mediation are today many (see Ervasti and Nylund 2014). One way to systematise approaches to mediation is the perspective of facilitative and evaluative orientations (presented by Leonard Riskin at the turn of the century (see Riskin 1996, 2003).[4] After the Riskin's grid, the orientations and approaches have been developed further and defined with various points emphasised. They have been criticised, as well. The dichotomy has thus had an important impact in the field of mediation and has landed in Finland, as well as the theoretical background for court-connected mediation. The approaches can further be defined as narrow or broad, and the degree of facilitation and evaluation may vary (see e.g. Riskin 1996; Lowry 2004; Mayer 2004; Ervasti and Nylund 2014). The division is somewhat simplified but it clarifies discussions and it is pedagogically effective. The line between facilitative and evaluative mediation is, however, not always clear (Riskin 1996, 2003; Ervasti and Nylund 2014; Lowry 2004).

By definition a facilitative mediator's main task is to facilitate the negotiations and the problem solving process between the conflicting parties, here, the

---

[4]Since the Finnish court-connected family mediation is built around these two orientations, they frame the discussion on mediation in this article.

parents (or other person having the custody). The facilitative mediator facilitates the communication between the parties and empowers them typically in a structured process to articulate their own interests, concerns, needs and solutions and to genuinely listen to and understand each other's. Facilitative mediation is usually interest-based. The focus is not on claims and legal definitions. A facilitative mediator does not direct the parties to a certain outcome and does not provide information. A facilitative mediator does not express his or her own opinion or suggestion for resolution in the matter and does not evaluate how a third person would resolve the case. The mediator does not evaluate the parties' views or proposals. The mediator is responsible for the process and the parties for the content and the outcome. The mediator supports the parties to find their own solutions. A facilitative mediator is neutral and objective, and the parties themselves carry the keys for resolution in their conflict (Riskin 1996; Mayer 2004; Ervasti and Nylund 2014, see also Lowry 2004).

The facilitative mediator "assumes that the parents are the most equipped agents to make good decisions about the needs of their children" and "even if parents want to make child-rearing decisions with which the facilitative mediator does not personally agree, his or her job is not to interfere" (Mayer 2004). The job for the facilitative mediator is to focus on helping the parents articulate and evaluate their own concerns (Mayer 2004).

In facilitative mediation it is up to the parties to decide what is the content of the discussions and if there is, for example, need for a legal discussion (see Adrian 2012; Ervasti and Nylund 2014). The mediator can support the parties to widen their perspectives and find alternatives (Ervasti and Nylund 2014). Also, new and creative outcomes are possible (Adrian and Mykland 2014). The purpose of facilitative mediation is for the parties to find a resolution that best serves their own and their common interests and they are satisfied with. In Finnish mediation research the baseline for mediation is facilitative (Ervasti and Nylund 2014).

How can then facilitative mediation promote the fulfilment of the child's legal rights and the best interests of the child? From the perspective of the best interests assessment, the first benefit is the individual and contextual discussions that aim to serve the parties' interests and needs. This promotes the individual, contextual and case-by-case solutions that are according to the CRC central in the best interests assessment. The other benefit is that the level of the conflict may diminish since the focus on is on the individual reasons, interest and needs behind the conflict. In this way, facilitative mediation may promote the parent's co-operation, turn the level and nature of their conflict more positive and spare the child from the conflict. This can protect the child's rights set forth in the UNCRC to e.g. the right to be protected from all forms of physical or mental violence, injury or abuse, neglect or negligent treatment, maltreatment or exploitation (article 19); the right to a standard of living adequate for the child's physical, mental, spiritual, moral and social development (article 27); and the to maintain personal relations and direct contact with both parents on a regular basis (article 9). When the negative conflict is erased from the child's growth environment, the child's right to rest and leisure, to engage in play and recreational activities (article 31) has better possibilities to be recognised and fulfilled as well.

The way for a facilitative mediator to support the best interests of the child is to help the parents identify the information they need to make informed decisions and consider how they might obtain it. The substantive expertise of the mediator may help him or her ask useful questions and frame issues in a constructive and meaningful way, as well as address the possibility that mediation is not the best way to get the family's needs met (Mayer 2004). From the child law perspective, it would be thus important to raise awareness about the modern child law perspective among family mediators, as well as family lawyers, who often support the parents in the Finnish court-connected family mediation.

The facilitative orientation may be tested if the parties are agreeing to something illegal or are breaching a third person's rights, here, it would be the child's rights. If the mediator informs the parents that their view or agreement is against the law, the mediator is opting out of the facilitative role. The other option would be to keep on proposing questions to, reframing and challenging the parents on their views (Mayer 2004). The challenge in facilitative mediation from the child law perspective is the best interests assessment. Typically, the child is the common interest of the parents (Roberts 2008). However, the fulfilment of the child's legal rights is in the end dependent on the parents, their knowledge about the child's rights and what they find relevant. Many parents are facing questions relating the rights of the child in a separation situation for the first time (Lowry 2004), and they may not be aware of the child's rights and their application. This may be problematic also for the self-determination and the informed consent of the parents (Mayer 2004).

From the child law perspective, challenges arise if the child's rights are not part of the discussions, no best interests assessment is conducted and the child's right to participate is not considered. The mediator's neutrality and objectivity as well as confidentiality are limiting the role of the facilitative mediator. The mediator should focus on neutrally presenting questions to the parents, ease their communication and help them understand their own and each other's interest. Even though the facilitative approach may vary between highly structured, open ended and process or outcome oriented the mediator should not educate or advise the parents, provide information about the child's rights or conduct the best interests assessment (Mayer 2004). The facilitative mediator should not be the child's lawyer.[5] Since the topics of discussion and the production of information are dependent on the parents, facilitative mediation may actually ignore the best interests assessment and the protection of the child's rights partly or completely.

---

[5]In Finland, the child is not a legal party in custody proceedings. The parents represent the child in these issues and no third-party child representatives to promote the child's legal rights in court emerge yet in Finland, see Tolonen (2015).

5 Evaluative Mediation Approach to the Best Interests of the Child

Evaluative (or directive, see Riskin 2003) approach is another possible orientation, when systemising mediation models with problem-solving focus (Riskin 1996; Lowry 2004; Ervasti and Nylund 2014). The level of evaluative approach may vary between moderate and strong (Riskin 2003). The more evaluative the role and approach of the mediator, the more evaluative the mediation becomes (Lowry 2004; Mayer 2004; Ervasti and Nylund 2014).

Evaluative mediation is defined as an analytical process that focuses the mediator's attention on the substance of the conflict and what would be necessary in order to achieve a settlement (Lowry 2004). The evaluative orientation to mediation assumes that the mediator is capable of both facilitating the mediation process and making judgments about its contents. Evaluative mediator provides information to the parties and focuses on reaching an agreement. The parties can be directed to certain resolution that by the mediator is considered to the best or the right one. In addition to directions and providing information, the evaluative mediator can make evaluations. The evaluations can focus on (1) the parties' positions and claims, (2) how a third person such as a judge would resolve the questions and (3) giving or evaluating proposals for solution (Ervasti and Nylund 2014; Riskin 1996; Mackie 1997). Evaluative mediation is settlement and agreement focused and an effective way to reach an agreement as such (Riskin 1996; Lowry 2004).

The evaluative mediator has two different roles: the role of a facilitator and the role of an evaluator (Shienvold 2004). The evaluative mediator typically uses many facilitative techniques (Riskin 2003). The challenge in evaluative and directive approach is that it may endanger the neutrality of the mediator (Love 1997; Kovach and Love 1998; Ervasti and Nylund 2014). The evaluative mediator is not in the same manner limited by objectivity as is the facilitative mediator. The evaluative approach tends to undermine the focus on the process of interaction, communication, negotiation and decision making that is the main role of a facilitative mediator. If the parents see the mediator as an information provider, the mediator's role as a facilitator can become undermined (Mayer 2004).

How can then evaluative mediation promote the fulfilment of the child's legal rights and the best interests of the child? From the child law perspective, the benefit is that the mediator can provide the parents information about the child's rights and that a best interests assessment should be made. As mentioned above, many parents are facing the questions relating the rights of the child in a separated family for the first time, and they need information and expertise (Lowry 2004). The evaluative mediator can make sure that the rights of the child are not ignored. The evaluative mediator can also evaluate how the parents are supporting the rights of the child, direct them to focus on their child and provide information and proposals for solutions.

The evaluative mediator takes responsibility for the outcome and directs the parties to an agreement. Evaluative mediation can save the parties faces from not going too deep into the reasons behind the conflict and neutral proposals can be an excuse to agree. It might also open the parent's eyes to see the their positions differently. By this way evaluative mediation can support the family to move on rather quickly, avoid the court room and settle their case (Lowry 2004). Since the nature and level of conflicts are different for some families this might be the way out of the conflict. In this way the child's rights set forth in the UNCRC to e.g. maintain personal relations and direct contact with both parents on a regular basis (article 9) may be promoted.

The challenge with evaluative family mediation is that there is, however, a risk that the conflict remains if the reasons, needs and interest are not individually addressed and the agreement does not reach the real problems that should be agreed on. The evaluative approach can for some families be too agreement focused (Love 1997). If the conflict is ongoing and enduring the problem solving purpose and focus are narrow in that sense that they are not providing the parents tools for constructive engagement. The narrow approach may also ignore some severe problems in the family that infringe the rights of the child (such as family violence that needs special attention, see Nylund 2012, 2016). If the mediation does not reach the roots of the parent's conflict the parents may not be committed to their agreement, they may continue their fighting and are not able to co-operate, even though they have an agreement on paper. The child's rights set forth in the UNCRC to e.g. maintain personal relations and direct contact with both parents on a regular basis (article 9), to the enjoyment of the highest attainable standard of health (article 24), to rest and leisure, to engage in play and recreational activities (article 31), to not be subjected to degrading treatment or punishment (article 37), to be protected from all forms of physical or mental violence, injury or abuse, neglect or negligent treatment, maltreatment or exploitation (article 19) and to a standard of living adequate for the child's development (article 27) may be under risk. The same applies to families with problems of violence, since in quick and narrow focused mediation many problems may be ignored (Nylund 2016).

The mechanisms for evaluations may vary between instructions and suggestions, as well as between statements and questions and evaluations can be strategic (Lowry 2004). No commonly agreed mechanisms exist (Ervasti and Nylund 2014; Lowry 2004; Riskin 1996). One important question is on what information are the evaluations based on. Typically no evidence material is presented in mediation. The challenge is if the parents experience the mediator as an authority; the parents trust on the evaluations, the evaluations may be based on more or less general or standardised information, on narrow, inadequate or lacking material or even false information. This may also lead to competition between the parents if they are trying to affect the mediator's proposals and evaluations. The parents may also feel pressure under directive mediation, and they agree since they feel that they have to. The family does not necessarily share the mindset of the mediator as to what is relevant in mediation. The real and individual problems may be thus unsolved and the problems may remain. The mediator takes over the parent's conversation and their opportunity and responsibility to solve their problems (Problems in evaluations, see Ervasti and Nylund 2014; Taylor 2002; Lowry 2004; Menkel-Meadow 1996).

The child's individual needs and hopes may be ignored especially if the child is not participating. The mediator's influence may lead to too quick and narrow closure and dissatisfaction to both result and the process (Lowry 2004).

Evaluative mediation orientation may ignore the individual assessment of the best interests of the child (article 3 of the UNCRC) if the focus is on general and standardised information relating to children. Evaluative approach might not lower the level of conflict and by this way may ignore the child's rights set forth in the UNCRC to e.g. maintain personal relations and direct contact with both parents on a regular basis (article 9), to the enjoyment of the highest attainable standard of health (article 24), to rest and leisure, to engage in play and recreational activities (article 31), to not be subjected to degrading treatment or punishment (article 37), to be protected from all forms of physical or mental violence, injury or abuse, neglect or negligent treatment, maltreatment or exploitation (article 19) and to a standard of living adequate for the child's development (article 27). Evaluative mediation may have a general or standardised approach to the child's right to participate, which is problematic especially if the participation right (article 12) is ignored. Evaluative approach may limit the parent's self-determination and the primary responsibility to decide over their children (article 18).

6 Conclusion

This article has focused on the best interests of the child in facilitative and evaluative mediation. From the child law perspective, the best interests of the child can be reached in mediation if the best interests assessment is conducted and all of the rights belonging to the child are taken into consideration, including the right to participate. In other situations, from the child law perspective, we have not reached the best interests of the child (Nieminen 2013).

The best interests of the child is, however, a complex and interdisciplinary concept. A lawyer and a psychologist, for example, see and understand the best interests of a child in mediation somewhat differently (see also Toivonen 2017). We need different tools to reach different elements of the whole. The legal perspective is one of the elements, and as described above, the best interests assessment provides a legal method—a legal checklist—to promote the best interests of the child. Standard-ised *methods* are seen as one tool to take the best interests of the child into account and to promote the child's legal security (Toivonen 2017; Kaldal 2012).

As discussed in this article facilitative and evaluative mediation orientations have somewhat different approaches to conflict resolution and, in this case, also to the child's rights. What is common for both approaches and mediation in general is that the parents are the ones who make the decisions. However, the mediator's role and approach affect the way the decisions are reached. The two mediation orientations were not developed to ensure the full and effective enjoyment of the rights of the child recognised in the UNCRC and the holistic development of the child. Thus the child law perspective and the best interests assessment require special attention in the traditional facilitative and evaluative mediation orientations. The child law approach creates an additional special element to facilitative and evaluative mediation.

Finnish court-connected family mediation is a combination of facilitative and evaluative mediation orientations and, in addition, the mediator is obliged to secure the best interests of the child. From a theoretical point of view, this seems to be a challenging combination. The Finnish mediator is firstly balancing between the two mediation orientations. Secondly, the mediator is balancing between the various definitions of the best interests of the child that in the Finnish court-connected family mediation is connected to (1) the National Act on Child Custody and Right of Access that represents the more traditional child law and not directly to the modern rights-based child law approach and (2) the UNCRC to which Finland is committed to. From the perspective of this article, Finnish court-connected family mediation meets challenges with the best interests standard and needs further research.[6]

References

Adrian L (2012) Mellem retssag og rundbordssamtale: retsmægling i teori og praksis. Jurist- og Økonomforbundets Forlag, København

Adrian L, Mykland S (2014) Creativity in court-connected mediation: myth or reality? Negot J 30(4):421–439

Auvinen M (2006) Huoltoriidat tuomioistuimissa. Sosiaalitoimi selvittäjänä, sovittelijana, asiantuntijana. Suomalainen lakimiesyhdistys, Helsinki

Aaltonen AK (2000) Tuomari sovinnontekijänä perheoikeusasioissa. Lakimies 98(7-8):1320–1324

Aaltonen AK (2015) Huoltoriitojen sovittelu tuomioistuimessa. Kauppakamari, Helsinki

Bendiksen L, Haugli T (2014) Sentrale emner i barneretten. Universitetsforlaget, Oslo

Bush RAB, Folger JP (2005) The promise of mediation. the transformative approach to conflict. Jossey-Bass, San Francisco

CRC General Comment 12 (2009) Committee on the Rights of the Child. General comment No. 12 (2009): The right of the child to be heard, 12.2.2009

CRC General Comment 14 (2013) Committee on the Rights of the Child. General comment No. 14 (2013) on the right of the child to have his or her best interests taken as a primary consideration (article 3, para. 1), 29.5.2013

Ervasti K (2011) Tuomioistuinsovittelu Suomessa. Helsinki, Oikeuspoliittinen tutkimuslaitos

Ervasti K, Nylund A (2014) Konfliktinratkaisu ja sovittelu. Helsinki, Edita

Freeman M (2012a) Introduction. Law Child Stud Curr Legal Issues 14:1–9

Freeman M (2012b) Towards a sociology of children's rights. Law Child Stud Curr Legal Issues 14:29–38

Gottberg E (2006) Yksityisen ja julkisen rajapintoja. Lapsen läheissuhteet yksityisen ja julkisen rajapinnassa. Lakimies 104(7–8):1225–1239

Haavisto V (2018) Developing family mediation in Finland: the change process and practical outcomes. In: Nylund A, Ervasti K, Adrian L (eds) Nordic Mediation Research. Springer, Cham, pp 41–66

---

[6]The empirical qualitative data of my dissertation focuses on how mediators are conducting mediation and supporting the best interests of the child in practice. The data consist of observations and interviews.

Hakalehto-Wainio S (2013) Uusi lapsioikeus. In: Husa J, Keskitalo P, Linna T, Tammi-Salminen E (eds) Oikeuden avantgarde. Juhlajulkaisu Juha Karhu 1953 – 6/4 – 2013. Talentum, Helsinki, pp 59–76

HE 114/2004 vp (2004) Hallituksen esitys eduskunnalle riita-asioiden sovittelua ja sovinnon vahvistamista yleisissä tuomioistuimissa koskevaksi lainsäädännöksi

Johnston J, Roseby V, Kuehnle K (2009) In the name of the child. A developmental approach to understanding and helping children of conflict and violent divorce. Springer, New York

Kaldal A (2012) Standardiserade metoder för att bedöma risk i ärenden om vårdnad, boende och umgänge. Juridisk Tidskrift 24(3):540–562

Kangas U (2013) Perhe- ja jäämistöoikeuden perusteet. Helsinki, Talentum

Karttunen R (2010) Isän ja äidin välissä. Lapsen kuulemisen psykologinen kehys huolto- ja tapaamisriidoissa. Tampere University Press, Tampere

Kovach K, Love L (1998) Mapping mediation: the risks of Riskin's Grid. Harv Negot Law Rev 3:71–110

Love LP (1997) The top ten reasons why mediators should not evaluate. Fla State Univ Law Rev 24:937–948

Lowry RL (2004) Evaluative mediation. In: Folberg J, Milne A, Salem P (eds) Divorce and family mediation. models, techniques, and applications. The Guilford Press, New York, pp 72–91

Mackie K (1997) Mediation futures. In: Macfarlane J (ed) Rethinking disputes: the mediation alternative. Cavendish, London, pp 371–379

McIntosh J (2000) Child-inclusive divorce mediation: report on a qualitative research study. Mediat Q 18(1):55–69

McIntosh J, Wells YD, Smyth BM, Long CM (2008) Child-focused and child-inclusive divorce mediation: comparative outcomes from a prospective study of postseparation adjustment. Family Court Rev 46(1):105–124

Mayer B (2004) Facilitative mediation. In: Folberg J, Milne A, Salem P (eds) Divorce and family mediation. models, techniques, and applications. Guilford Press, New York, pp 29–52

Menkel-Meadow C (1996) Is mediation the practice of law? Altern High Cost Litig 14:57–61

Mueller-Johnson K (2005) Supporting conflicted post-divorce parenting. In: Maclean M (ed) Family law and family values. Hart, Oxford

Nieminen L (1992) Objektista subjektiksi. Perus- ja ihmisoikeusjärjestelmän sukupuolisidonnaisuudesta. In: Turunen R (ed) Naisnäkökulmia oikeuteen. Gaudeamus, Helsinki, pp 58–84

Nieminen L (2013) Perus- ja ihmisoikeudet ja perhe. Helsinki, Talentum

Nolan-Haley JM (1999) Informed consent in mediation: a guiding principle for truly educated decisionmaking. Notre Dame Law Rev 74(3):775–840

Nylund A (2012) Barnefordelingssaker og familier med høyt konfliktnivå. Tidsskrift for familierett, arverett og barnevernrettslige spørsmål 10(3–4):215–235

Nylund A (2016) Tilpasset mekling som konfliktløsningsmetode i konflikter om omsorgsorganisering. Tidsskrift for familierett, arverett og barnevernrettslige spørsmål 12(2):106–124

OM 25/2013. Oikeusministeriön Mietintöjä ja lausuntoja 25/2013. Asiantuntija-avusteista huoltoriitojen sovittelua koskeva kokeilu käräjäoikeuksissa 1.1.2011-31.12.2013. Loppuraportti

Pajulammi H (2014) Lapsi, oikeus ja osallisuus. Helsinki, Talentum

Parkinson L (2011) Family mediation. Appropriate dispute resolution in a new family justice system. Family Law, Bristol

Parkinson P, Cashmore J (2008) The voice of a child in family law disputes. Oxford University Press, Oxford

Rejmer A (2003) Vårdnadstvister. En rättssociologisk studie av tingsrätts function vid handläggning av vårdnadskonflikter med utgångspunkt från barnets bästa. Lund Studies in Sociology of Law, Lund

Riskin L (1996) Understanding mediators' orientations, strategies, and techniques. Harv Negot Law Rev 1:7–51

Riskin L (2003) Decisionmaking in mediation: the new old grid and the new new grid system. Notre Dame Law Rev 79(1):1–54

Roberts M (2008) Mediation in family disputes. Principles of practice. Ashgate, Aldershot

Salminen K, Ervasti K (2015) Tuomioistuinsovittelun yleistyminen ja tuomioistuimen tehtävät. Lakimies 113(5):591–612

Saposnek DT (2004) Working with children in mediation. In: Folberg J, Milne A, Salem P (eds) Divorce and family mediation. Models, techniques, and applications. The Guilford Press, New York, pp 155–179

Shienvold A (2004) Hybrid processes. In: Folberg J, Milne A, Salem P (eds) Divorce and family mediation. Models, techniques, and applications. The Guildford Press, New York, pp 112–126

Sinkkonen J (2011) Kiintymyssuhdenäkökulma vanhempien avo- tai avioeroon. In: Sinkkonen J, Kalland M (eds) Varhaislapsuuden tunnesiteet ja niiden suojeleminen. Helsinki, WSOYpro

Skjørten K (2005) Samlivsbrudd og barnefordeling. Gyldendal Akademisk, Oslo

Taylor A (2002) Family dispute resolution. Mediation theory and practice. Jossey-Bass, San Francisco

Toivonen V (2017) Lapsen oikeudet ja oikeusturva. Lastensuojeluasiat hallintotuomioistuimissa. Alma Talent, Helsinki

Tolonen H (2015) Lapsi, perhe ja tuomioistuin. Lapsen prosessuaalinen asema huolto- ja huostaanotto-oikeudenkäynneissä. Suomalainen lakimiesyhdistys, Helsinki

Welsh N (2004) Reconciling self-determination, coercion, and settlement in court-connected mediation. In: Folberg J, Milne A, Salem P (eds) Divorce and family mediation. Models, techniques, and applications. The Guilford Press, New York, pp 420–443

Part IV
Mediation in Theory and Practice

Past, Present and Future of Mediation in Nordic Countries

Kaijus Ervasti

Contents

Abstract In this article, I argue that it is useful to make a distinction between theoretical models of mediation, practical systems of mediation in context, and mediation in action. Using this distinction makes it possible to examine the relationship of the model of mediation, the context in which mediation is practiced and mediator behaviour, and to analyse the field of mediation and obtain a better understanding of mediation, as such, as a result. First, I offer a brief historical overview of how mediation has developed in the Nordic countries on a theoretical, institutional and practical level. Then, I unfold and examine which theoretical models are at play, what the different areas of practice are and how mediators interpret and implement theoretical models in their practice. One main problem is that mediators in their everyday work sometimes act in a different way than they think themselves or what theory of mediation postulates. In conclusion, I point to the

K. Ervasti (✉)
Faculty of Social Sciences, University of Helsinki, Helsinki, Finland
e-mail: kaijus.ervasti@helsinki.fi

© The Author(s) 2018
A. Nylund et al. (eds.), *Nordic Mediation Research*,
https://doi.org/10.1007/978-3-319-73019-6_12

need for further empirical and theoretical studies, as well as the development of mediation training in Nordic countries.

1   History of Mediation in Nordic Countries

In the last 50 years, there has been a significant number of writings on conflict resolution and mediation. There are a wide range of theoretical constructions, concepts and models dealing with these topics. In practice, there is also a huge number of new conflict resolution systems in Western countries. More and more conflicts will be resolved in an out-of-court system. Particularly mediation is today a widely used method to resolve conflicts in Western countries, including the Nordic countries.

In this article, I will introduce mediation systems in Nordic countries. At first there are some historical remarks on the development of mediation in Nordic countries. After that I will handle mediation as a system that has three elements: theoretical models of mediation, practical systems of mediation in context, and mediation in action. Finally, I will handle separately each of these elements.

Mediation has old roots in Nordic countries. Modern law, a trained legal profession and jurisprudence are phenomenon of the late eighteenth and nineteenth centuries in Nordic countries. In pre-modern time, legal, administrative issues and common things of the people were handled in a local assembly called *ting*. Criminal cases, civil cases, disputes concerning ownership of land and the like were all handled in *ting*. A large part of the local people took part in the decision making process. Decision making was based on consensual negotiation of local people. For example, resolution in homicide cases often entailed compensation to the family of the victim. It is not difficult to see similarities between pre-modern conflict resolution systems and late modern or post-modern conflict resolution system and mediation systems in Nordic countries (Letto-Vanamo and Tamm 2017).

The late eighteenth and nineteenth century saw the appointment of special conciliation boards in Denmark, Norway and Iceland, but not in Finland or Sweden. According to the regulation of 1795 in Denmark and Norway, all civil case, in general, should be subject to settlement efforts prior to going to court. These conciliation boards handled mostly civil cases, but also cases of defamation, debt, marriage and violence. This system has been abolished in Denmark and Iceland, but it is working still in Norway (Vindeløv 2012; Nylund 2014). Norwegian boards try to get settlement in civil cases but gives also judgments. Members of boards are laymen. The conciliation boards handle about 80,000 cases per year.[1] Nordic conflict

---

[1] See http://www.forliksraadet.no/index.php?page_id=2032.

resolution systems have had also an impact on the US system of the turn of the century 1900. In Galanter's (1986) words:

> Before the turn of the century, conciliation model after the conciliation courts of Norway and Denmark had been urged on American as a superior way of dealing with disputes. Although its proponents emphasized conciliation tribunals as informal forums for producing mutual accord, separate from the ordinary courts, the conciliation idea became linked with the notion of providing accessible and inexpensive justice to small claimants in the courts.

It has been also said that Nordic court procedure, especially in Finland and Sweden, has been almost until into modern time "peasant". For example, in Finland, there was a board of lay judges both in civil and criminal cases in the countryside at the end of the 1900s. Today, lay judges are used only in some criminal cases. Court proceedings are also less formal in Nordic countries, as in many other countries. In Finland and Sweden, judges or lawyers do not have any specific clothing like a cloak and wig. It is also not mandatory to use a lawyer in court cases in Finland. It has been also said that Nordic conflict resolution culture and court culture has been very pragmatic in promoting settlement and avoiding full-scale trial.

In the early 1980s the modern mediation movement has risen in Nordic countries, especially in Norway and Finland. Both countries introduced new victim offender mediation systems. The background of this movement was the thinking of Norwegian sociologist Nils Christie (Nylund 2014). Nordic welfare states include several institutions that, among other tasks, aim to resolve conflicts such as different kind of advisory services, boards, ombudsmen, and self-regulatory systems. Mediation systems exists in both the public and private sectors.

Conflict resolution systems are always culturally specific and chosen (Menkel-Meadow 1996). In the last 20 years alternative conflict resolution systems in Nordic countries have become more common. Mediation has increased strongly in the Nordic countries especially in the 2000s. New mediation systems have developed and also the caseload in mediation has increased (see e.g. Nylund 2010; Vindeløv 2012; Adrian and Mykland 2014; Ervasti and Nylund 2014; Ervasti and Salminen 2017). Finland, Norway and Denmark, for example, have introduced new court connected systems (see Bernt 2011; Mykland 2011; Adrian 2012; Ervasti 2014; Ervasti and Nylund 2014; Ervo and Nylund 2014).There is also a lot of interaction amongst researchers in these countries. Sweden and Iceland has not been as active in this area. There are not such court-connected mediation systems in Sweden and Iceland as exists in other Nordic countries.[2]

---

[2]Social democrats have been for a long time Sweden's largest political party. The party has been against privatisation of infrastructure. According Lindel (2004): "private ADR would probably be seen as a risk to the welfare system" in Sweden. That can be one reason why Sweden do not pass the same pace with other Nordic countries.

2 Mediation as a System

Mediation is one of the basic conflict resolution systems.[3] There are several definitions of mediation. There is also a wide range of views on mediation.[4] Discussion has spoken of ideologies, policies, processes, institutions, models, practices and applications of mediation. Often are made a distinction between theoretical models of mediation and mediation in practice. That distinction has used in the names of many books and articles (e.g. Folberg and Milne 1988; Alfini et al. 2001; McCorkle and Reese 2005; Adrian 2012). Sometimes this categorisation refers to the distinction between theoretical questions of mediation and more practical issues—such as mediation techniques. Sometimes it has used as an analytical tool in empirical studies to make a distinction between theoretical models of mediation and mediation in reality.

It is useful to make a distinction between theoretical models of mediation, practical systems of mediation in context, and mediation in action.[5] Using three categories makes it possible to get more analytical power to view mediation as a system. Sometimes it is difficult to follow the discussion of mediation because writers are not always telling the context of their approach. Discussion is more rational if the theoretical and practical as well as action level context are clear.

All these dimensions of mediation are in interaction with each other. Theoretical models of mediation have an influence to practical mediation systems and to mediation in action. Also practical mediation systems effects to theoretical models and mediation in action. Mediation in action has own influence also to theoretical models and practical systems.

This model is heuristic. It is useful for comparing how different elements (theoretical models, practical systems, mediation in action) are interacting each other, e.g. how theoretical models are influencing—or not—to the practical mediation systems and mediation in action. It can be also useful in comparing different mediation systems and mediation in different countries and cultures. It can be used as a tool in critical research by disclosing what kind of gaps and lacks there is between theoretical models, practical systems and mediation in action (Fig. 1).

There is many kind of *theoretical models of mediation*. In this time there is many kind of theoretical discussion concerning mediation in Nordic countries like theoretical models of mediation and taxonomy of them (Ervasti and Nylund 2014), Vindeløvs "reflexive mediation" (Vindeløv 2012), creativity of mediation agreements (Adrian and Mykland 2014), mediation in the light of understanding of identity (Asmussen 2018) and meaning of restorative approach in mediation (Rasmussen 2018).

---

[3]According Goldberg et al. (1999), there is three primary processes of conflict resolution: negotiation, mediation and adjudication. They have called variants of arbitration, mini-trial, summary jury trial and ombudsman as a hybrid processes. Ervasti and Nylund (2014), have seen also evaluation as a primary process of conflict resolution.

[4]In Nordic countries mediation is often defined very broadly and there is not different words for "mediation" and "conciliation". See Nylund 2018.

[5]Originally this categorising has been made by Ervasti and Nylund (2014), but they have the categories of theoretical models of mediation, applications of mediation, and mediation in action.

Fig. 1 Mediation as a
system

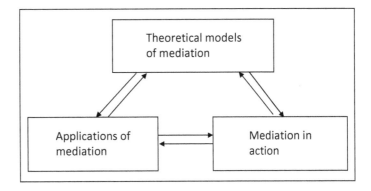

There is also a great variety of different applications,[6] programmes or *practical systems of mediation in context*. In Nordic countries there exists community mediation, school mediation, neighbourhood mediation, multicultural mediation, court-connected mediation, workplace mediation, commercial mediation and international peace mediation. In the European Union there has been discussion of the possibilities of alternative dispute resolution (ADR) and mediation in administrative law (Dragos and Neamtu 2014). In Nordic countries there is not yet institutionalised mediation systems in the field of administrative law.

The third level is *mediation in action*. There are thousands of mediators in all Nordic countries who are working as professional mediators or as laymen in different kinds of practical mediation systems. They have many kind of theoretical and practical training in different systems. Moreover, there is a great variety in their activities and behaviour. One very interesting research topic is how is the relationship between theoretical model, practical system and mediation in action in different contexts.

3   Theoretical Models of Mediation

Often mediation has been understood as an assisted negotiation or facilitation of negotiation. The "purest" form of mediation is facilitative mediation where a mediator helps the parties to find their own solution. The facilitative model of mediation is the most common model of mediation in civil cases also in Nordic countries like in other Western countries.[7]

---

[6]E.g. Menkel-Meadow (2016), Umbreit (1988), Folberg and Milne (1988) have used the term "applications".

[7]Discussion of the theoretical models of mediation (in civil cases) has been dominated by division of mediation into a facilitativeand evaluative model made by Leonard Riskin (1996) 20 years ago. Since then transformative mediationhas become the third primary model of mediation in civil cases. For a discussion of mediation models, see Menkel-Meadow (1984), Bush and Folger (2005), Winslade and Monk (2001).

Mediation and conflict resolution in Nordic countries have been greatly influenced by theories prevalent in the United States at this time. However, there is also old indigenous mediation systems in Nordic countries as well as theoretical models of conflict resolution and mediation. In Nordic countries conflict resolution research has been strongly linked to sociology of law or socio-legal studies. Especially in the Norway, there has been many well-known theoretical researchers in this area.[8]

Norwegian professor Wilhelm Aubert (1922–1988) has developed conflict theory in Nordic countries in the 1960s and 1970s. He made a distinction of two types of conflict and conflict resolution: competition and dissensus (Aubert 1963; Aubert 1967) Another Norwegian professor, Torstein Eckhoff (1916–1993) has also had significant influence on Nordic conflict resolution research. He has analysed the roles of judges, mediators and administrators in conflict resolution. In his quite well known article from the 1960s Eckhoff handles key concepts of conflict resolution such as "conflict", "dispute", "solution", "outcome", "opinions" and "interests". He makes also a distinction between three types of conflict resolution methods: "to mediate", "to judge" and "to administer". According Eckhoff: "the third party's interest in the outcome and the power-relationship between him and the parties are important factors which will be considered". There can be various reasons for the participation of a third party in the conflict resolution. In mediation the parties try to get an agreement by appealing to their own interests. The activity of a judge is related more to the level of norms rather than the level of interests. The administrator decides how three conflict should be resolved—like also the judge. According Eckhoff, in contrast, the judge "who merely pretends to determine what already is right, the administrator establishes an arrangement which is character of being new"—in other words, what the rights and duties should be in the future (Eckhoff 1966).

A third Norwegian professor, Johan Galtung (1930–), is known as the principal founder of the discipline of peace and conflict studies (see e.g. Galtung 2000). A fourth Norwegian professor, Thomas Mathiesen (1933–), is best known as a criminologist, but has also some studies in conflict resolution. According to Mathiesen, conflict of interests and use of power will transform to conflict of norms when the conflict is indispensable in public forum. Courts and university lawyers develop conversion of conflict of interests to conflict of norms (Mathiesen 1979).

Especially a fifth Norwegian professor, Nils Christie (1928–2015), has had a great significance in building victim offender mediation systems in different Nordic countries in the 1980s and early 1990s. It is his influence that the mediators in victim offender mediation (VOM) are laymen in Nordic countries. In many other countries, mediators are professionals and work in probation service, for instance. He has had great influence also in many other mediation systems such as community mediation, school mediation and workplace mediation in Nordic countries.

Christies' article *Conflict as Property* (1977) has inspired many researchers, practitioners and system designers in Nordic countries and also in other Western countries

---

[8]For trends in sociology of law in Scandinavia see Hammerslev (2010), and Hammerslev and Madsen (2014).

(Albrecht 2010). The thinking of Christie lies in the idea of communities, where people should handle their own problems and conflicts so that they can growth as a humans. He has seen conflicts as a potential for activity and participation. According to Christie, lawyers in reality steal conflicts of people in Western countries. According to Christie, courts in criminal cases are victim-oriented organisations where the victim has been left behind. He has been an advocate of lay-oriented court system.

In this time, the common theoretical approach in victim offender mediation in Nordic countries is restorative justice. It means that the theoretical basis of VOM has changed. The thinking of Christie has influenced restorative justice theory (Braithwaite 1996). But there are also some differences.

Nowadays a facilitative mediation model combined with an interest-based approach is the common model of mediation in civil cases in Nordic countries like also in other Western countries (Vindeøv 2007, 2012). Denmark has generated "reflexive" mediation, which is a (non)model of sorts, as a new perspective on conflict resolution and mediation. The model has great importance in Denmark today. The key to reflexive mediation lies in the values and understandings of conscious mediation practice. Reflexive mediation is eclectic and allows inspiration to be drawn from different mediation models. However, the process is not anything goes. The basic values of mediation must be respected to call the process mediation.

4 Practical Mediation Systems in Context

There are many kind of practical mediation systems in Nordic countries (Ervasti and Nylund 2014). There are some differences but also some similarities between different countries. Figure 2 describes practical mediation systems in Nordic countries.

4.1 Communal Mediation Systems

Many new mediation systems were introduced in the Nordic countries in 1980s, 1990s, and 2000s.Those systems, such as victim offender mediation and court-connected mediation, have risen in legal context. It is very interesting that there has not been much private mediation systems out of the legal context before the 2000s.

In these days, there is in Finland, like also in other Nordic countries, *communal mediation systems*. In early 2000s there was some experiments of mediation in multicultural conflicts in Finland. In 2014, the Finnish refugee Council founded the Centre for *Community mediation*. That system has handled many kinds of conflicts in neighbourhoods and local communities. The background of that system is community mediation model from the United States. But also the thinking of Christie and restorative justice model are included. In Finland, there is about 100–200 cases per year in community mediation. In Norway, the National Mediation Office provides

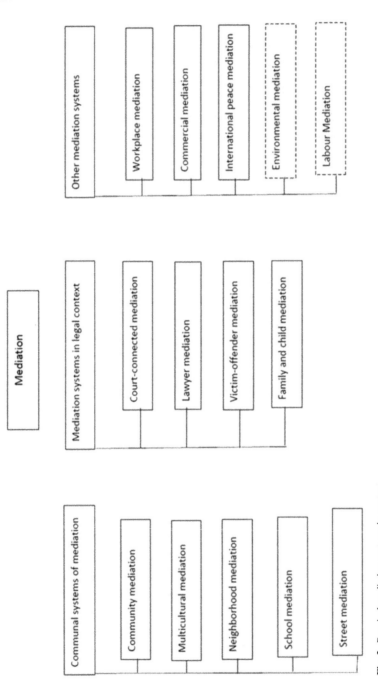

Fig. 2 Practical mediation systems in context

community mediation. That service uses interest-based, facilitative mediation (Nylund 2014). The background of this system is also the thinking of Christie.

School mediation started in Finland in 2000. The theoretical basis of that system is a restorative approach. The objective is to resolve conflicts directly with the help of a trained pupil or teacher. In the mediation young pupils face each other, take responsibility for their actions and can contribute to creating a better atmosphere in the school. For example, cases of bullying and name-calling have been handled in mediation (Gellin 2018). In Finland, there are over 10,000 mediated cases each year. Developers of communal mediation and school mediation have had background in victim offender mediation. In Norway, there is also a comprehensive school mediation programme. The first project of school mediation was in Norway in the mid-1990s. Behind the Norwegian system is the thinking of Christie and the Restorative Justice model (Vestre 2005; Norman and Öhman 2011).

There has been also some school mediation projects in Sweden. In this time, over 100 schools are using mediation as a tool in conflict situations (Norman and Öhman 2011). In Sweden, Marklund (2007) has conducted a case study research of school mediation. The theoretical background was also restorative justice and the thinking of Christie.

In Norway, Finland and Denmark there are also *street mediation* systems. The idea is to stop a young person when she or he does wrong or behaves in a disorderly manner. The goal is to encourage young people to understand their own blunders, take responsibility for them and correct them. In street mediation, meeting the young person meets the complainant in a safe environment in the presence of his or her parents and the mediators.

4.2   Mediation in Legal Context

In Nordic countries, there is also *mediation systems in legal context*. All mediation systems in Western countries are acting somehow "in the shadow of the law", even community mediation systems (Merry 1982). In this context, mediation system can be categorised to the legal context if there is regulating of mediation or lawyers are involved in mediation.

4.2.1   Victim Offender Mediation

In Finland, Norway, Denmark and Sweden the best known mediation system is *victim offender mediation*. The first victim offender mediation experiment started in Finland in 1983. The Act on Mediation in criminal and certain civil cases came into force in Finland in 2006. The focus of the mediation has been on juvenile crime, and most cases have concerned assaults, criminal damages and thefts. In about one-half of the cases, the offender is under the age of 21 years. The mediators are volunteers who receive a brief training before they start working. Victim offender mediation is always voluntary and there is not mandatory mediation. Most of the cases comes to mediation from police and prosecutors. In Finland, there is about 12,000 cases in victim offender mediation per year. That is quite high, because criminal proceedings total about 60,000 cases per year in district courts (Grönfors 1989; Iivari 2010; Lappi-Seppälä 2015).

In Norway, the first victim offender mediation project started in 1981.The Act on Mediation came into force in 1991. The great majority of offenders in mediation are young people. In Norway, there are about 9000 cases in victim offender mediation per year.[9] (Lundgaard 2015).[10]

In Denmark, the first experiments of victim offender mediation started in the mid-1990s. The Act on Mediation came into force in 2010. In Denmark, mediation is an option for parties in all criminal cases that are found suitable for mediation. In 2016, there was 560 cases in victim offender mediation.[11] In Denmark, VOM can supplement criminal procedure but not replace it (Stoorgaard 2015). In Finland, on the other hand, mediation can in many situations replace criminal procedure in practice. Criminal law in Finland gives a possibility for prosecutors to waive charges, for courts to waive punishment and mitigate sentencing if the parties have reached settlement or agreement in case (Lappi-Seppälä 2015).

In Sweden, the first victim offender mediation experiment started in 1987. The Act of Mediation came into force 2002. In 2008, it became mandatory to offer mediation to young offenders under the age of 21 years. There is still some problems in the Swedish system. According to Marklund (2015) "[t]here is quite widespread frustration in the mediation services over the state of affairs that is exacerbated further when one sees how well it can work in both Norway and Finland."[12] (Marklund 2015).

The builders of VOM in the beginning were sociologists. The building of VOM was part of a movement that criticised the criminal justice system and was seeking alternatives to retributive system. In Nordic countries, the sentencing systems place high value in consistency and uniformity in sentencing. There is not, for example, "problem solving courts" in Nordic countries.[13] The ideological background in Finland has been "humane neoclassicism". This stressed legal safeguards and repressive measures. Individualised sentencing was de-emphasised (Hinkkanen and Lappi-Seppälä 2011). In VOM the idea is to seek more individualised solutions

---

[9]About one-half of the cases in Norway are civil cases. Mediation service in Norway, like also Mediation offices in Finland, can handle also civil cases. Most of them are compensation of crime and only a few cases in both countries do not have any connection to crime.

[10]For more information on Norwegian victim offender mediation, see Ervasti and Nylund (2014) and Lappi-Seppälä and Tonry (2011).

[11]http://konfliktraad.dk/konfliktraad-i-tal.aspx.

[12]See also Jacobsson et al. (2012).

[13]A "problem solving court movement" developed in the United States in the 1980s, and there are, for example, drug courts, community courts, domestic violence courts and mental health courts. Today, there is problem solving courts also in Canada, Ireland and Scotland. See e.g. Lane (2003) and Boldt (2014).

to problems or misbehaving of the people. In the background of developing VOM was the thinking of Christie. Researchers were also inspired by the reflexive law of Günther Teubner, at least in Finland and Denmark.

4.2.2 Judicial Settlement Efforts and Court-Connected Mediation

Judicial settlement efforts in civil procedure plays an important role in all Nordic countries (Ervasti 2014; Ervo and Nylund 2016). For example, according to Finnish legislation, a judge is required to investigate the prospects for settling a civil case during its preparation and pursue an amicable resolution of the matter. A judge may also make a proposal for a settlement. The promotion of settlement in civil proceedings is not a matter of mediation as such, but a matter of promoting an amicable resolution in judicial proceedings. Many provisions on judicial proceedings restrict the actions of the judge in promoting a settlement. The objective is also that the reached settlement complies with the substantive law.

In Finland, the number of settlements certified by the district courts has risen nearly to 2500 per year. Moreover, not all of parties who reach settlements request they be certified. Many judges surmise that almost one-half of the cases that they deal with end in one or another sort of settlement. According to empirical studies, some judges are promoting settlement very strongly and some others are quite passive in that area (Ervasti 2004; Adrian 2016).

Theoretically settlement promotion can describe some kind of compromising or conciliation system or "settlement driven mediation". It is not really mediation. A judge most follow the rules of fair trial in civil process and she or he cannot be mediator and use mediation techniques, such as private meetings, in that process. In the word of Nylund: "Judicial settlement activities should not be called mediation in English. The process is strictly settlement focused; the judge is, in my opinion, correctly prohibited from using mediation techniques and, therefore, the ability to generate 'better' outcomes." (Nylund 2014).

In Denmark, there is a specific system in civil cases where a judge tells after a main hearing what kind of judgement he or she probably will give and the parties will make a settlement grounding to that approximation. Over 90% of all cases will be settled in that way. There is not any regulation of such activities. Judges has developed that system in their everyday work (von Eyben 1987).

One problem with discourse in Nordic countries is that in Danish and in Norwegian has been used term "mediation" (*mekling/mekling*) also of judicial settlement efforts or promoting settlement in civil procedure.

Finland, Norway and Denmark has introduced a *court connected mediation system*. In Norway, there started an experiment of court connected mediation in 1997. It has been a permanent system from 2008 (Bernt 2011; Nylund 2010) after an evaluation of the experiment (Knoff 2001). Denmark started an experiment in 2003 and a system has been permanent from 2008 (Adrian 2012) after evaluation of the experiment (Roepstoff and Kyvsgaard 2005).

In Finland, there was not any experiments. In the beginning of 2006, the Act on court-connected mediation entered into force. Court-connected mediation is a procedure, voluntary to the parties and managed by a judge, aiming at a situation where parties themselves can find a satisfactory resolution to their conflict.

The court decides whether mediation is to be undertaken. The court proceedings are interrupted for the duration of the mediation. When a judge decides to refer parties to mediation, another judge of same district court act as a mediator.

The theoretical basis of Nordic court-connected mediation is a facilitative mediation model. In Finland, nobody else other than a judge can act as a mediator in court connected mediation. In Denmark, court-connected mediators are judges and lawyer. In Norway, primarily judges act as mediators but others are allowed, too. In this time there are about 2000 cases in court connected mediation per year in Finland. It is quite a lot, because there are about 8000 disputed civil cases in district courts per year (Ervasti 2014, Salminen and Ervasti 2015). In Denmark, 1146 cases were referred to mediation in 2016,[14] which amounts to about 2% of eligible cases. There is large variation in the number of settled cases in court-connected mediation in Nordic countries (Adrian 2016). Norway has seen been over 400 cases referred to mediation per year (Lundström 2013).

In Sweden, there is not the same kind of court-connected mediation system than in Finland, Norway and Denmark. There is possible also in Sweden to use "special mediator" in civil process, but it has been used very rare (Dahlqvist 2014). It has been said that the main reason why there is not court-connected mediation system in Sweden is simply the significant role of judicial settlement efforts in that country (Lindell 2004; Ficks 2008).

A Nordic court connected mediation model where judges are acting as mediators is quite unique. In many countries, there is a referral-system where courts can send a case to out-off-court mediation. In Norway and Finland some judges, advocates and researchers was inspired by mediation and started to lobby system to law makers and politicians. Some judges had also unofficial experiments in the court system. For example, in Finland, law makers and state officers were not very enthusiastic to build a new system, but the Minister of Justice was interested in the proposal of judges. So, the system has come to Nordic countries from the down to up. In background there was also efforts to limit the amount of court cases and the costs of court system (see e.g. Reform af den civile retspleje V 2006).

---

[14]http://www.domstol.dk/om/talogfakta/statistik/Documents/Civile%20sager/2016/Byretter_civile_sager_retsmaegling_2016.pdf.

4.2.3 Lawyer Mediation

There is also *lawyer mediation* in Nordic countries. In order to resolve different kind of conflicts the Finnish Bar Association founded its own mediation system in 1998. At the same time, its mediation rules were approved. The system is based on voluntariness. The parties to the conflict appoint an advocate to act as a mediator between them. In mediation by lawyers facilitative approach has been adopted. The Norwegian Bar Association founded mediation system in the year 2000. (Austbø and Engerbretsen 2003). In the year 2003 Danish Bar and Law Society established an Association of Danish Mediation Advocates (Vindeløv 2013). At least in Finland but also in other Nordic countries the whole culture of lawyers like also court culture is changing to direct of "negotiated law".

4.2.4 Family Mediation

There is also *family mediation* in all Nordic countries. For example, in Finland, regulation on mediation in divorce matters has existed for over 60 years. Family mediators can provide help and support in the event of family disputes and conflicts that concern compliance with decisions and agreements on child custody and right of access. The primary aim of mediation is to protect the best interests of children. Family mediation is mainly the responsibility of municipal social welfare authorities who typically have a university-level education. They help the parties to divorce cases agree on the custody of the children and the right of access (Haavisto 2018). Sweden has quite the same system (Norman and Öhman 2011). Family cases can be mediated also in court-connected mediation (Salminen 2018) but also during the court process in Norway (Bernt 2018).[15]

The roots of family mediation in Nordic countries rests originally in Christian values. The main effort earlier was to keep the family together and prevent divorce. Even in this time there is obligatory family mediation in Norway in divorce situations. In this time it has been stressed more the welfare of the child or best interests of the child. In theoretical discussion in Nordic countries, the best interests of the child is one of the main questions in the field of family mediation.

4.3 Other Mediation Systems

There are also many *other mediation systems* in Nordic countries. *Workplace mediation* is a new phenomenon. In workplace mediation, a company employs a mediator to assist in resolving conflicts within the work community. Conflicts can, for instance, relate to bullying. Conflict in a work community can in many ways be

---

[15]For family mediation in Sweden, see Rystedt (2012).

counter-productive for the operation and performance of the work community. In Finland, there are about 100 to 200 cases per year in that system. In Finland, workplace mediation has developed primarily on the basis of the victim offender mediation and restorative justice model.

There is also *commercial mediation* or business mediation in Nordic Countries.[16] For example, the Finland Arbitration Institute of the Finland Chamber of Commerce has had its own mediation system from 2016 akin to the Arbitration Institute of the Stockholm Chamber of Commerce, the Arbitration Institute of Oslo Chamber of Commerce and the two arbitration institutes in Denmark. The theoretical basis of the mediation of the Finnish Arbitration Institute is a facilitative mediation model.

Mediation by the Finnish Association of Civil Engineers deals mostly with disputes concerning building projects. The building trade is an industry prone to conflicts as the projects often involve a network of multiple actors. Experts in the industry as well as lawyers can act as mediators. In connection with the mediation, it is also possible to choose a procedure that is based on an arbitration agreement and concludes when a settlement is reached.

International peace mediation, on the other hand, is a widely used procedure. Mediation cases have increased radically since the mid-1990s. Norway has been a pioneer in international mediation in the early 1990s. Also, Finland and Sweden have been very active in this area. There have been several internationally acknowledged peace mediators in Nordic countries, such as Finnish Martti Ahtisaari, who has awarded the Nobel Prize. International peace mediation focuses on international crisis management and prevention of violence. Peace and conflict research is also very dynamic in Nordic countries (see e.g. Lehti 2014).

In recent years, a possibility for *environmental mediation* has also been discussed. In 2009, there was also an experiment of environmental mediation in Finland. Mediation has not been taken into account in planning or in the permit procedure concerning changes in land use, although it could be used as a conflict-solving method. When it comes to administrative matters, there is no organised mediation in Finland.

In Nordic countries in *labour mediation* can be handled conflicts between trade unions and employer's organisations. At least in Finland it is a mixed conflict resolution system and not a "pure" mediation system.

5 Mediation in Action

Mediation in action is based always on some theory and some practical system of mediation. The underlying theory is direct mediation on a practical level. Different theories of mediation requires different mediation style and techniques. In literature has been discussed plenty of different kind of styles and techniques in mediation

---

[16]For commercial mediation in Europe, see Richbell (2014).

(see e.g. Alfini 1991–1992; Oberman 2008; Charkoudian et al. 2009; Marcum et al. 2012; Kressel et al. 2012; Baitar et al. 2013; Ervasti and Nylund 2014). According to Menkel-Meadow (1984), the *orientation* in negotiation leads to a *mindset* about what can be achieved, which, in turn, affects the *behaviour* chosen, which, in turn, affects the *solution* arrived at.

Typically techniques in mediation are, for example, active listening, questioning, caucuses (separate meetings), reality testing and brainstorming. Using a variety of techniques constitutes a wholeness, which one can call a "mediation style". Different mediation theories requires different mediation styles. Figure 3 shows what kind of techniques are typical in different models of mediation and conciliation.

For the *evaluative* mediation style, it is typical to evaluate the case, provide information, make proposals for settlement—like also reality testing—and to use caucuses. For the *compromising style*, it is typically shuttle mediation where the parties are in different rooms and a mediator delivers offers and counter-offers between the parties. That kind of activity can be called strategic bargaining. For the *facilitative style*, typical use includes such techniques as active listening, questioning and brainstorming. For the *transformative style*, typical use includes empowering, recognition and supporting self-determination of the parties. In transformative mediation, the parties are controlling the process and results. In facilitative mediation, the mediator is the leader of the process and the parties have responsibility of the results. In evaluative mediation, the mediator has a responsibility of the process but also at least in part of the results.

The problem is that mediators in their everyday work are many times acting in a different way that they think themselves or what theory of mediation postulates. For example, mediation in victim offender mediation is not always following the theory of the restorative justice model and court connected mediation is not always

Evaluative	Compromising	Facilitative	Transformative
Evaluation	Forwarding offers and counter offers	Improving communication	Empowering
Provision of information	"Shuttle mediation"	Active listening	Recognition
Proposals for settlement	Promoting middle range solutions	Replacement of terms	Supporting self-determination and self-confidence
Reality testing	Highlighting the benefits of quick solution	Questioning	Helping parties activate their inherent capacity for deliberation and decision making
Caucuses	Highlighting weakness of other processes and solutions	Brainstorming/ development of alternatives	Enhancing interpersonal communication

Fig. 3 Typical techniques in different mediation models

following facilitative model. Especially legal context mediation systems evolve often mixed systems. In practice, it means that used mediation styles and mediation techniques will diverge from what theory requires. In that case, the quality of the mediation process or outcome is not necessarily so good than it could or should be. This kind of action has been called "stylistically flexible", "eclectic style", "situational style" and "hybrid" or "mixed" conflict resolution system (Imperati et al. 2007; Kressel et al. 2012; Marcum et al. 2012; Ervasti and Nylund 2014; Ervasti and Salminen 2017). In mixed or hybrid conflict resolution systems ethical principles of mediation are, in fact, always not realised and, on the other hand, people do not get even a formal legal protection—instead, it can be a semi-legal system or semi-mediation (Ervasti and Nylund 2014).

Legislation in Nordic countries concerning mediation (court-connected, VOM, family) gives a frame for mediation but there is not detailed regulation or orders on how the mediation process should be. So, mediators have many possibilities to choose a mode of action.

In many studies in Nordic countries has founded gap between the theoretical basis of a mediation system and the behaviour of mediators. Here are examples from Finland, Denmark, Sweden and Norway.

In Finland, Elonheimo (2004) has conducted research on the victim offender mediation in Finland. In that study it has been observed 16 mediation cases in a mediation office of the Turku district (nine assaults and seven property crimes). The research found a gap between the restorative mediation model and actual behaviour of mediators. There was a lack of dialogue and lack of producing "re-integrative shame."[17]

Adrian (2012) has conducted research of court-connected mediation in Denmark. She has used observations (n = 20), interviews of mediators (n = 20) and the parties (n = 35) and documents (n = 42) as research material. According to Adrian, in many cases interests and needs was not on focus in mediation like the theoretical basis of mediation demands. In some cases, the mediator had an evaluative mediation style and mediators were not always neutral. Some of mediators and also parties have had difficulties in court-connected mediation to get free of the roles they have usually in litigation.

Jacobsson et al. (2012) have conducted research of victim offender mediation in Sweden. They have analysed 25 mediation meetings, which were recorded and transcribed. According to researchers, the Swedish mediation policy in practice seems "not to be fully congruent with restorative justice ideology". Mediation also seems to be quite offender-focused. There is also "risk that victims in some cases can feel that they are forces to act in line with the offender's will, with or not, personal benefit".

Mykland (2011) has conducted research of court-connected mediation in Norway. She has observed 15 mediation cases. The basis of Norwegian court-connected mediation is facilitative interest based mediation. According to Mykland, many mediators have used power and had an evaluative style. Sometimes they have

---

[17]Takala (1988) and Mielityinen (1989) has the same results in their studies.

combined mediation and arbitration together. There is also lot of variation in the behaviour and styles of mediators. So, there is a gap between mediator style and the theoretical basis of mediation.

There can be many reasons why the mediator behaves differently than the underlying theory postulates. Maybe the mediator does not know what he or she really are doing or does not care of theory or does not consider theory as important. It is very important to take care of education of mediators so that they can recognise what they are doing and to reflect on it. It is also very important to conduct empirical studies and research on mediation in order to develop the system.

Vibeke Vindeløv (2013), has stressed that "mediator must take on the role of the reflective practitioner" who "trusts the parties to bring their knowledge and skills to bear on the problem". She emphasises that the parties must define how broad the mediation should be. This flexibility does not mean that "anything goes".[18]

6 Conclusions

As a whole there are many kinds of conflict resolution systems and mediation systems in a complex and multidimensional postmodern society. In Nordic countries, especially in the 2000s, mediation systems have increased rapidly. At the same time, the research community in this area has become quite dynamic. There is increasingly more research in the field of conflict resolution and mediation in Nordic countries and lot of co-operation amongst researchers in these countries. Nonetheless, there is still a lack of empirical studies and evaluations of the systems and, at least in Finland, there is also a lack of sufficient training in many areas of mediation.[19] It is, for example, very difficult to find usable and comparable information of the rates of mediation cases in different mediation systems. Both empirical and theoretical studies are needed. Also needed is the development of mediation training.

References

Adrian L (2012) Mellem retssag og rundbordssamtale: Retsmægling i teori og praksis. Jurist- og Økonomforbundets Forlag, København
Adrian L (2016) The role of court-connected mediation and judicial settlement efforts in the preparatory stage. In: Ervo L, Nylund A (eds) Current trends in preparatory proceedings. A comparative study of Nordic and former communist countries. Springer, Cham, pp 209–231
Adrian L, Mykland S (2014) Creativity in court-connected mediation: myth or reality? Negot J 30:421–439

---

[18]Vindeløv (2013).

[19]The University of Copenhagen has a master's degree programme in mediation. http://jura.ku.dk/uddannelser/efterogvidereuddannelse/master.

Albrecht B (2010) Multicultural challenges for restorative justice: mediators' experiences from Norway and Finland. J Scand Stud Crim Crime Prev 11:3–24

Alfini J (1991) Trashing, bashing, and hashing it out: is this the end of 'good mediation'? Fla State Univ Law Rev 19:47–75

Alfini J, Press S, Sternlight J, Stulberg J (2001) Mediation theory and practice. LexisNexis, Newark

Asmussen IH (2018) Modern view of identity change - what is going on in mediation. In: Nylund A, Ervasti K, Adrian L (eds) Nordic mediation research. Springer, Cham, pp 133–143

Austbø A, Engebretsen G (2003) Mekling i rettskonflikter. Retsmekling, mekling ved advokater og mekling i forliksrådene og konfliktrådene. Cappalen Akademisk Forlag, Oslo

Aubert V (1963) Competition and dissensus: two types of conflict and conflict resolution. J Confl Resolut 7:26–42

Aubert V (1967) Courts and conflict resolution. J Confl Resolut 11:40–51

Bernt C (2011) Meklerrollen ved mekling i domstolene. Fagbokförlaget, Bergen

Bernt C (2018) Custody mediation in Norwegian courts: a conglomeration of roles and processes. In: Nylund A, Ervasti K, Adrian L (eds) Nordic mediation research. Springer, Cham, pp 105–133

Boldt R (2014) Problem-solving courts and pragmatism. Maryland Law Rev 73:1120–1172

Braithwaite J (1996) Restorative justice and a better future. Dalhousie Rev 76:9–31

Bush R, Folger J (2005) The promise of mediation. New and Revised edn. Jossey-Bass, San Francisco

Christie N (1977) Conflicts as property. Br J Criminol 17:1–15

Charkoudian L, de Ritis C, Buck R, Wilson C (2009) Mediation by any other name would smell as sweet – or would it? Confl Resolut Q 26:293–316

Dahlqvist A (2014) Mediation in Swedish courts: change by EU directive? In: Ervo L, Nylund A (eds) In the future of civil litigation. Access to court and court-annexed mediation in the Nordic countries. Springer, Cham, pp 137–156

Dragos D, Neamtu B (eds) (2014) Alternative dispute resolution in European administrative law. Springer, Heidelberg

Eckhoff T (1966) The mediator, the judge and the administrator in conflict resolution. Acta Sociol 10:148–172

Elonheimo H (2004) Restoratiivinen oikeus ja suomalainen sovittelu. Oikeus 33:279–299

Ervasti K (2004) Käräjäoikeuksien sovintomenettely. Empiirinen tutkimus sovinnon edistämisestä riitaprosessissa. Oikeuspoliittinen tutkimuslaitos, Helsinki

Ervasti K (2014) Court-connected mediation in Finland: experiences and visions. In: Ervo L, Nylund A (eds) In the future of civil litigation. Access to court and court-annexed mediation in the Nordic countries. Springer, Cham, pp 121–135

Ervasti K, Nylund A (2014) Konfliktinratkaisu ja sovittelu. Helsinki, Edita

Ervasti K, Salminen K (2017) Conflict resolution in the garden of forking paths. In: Rønne A, Adrian L, Nielsen L (eds) Fred, forsoning og mægling. Festskrift til Vibeke Vindeløv. Jurist og økonomforbundets forlag, København, pp 95–110

Ervo L, Nylund A (eds) (2014) The future of civil litigation – access to courts and court – annexed mediation in the Nordic countries. Springer, Cham

Ervo L, Nylund A (eds) (2016) Current trends in preparatory proceedings. A comparative study of Nordic and former communist countries. Springer, Cham

Ficks E (2008) Models of general court-connected conciliation and mediation for commercial disputes in Sweden, Australia and Japan. J Jpn Law 25:131–152

Folberg J, Milne A (1988) Divorce mediation. Theory and practice. Guiford Press, New York

Galanter M (1986) The emergence of the judge as a mediator in civil cases. Judicature 69:257–262

Galtung J (2000) Conflict transformation by peaceful means (the transcend method). United Nations disaster management training programme. http://www.transcedn.org/pctrcluj2004/TRANSCEND_manual.pdf

Gellin M (2018) Restorative approach and mediatoin in Finnish schools: from conflicts to restoration. In: Nylund A, Ervasti K, Adrian L (eds) Nordic mediation research. Springer, Cham, pp 247–266

Goldberg S, Sander F, Rogers N (1999) Dispute resolution. Negotiation, mediation and other processes, 3rd edn. Aspen Law & Business, New York

Grönfors M (1989) Mediation – experiment in Finland. In: Albrecht PE, Bakes O (eds) Crime prevention and intervention. Walter de Gruyter, Berlin – New York

Haavisto V (2018) Developing family mediation in Finland: the change process and the practical outcomes. In: Nylund A, Ervasti K, Adrian L (eds) Nordic mediation research. Springer, Cham, pp 41–66

Hammerslev O (2010) Convergence and conflict perspectives in Scandinavian studies of the legal profession. Int J Leg Prof 17:135–152

Hammerslev O, Madsen MR (2014) The return of sociology in Danish socio-legal studies: a survey recent trends. Int J Law Context 10:397–415

Hinkkanen V, Lappi-Seppälä T (2011) Sentencing theory, policy, and research in the Nordic countries. In: Tonry M, Lappi-Seppälä T (eds) Crime and justice in Scandinavia, vol 40. Crime and Justice, Chicago, pp 349–404

Iivari J (2010) Providing mediation as a Nationwide Service. Empirical research on restorative justice in Finland. In: Vanfraechem I, Aertsen I, Willemsens J (eds) Restorative justice realities. Empirical research in a European context. Eleven, The Hague, pp 95–119

Imperati S, Brownmiller D, Marshall D (2007) If Freud, Jung, Rogers, and Beck were mediators, who would the parties pick and what are the Mediator's obligations? Idaho Law Rev 43:643–708

Jacobsson M, Wahlin L, Andersson T (2012) Victim-offender mediation in Sweden: is the victim better off? Int Rev Victimol 18:229–259

Knoff RH (2001) Baskere? Billigare? Vennligere? Evaluering av prøveordningen med rettsmekling. Rapport for justisdepartementet

Kressel K, Henderson T, Reich W, Cohen C (2012) Multidimensional analysis of conflict mediator style. Confl Resol Q 30:135–171

Lane E (2003) Due process and problem-solving courts. Fordham Urban Law J 30:955–1026

Lappi-Seppälä T, Tonry M (2011) Crime, criminal justice and criminology in Nordic countries. In: Tonry M, Lappi-Seppälä T (eds) Crime and justice in Scandinavia. Crime and justice, vol 40. The University of Chicago Press, Chicago, pp 1–32

Lappi-Seppälä T (2015) Finland. In: Dünkel F, Grzywa-Holten J, Horsfield P (eds) Restorative justice and mediation in penal matters. A stock-taking of legal issues, implementation strategies and outcomes in 36 European countries, vol 1. Forum Verlag Godersberg, Mönchengladbach, pp 243–266

Lehti M (ed) (2014) Nordic approaches to peace mediation. Research, practices and policies. Tapri Studies in Peace and Conflict Research No 101, Tampere

Letto-Vanamo P, Tamm D (2017) Adjudication or negotiation. Mediation as a non-modern element in conflict resolution. In: Rønne A, Adrian L, Nielsen L (eds) Fred, forsoning og mægling. Festskrift til Vibeke Vindeløv. Jurist og økonomforbundets forlag, København, pp 213–225

Lindel B (2004) Mediation in Sweden. ADR Bull 7(5):1–8

Lundgaard JM (2015) Norway. In: Dünkel F, Grzywa-Holten J, Horsfield P (eds) Restorative justice and mediation in penal matters. A stock-taking of legal issues, implementation strategies and outcomes in 36 European countries, vol 2. Forum Verlag Godersberg, Mönchengladbach, pp 619–636

Lundström B (2013) Mediationens gennembrud. Advokaten 13(3):37–39

Marcum T, Stoner C, Perry S (2012) Reframing the mediation lens: the call for a situational style of mediation. South Illinois Univ Law Rev 36:317–334

Marklund L (2007) Skolmedling i teori och praktik. Licentiate's Dissertation, Uppsala Universitet, Uppsala

Marklund L (2015) Sweden. In: Dünkel F, Grzywa-Holten J, Horsfield P (eds) Restorative justice and mediation in penal matters. A stock-taking of legal issues, implementation strategies and outcomes in 36 European countries, vol 2. Forum Verlag Godersberg, Mönchengladbach, pp 917–933

Mathiesen T (1979) Ideologi og motstand. Elementer til en politisk strategi. Pax forlag, Oslo

McCorkle S, Reese M (2005) Mediation theory and practice. Pearson Education Inc., Boston

Menkel-Meadow C (1984) Toward another view of legal negotiation: the structure of problem solving. UCLA Law Rev 31:754–842

Menkel-Meadow C (1996) The trouble with the adversary system in a postmodern, multicultural world. William Mary Law Rev 38:5–44

Menkel-Meadow C (2016) Mediation and its applications for good decision making and dispute resolution. Honorary doctorate in human sciences KU Leuven 9 February 2016. Acta Falconis. Intersentia, Cambridge

Merry S (1982) The social organization of mediation in nonindustrial Societys: implications for informal community justice in America. In: Abel R (ed) The politics of informal justice. Academic Press, New York

Mielityinen I (1989) Rikos ja sovittelu. Valikoituminen, merkitys ja uusintarikollisuus. OPTL, Helsinki

Mykland S (2011) En studie av mekleratferd i norske rettsmeklinger. NHH. Institutt for strategi og ledelse. Ph.D. thesis No 2011/02

Norman J, Öhman L (2011) Medling och andra former av konflikthantering. Iustus Förlag, Uppsala

Nylund A (2010) Meklingsmodeller i tvisteloven: terapi, tvekamp eller kreativ problemløsning? Lov og Rett 49(5):272–284

Nylund A (2014) The many ways of civil mediation in Norway. In: Ervo L, Nylund A (eds) In the future of civil litigation. Access to court and court-annexed mediation in the Nordic countries. Springer, Cham, pp 97–119

Nylund A (2018) A dispute systems design perspective on Norwegian child custody mediation. In: Nylund A, Ervasti K, Adrian L (eds) Nordic mediation research. Springer, Cham, pp 9–29

Oberman S (2008) Style vs. *Model*: why quibble? Pepperdine Dispute Resolut Law J 9:1–62

Rasmussen KB (2018) When is restorative justice? In: Nylund A, Ervasti K, Adrian L (eds) Nordic mediation research. Springer, Cham, pp 145–179

Reform af den civile retspleje V (2006) Retsmægling. Betænkning nr. 1481. København

Richbell D (2014) How to master commercial mediation. Bloomsbury, London

Riskin L (1996) Understanding mediators' orientations, strategies, and techniques. Harv Negot Law Rev 1:7–51

Roepstorff J, Kyvsgaard B (2005) Forsøg med retsmægling – en evalueringsrapport. Justitsministeriets Forskningsenhed, København

Rystedt E (2012) Mediation regarding children – is the result always in the best interest of child? A view from Sweden. Int J Law Policy Family 26:220–241

Salminen K (2018) Is mediation in the best interests of a child from the child law perspective? In: Nylund A, Ervasti K, Adrian L (eds) Nordic mediation research. Springer, Cham, pp 209–222

Salminen K, Ervasti K (2015) Tuomioistuinsovittelun yleistyminen ja tuomioistuimen tehtävät. Lakimies 113(5):591–612

Stoorgaard A (2015) Denmark. In: Dünkel F, Grzywa-Holten J, Horsfield P (eds) Restorative justice and mediation in penal matters. A stock-taking of legal issues, implementation strategies and outcomes in 36 European countries, vol 1. Forum Verlag Godersberg, Mönchengladbach, pp 183–202

Takala J-P (1988) Moraalitunteet rikosten sovittelussa. OPTL, Helsinki

Umbreit M (1988) Mediation of victim offender conflict. J Dispute Resolut 85:1–21

Vestre M (2005) Konfliktløsning gjennom elevmedgling. En kvalitativ studie av tre meglingssaker. Hovedoppgave i sociologi. Universitetet i Oslo, Oslo

Vindeløv V (2007) Mediation – a non-model. Djøf Publishing, Copenhagen

Vindeløv V (2012) Reflexive mediation. With a sustainable perspective. Jurist- og Økonomforbundets Førlag, København

Vindeløv V (2013) Konfliktmægling. En refleksiv model. 3. reviderede udgave. Jurist- og Økonomforbundets Førlag, København

von Eyben WE (1987) Dommertilkendegivelser. København
Winslade J, Monk G (2001) Narrative mediation. A new approach to conflict resolution. Jossey-Bass
Publishers, San Francisco

Mediation in Finnish Schools: From Conflicts to Restoration

Maija Gellin

Contents

Abstract In his article, I describe the basis, progress and models of mediation in Finnish schools. Mediation has been offered as an alternative and restorative conflict management practice for intervention of misbehaviour and bullying since 2001. I present participation and learning approaches along with relevant literature as this constitutes the basis for the development and implementation of school mediation programmes. In the article, I also discuss how misbehaviour and bullying can be prevented by improving social skills and pupil participation in school with a restorative approach and mediation. In the last part of the article, I describe mediation practices in Finnish schools and present the latest statistics on school mediation training, the use of school mediation and surveys on user satisfaction. In conclusion, I discuss the impact of mediation and restorative practices. The article is connected to the discourse in the field of education about increasing pupil participation and strengthening children's rights by implementing child-friendly methods to conflict management in schools.

M. Gellin (✉)
Finnish Forum for Mediation, Helsinki, Finland
e-mail: maija.gellin@sovittelu.com

1 Introduction

In the Finnish school context, restorative practices and mediation are used as an alternative and child friendly process when managing challenging situations, misbehaviour and bullying in schools. Basically, the aim is to increase democracy and pupil participation, strengthen relationships and improve learning of social skills even in conflict situations. Conflicts are seen as learning possibilities, and pupils are understood as an active and capable experts in their peer groups when solving different kind of social situations. In Finland, a restorative approach and mediation have been implemented in schools since 2001 when the programme for mediation in basic schools was established. In Sect. 2, some perspectives from literature and research reports on restorative approach in schools are discussed. In Sect. 3, the history, programme and practices of mediation in Finnish schools are described with the outcomes of mediation activity according the statistics from year 2016. The last section provides conclusions and summary insight.

2 Restorative Justice in the School Context

A restorative approach in schools has its backgrounds in restorative justice. Restorative justice is said to have its roots in many cultures' traditional interaction patterns, in which participation and face-to-face encounters have played a significant role in solving different situations. Often mentioned as a first stage is the development of conflict management with young people in New Zealand: Maori communities were unhappy with the way their young people, who were in trouble because of criminal behaviour, were dealt by the criminal system. The Maori people felt that the system was against their own traditional custom of involving friends and family in resolving the situation. Instead of excluding young people from the community, the Maoris preferred to strive together to discuss harmful behaviour to reach common understanding on how youngsters could be reintegrated to their community (Peachey 1989; Hopkins 2006; McCold 2006; van Wormer et al. 2012; Ervasti and Nylund 2014; Hopkins and Gellin 2016). McCold (2006), who has been one of the developers of restorative practices in schools in the United States, has claimed that in the beginning restorative justice was mediation and sees that practice actually precedes restorative justice. He says that mediation, circles and conferencing were the methods that developed at the same time and they influenced to each other (McCold 2006). Zehr (2002), for his part, shares the perspective that development of restorative justice has been affected by the way restorative circles were used in traditional cultures. However, Zehr states that mediation should not be considered self-evidently as a restorative method. It should rather be observed whether mediation practices do have restorative values and principles included or not before arguing mediation as a restorative process (Zehr 2002).

Although the origins or definitions of restorative justice or mediation are still under discussion, mediation has became a widely used alternative conflict resolution method in many levels of societies (Ervasti and Nylund 2014; Kinnunen 2012). Mediation is understood as a process where an impartial third party facilitates the conflict of parties, so that they can find a common and satisfactory solution to their conflict. In restorative mediation, the main purpose is to give the right of participation to parties in conflict to ensure that the parties can meet in a safe situation, they are heard and that they can influence the process and commit to the solutions (Elonheimo 2010; Pehrman 2011; Ervasti and Nylund 2014). Conflict is seen as a learning situation, which works both reactively as well as proactively. Individuals are seen as experts of their own living circumstances and, therefore, the important focus is to empower them for their lives and future just there where they live (Christie 1977; Poikela 2010; Gellin 2011).

Looking from the aspect of participation and child friendly approach, when using mediation in schools one basic focus is to give children information and experience of restorative practices. Mediation in schools can be seen as a learning situation where children learn not only to manage conflicts but also to use their right of participating and being heard, which are the rights especially addressed in the UN Convention on the Rights of the Child (CRC 1989, article 12) and in the Guidelines of the Ministers of the Council of Europe on Child Friendly Justice (2011). The Finnish National Core Curriculum for Basic Education (2014) addresses also the UN Convention on the Right of the Child by noting that the convention gives the judicial aspect to basic education. The core curriculum points out convention principles of equality and child's best and right to protection, as well as a child's right to be heard, opinions to be respected and a child's rights to good life and development (The Finnish National Core Curriculum 2014). Once the meaning and practice of mediation is learned and understood in a school, an individual can also in future turn to available mediation services in Finnish society, when needed. The other aim of restorative approach in schools is to empower children to participate actively in their local communities. When using mediation even among children in kindergartens and schools, common information of mediation processes can reach also the members of families and other citizens.

The Special Representative of the UN Secretary General (SRSG) on Violence against Children published in 2013 a document Promoting Restorative Justice for Children. Under the framework of International Juvenile Justice Observatory (IJJO), Chapman et al. (2015a) produced the European Model for Restorative Justice with Children and Young People, which built upon the content of the SRSG's report. The authors points out that the primary purpose of restorative justice is to restore justice. Moreover, it can be applied within families, schools, communities, organisations, civil society and the State to provide peaceful conflict resolution and contribute to cohesive and democratic societies. The approach for restorative justice with children and young people includes a holistic approach based upon the best interests of the child involving effective communication and co-ordination among different service providers. Restorative approach seeks to protect children from violence through restorative processes that are child-sensitive and respect the rights of children whether they are perpetrators of harm or victimised by others. The authors are under-lying three capitals that restorative approach produces: (1) Cultural capital: the key values and beliefs that inform the purpose, meaning and processes of restorative justice with children and young people in Europe. (2) Social capital: the key parties that engage in restorative processes and their needs and relationships that bring them together to prevent or repair harm. (3) Intellectual capital: the knowledge and expertise that is required to facilitate the restorative processes (Chapman et al. 2015a).

2.1 Mediation is Considered as a Method of Learning Conflict Management in Schools

Looking from the point of learning, the perspectives of Christie (1977, 1983) are significant particularly in the school context. He argued that conflicts should been seen as a learning processes for social skills. From that point, parties to the conflict should be supported—not punished or excluded. He stated that the criminal justice system has taken conflicts away from the parties and, thereby, they have became other people's property. He saw that by taking the ownership away from parties also the possibility for learning was missed. He outlined procedures that restores the participants' rights to their own conflicts and encouraged to search for alternatives for punishment, not only for alternative forms of punishment. Christie stated that both the offender and the surrounding community know what is wrong, and a crime should be considered a starting point for dialogue instead of being answered by causing pain. The key concepts of the restorative theory—repairing harm, human relations, chance and commitment—create a strong contrast with the traditional punishment-focused justice that delivers shame, exclusion and punishments (Christie 1977, 1983).

Poikela (2010) associates restorative approach with learning and argues that restorative learning has much to do with reflection. He divides restorative learning into two levels. Firstly, restorative learning takes place naturally in an individual's social context. A person's pervious experiences and education, as well as possible trainings, affect his or her ability to maintain and update his/her capabilities in constantly changing life situations. On this level, a person can maintain his/her focus and balance the relationship between himself or herself and the environment. As the second level, Poikela sees a situation where an individual is lacking the first level capabilities and is thus in need of support and guidance. When a person's focus resources have been stagnated, he/she needs support to solve conflicts, make decisions, and regain balance between himself or herself and the changing environment. Reflection, which means the reassessing of one's learning and capabilities, is a means of maintaining and updating learning. Poikela states that the core of learning is reflection that is the key to both directing activity and understanding the assessment (Poikela 2010). A concrete experience or observance is the starting point for learning, and reflection *on* action takes place in relation to reflection *in* action, i.e. behaviour and seen activity. Between observance and activity an understanding takes place, which is called reflection *for* action. Poikela emphasises the importance of reflection in all phases of learning (Poikela 2009).

Morrison and Vaandering (2012) sees that in school context the punitive regulatory framework has been for decades leaning on the form of exclusionary practices, such as referrals, suspensions and expulsions, even though evidence indicates clearly the ineffectiveness and damaging impact of exclusions. They argue that in contrast to a punitive approach a restorative justice framework employs a responsive regulatory approach that identifies social engagement as a key element for safe schools. Morrison and Vaandering emphasises that rather than focusing on external sanctioning systems such as rewards and punishment, restorative justice is focusing on a motivational lever that is embedded in the value base of conflict management. When the traditional approach investigate what law and code of conduct has been broken, who did it and what is a correct punishment, the restorative approach examines what happened, who has been affected and how to repair the harm done. The process includes those closest to the harm and those closest to the community affected. This is distinct to punitive process, where typically the problem and wrongdoer are sent away from the community where the harm occurred. Morrison and Vaandering argues that restorative justice in educational policy creates school communities that move from the predominant paradigm of regulatory formalism, to a paradigm that is more responsive because it enable a process to address the harm through nurturing a human capacity for restitution, resolution and reconciliation (Morrison and Vaandering 2012).

Also Chapman et al. (2015b) sees that restorative philosophy reframes school's curriculums into a policy where strengthening relationships is one of the main focus areas. The policy would not simply list rules that should not be broken, but would define how all members of the school should communicate with each other and how they should respond to harm and conflict. The policy would be an integration of restorative culture and practices. Restorative relationships between staff and children, between children and between staff members are based upon language and communication that expresses respect and assumes personal responsibility (Chapman et al. 2015b).

2.2 Mediation Strengthens Social Skills and Relationships

Mediation in schools is usually argued by a learning aspect as opened above, but also the aspect of strengthening social skills not only for school life but also for the future is often addressed. In several research studies, restorative practices are reported to strengthen a child's rights to be heard and participate, increase democracy and conflict management, improve a child's social skills, increase the capability to take responsibility, decrease social exclusion or labelling, and strengthen preventing misbehaviour and bullying in schools (Hopkins 2006; McCold 2006; Zehr 2002;

Thorsborne 2016; Gellin 2011; Gellin et al. 2012). However, there are challenges also reported. Also vital is the need to investigate more closely from different perspectives the results of research reports when developing mediation practices in Finnish schools, as described here.

Hopkins (2006) gives her view on what a restorative school is like. She says that the ethics of justice and caring should be the basis of all activity in the school community. Hopkins states that school communities today face many challenges and that restorative thinking can support and get results in the following issues: the increase of safety and peace as well as the improvement of the school climate, the decrease of isolation and exclusion, a grown sense of community, an increased participation, the decrease of bullying and other disturbing behaviour in the whole school community as well as the avoidance of exhaustion amongst the staff. Hopkins describes two different learning possibilities for pupils that depend on the approach that a teacher chooses in a conflict situation. Firstly, she argues that if a teacher starts a discussion with the word "Why?", the question causes a need to defend one's actions and the only thing that a pupil learns is that its better to not get caught in a similar situation or its best to learn to explain the situation in a way that oneself is presented in the best possible light, even if this means lying. Secondly, Hopkins describes practices in a restorative school where the teacher has already learned to apply restorative methods in a conflict situation. According to restorative thinking, the teacher sees a conflict as a learning situation and instead of punishment, the teacher is interested in solutions and supports the pupil in considering the situation from the point of view of the whole class. The teacher listens, but does not rate the situation on any scale of true-false or good-bad. With the restorative approach the teacher helps to reconnect the pupil with the community that he/she has been excluded from by supporting the pupil's own solutions affecting his/her behaviour in such a way that he/she is ready to return to class (Hopkins 2006).

Also, Bonafé-Schmitt (2012) sees that learning is an essential aspect of mediation in schools. He discusses the results of a school mediation programme in Lyon and argues the aim of mediation is not based on discipline. Instead, mediation gives an alternative process where social learning is addressed. Bonafé-Schmitt consider school as a forum to learn skills for citizenship. He notes that with the concrete conflict management method that mediation offers, an individual is not only learning to solve problems at school but also in future in any society he or she participates. As a critical point, Bonafé-Schmitt addresses the role of mediator in balancing the power in parties' relations, so that a satisfied agreement can be found. He points out that when understanding mediation as a co-operative negotiation, the motivation to participate to mediation can increase. Bonafé-Schmitt sees that because of participatory and co-operative aspects of mediation, the natural attitude to conflicts as a part of social life can be reached (Bonafé-Schmitt 2012). Marklund (2007) studied how the principles of mediation were followed in school mediation situations in one school mediation programme in northern Sweden. She states in her conclusion that it is often the adult mediator's burden to try to determine which of the parties is right and which one is wrong. Marklund states that the most difficult part of mediation for adult mediators was to maintain a facilitative role. She compared this to pupil mediator's mediation work and observed that the peer mediators had less difficulty in understanding and accepting the fact that there can be two equally "true" versions of the same story. Marklund describes how peer mediators felt proud of having helped their friends (Marklund 2007).

In the literary overview *Restorative Justice in U.S. Schools: A Research Review* writers Fronius et al. (2016) note that there are many different restorative practices used in schools, but in all of them the main basis is to give participatory methods as an alternative to punitive ones in schools. Restorative practices are used in conflicts of breaking school rules as well as in cases of bullying. After observing different research reports from the United States, they conclude that, according to the reports, the restorative approach had changed pupil's behaviour more effectively than punishments, teachers had better relations with their pupils, pupils respected school staff members more than earlier and there was less needs to intervene in social relationships in a classroom than before using the restorative approach. They found that in reports improvement of a positive school atmosphere, tolerance and support were also reported as impacts of restorative approach. However, they noticed that to reach these benefits restorative practices should be implemented in a school culture and ethics. They also criticised that any comparative research has not yet been completed in the field (Fronius et al. 2016).

2.3 Mediation in Schools Needs Commitment to Principles of Restorative Approach

Hopkins (2006) argues that commitment to a whole school approach is essential when implementing restorative practices in schools. She sees that it is important to produce a restorative "mindset" before starting to use restorative practices. Without understanding the values and principles of restorative approach, practices have no real effects, she states. She found as a critical point that there occurred resistance to a new way of thinking by some staff members and noticed also that lack of support by the head of a school created challenges when implementing the restorative approach. By proper training and careful information these barriers could be overcome, concludes Hopkins. She lists recommendations with which restorative practices can be implemented into the school's everyday life. Hopkins sees that it is important at first step to train the school leaders and senior staff to understand the restorative approach and restorative methods. After the training, this group can plan how to train the school's entire personnel and how all the pupils are informed of and trained in the new practices. Hopkins considers it of upmost importance that after the start-up of the activity, there is real follow-up and updates on it to support the restorative approach in the school's everyday life. Hopkins concludes by stating that the restorative approach and methods should be mentioned in the school curriculum, and it is useful for a school to build a network with other schools in which the restorative approach is being applied (Hopkins 2006).

Marklund (2007) has researched the results of one mediation programme in Swedish schools and sees that if we only observe conflict as a negative phenomenon with negative effects we cannot see the possibilities to transform hidden in conflicts. She defines that a conflict between parties as a situation where the needs of the parties has not been met or fulfilled. How conflicts are experienced varies from pupil to another and that is why dialogue is needed when solving problems. Through a structured mediation process learning can take place and lead to the growth of social skills. As a conclusion, Marklund argues that there is a need for effective methods to manage conflicts in schools and states that mediation could be such a method. In her research, she found that mediation was experienced as a suitable tool to manage conflicts in schools. She also found five principles that should be followed in mediation to achieve the benefits of mediation. At first mediation should be understood as a peaceful process where no power or forcing can be used. Secondly, parties should participate in mediation at their own will. Thirdly, Marklund underlines that mediation is confidential, which means that nothing said in mediation can later be used against to any party. She argues that in mediation, the aim is to find compensation to a conflict and solution that can be accepted by parties and their near society. As a fifth principle, Marklund addresses the role of mediator as a facilitator that helps the parties to go through the process and find the solution together (Marklund 2007).

3 School Mediation in Finland

3.1 History and Basic Elements of Mediation Activity in Finnish Schools

The Finnish Forum for Mediation (FFM) was founded in 2003 to act as a Finnish mediation co-operation organisation whose ideology is based on the modern mediation movement. Its board represents the entire mediation field though its members' expertise and activities outside the forum. FFM is a voluntary and independent non-governmental organisation that aims to participate and influence society development by reinforcing the civil society and bettering the society's well-being through mediation. School mediation, as well as the family mediation and workplace mediation, has been developed in separate projects in the framework of FFM. One important aspect for co-operation in the board has been to find the interfaces between the mediation work done in the different levels of society to strengthen conspicuousness and use of mediation nationwide. When looking from the field of education, it is essential to notice that by using mediation as a conflict management tool even in a school, the school societies are connected to the conflict management activities that are available in their local communities and also in the Finnish society, at large.

In Finland, progress of school mediation and restorative approach in schools started in 2000 when a group of youth workers under the Finnish Red Cross were invited by education officers of the City of Helsinki to develop a new participatory way to manage misbehaviour and bullying in schools. The programme was called VERSO (comes from the Finnish word *vertaissovittelu*, which means peer mediation, while *verso* as such means in Finnish a new tiny plant growing up from the soil) and, at the first stage, the programme developed a training to teach pupils act as peer mediators and adult staff members to mentor their practice in a school. First trainings were established in 2001 in a secondary school and, because of promising feedback (see the data later in this section), there were soon both primary and secondary schools asking for trainings to start the programme. In 2003, the VERSO programme was moved from the Finnish Red Cross to the framework of Finnish Forum for Mediation, just for having a closer connection to the co-operation of other mediation activities and projects in Finland. In 2005, the programme got funding from the Ministry of Education for 2 years and ever since there has been full time workers to develop, evaluate and offer trainings in the programme nationwide. In 2007, the programme got more permanent funding from the Ministry of Social Affairs and Health. According the statistics from 2007 to 2017, a total of 649 schools have been trained to use the VERSO programme in their schools, of which 609 are comprehensive schools and 40 are vocational institute departments. According to the Statistics Finland, there were 2339 comprehensive schools, 342 upper secondary schools and 99 vocational institutes in Finland for the year 2016, but the number of schools is still decreasing.[1]

Coming back to the Finnish school context, the Finnish National Core Curriculum for Basic Education (2014) was implemented from the beginning of autumn 2016. The Finnish National Core Curriculum provides a uniform foundation for local curricula, thus enhancing equality in education throughout the country. The curricula of each municipality and school steer instruction in more detail, taking local needs and perspectives into consideration. Some of the key goals of the new curricula include strengthening pupil participation, increasing the meaningfulness of study, making it possible for each pupil to experience success and giving lifelong and wide skills also for active citizenship in future. Children and youths are guided in taking more responsibility for their schoolwork, but also given more support in their studies. The pupils' experiences, feelings, interests and interaction with others lay the foundation for learning. The teacher's task is to guide the pupils into lifelong learning by taking the individual learning approaches of each pupil into consideration. The Finnish National Core Curriculum is giving strong support for increasing participation of children in their schools as well addressing the possibilities to learn mediation and negotiation during school years.

According the paragraph 3.3. one of the educational aims is that "*pupils learn to take responsibility, make decisions and keep agreements by experience. They learn the important role of rules, agreements and trust. They learn cooperation and they have opportunities to practice skills for negotiation, mediation and conflict management as well as critical thinking. Pupils are encouraged to see the other point of view when thinking of their own suggestions and especially notice equality, fairness*

---

[1]http://tilastokeskus.fi/til/kjarj/2016/kjarj_2016_2017-02-14_tie_001_en.html.

and meaning of sustainable development of life" (The Finnish National Core Curriculum 2014).

The fact that mediation is mentioned as a one social skill to learn in the Finnish National Core Curriculum (2014), as opened above, can been seen based on the previous 17 years of development and practice of mediation in schools. The aim of the VERSO programme is to implement mediation as a conflict management tool so that both pupil and staff members can work restoratively in daily co-operation. Pupils act as peer mediators with the support of trained school staff members that work as mediation advisors in their school. Teachers that have participated in advanced VERSO programme's mediation training can use mediation in different kind of conflict situations and can implement restorative methods, such as circles, also in their didactics so that pupil learn to participate, impress their ideas and thoughts and do co-operation as part of daily learning in classrooms. Like Kiilakoski (2009) notes schools should be seen not only a places of learning of academic skills but also a social spaces where interaction and communication are in important role. Doing together during lessons is one way to learn these social skills. Thus, restorative practices are giving valuable methods for this co-operation. When a pupil get used to work together it is easier to manage also conflicts together whenever they occur. One aim of the restorative approach in schools is to understand conflicts as a learning situations, where by using mediation parties of a conflict can meet and discuss in safe situation to find a common solution to their conflict. The idea is to notice and work with the conflict as soon as possible so that a conflict will not escalate to more serious one. However, even in serious issues mediation can be used to solve the situation with the support and participation of all those that are involved in and affected by the case (Gellin 2007, 2010; Gellin et al. 2012).

In Finland, mediation in schools is facilitated by trained pupils (peer mediators) or by trained staff members (adult mediators). In Fig. 1 describes the case flow in daily practice.

In the case of conflict, the person that notices the situation or does the intervention or who is a party in that conflict can make the referral to mediation. There is always a team of adult school staff members—called mediation advisors or mentors—that mentor the practice and evaluate the case to decide in what process a case will be managed.

Peer mediation as a method follows a clear process in which trained pupil mediators slightly older than the parties of a conflict help the parties to themselves find a solution to their conflict. During the mediation, the parties get to tell their side of the conflict, describe their feelings and think about different solutions to the conflict. The mediators have no power to give out punishments and are bound to confidentiality. Typical cases mediated in peer mediation are verbal such as nicknaming or spreading rumors, physical such as slapping and pushing, or others such as threatening, isolating, forcing, borrowing or hiding property without permission.

In adult-led mediation one or two trained adult mediators facilitate a conflict that has observed to be better suitable for adult-led mediation process. Parents and headmasters are informed about the case and are also invited to participate to the process. It is addressed to take care that the principles of restorative approach are followed during the process. The conflicts that are referred to adult-led mediation are, for

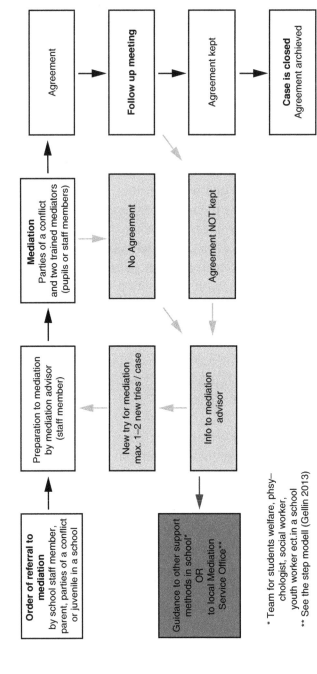

Fig. 1 The process of mediation practice in Finnish schools

example, bullying cases that have been going on for long, property violations when financial compensation have to also be discussed, conflicts between a teacher and a pupil or conflicts between a teacher and parents.

In any event, regardless if mediation is led by peer mediators or adult mediators, in the end of mediation situation the parties are making an agreement. After decided period, usually after 1 or 2 weeks, the mediators and parties meet again for a follow-up meeting. If the follow-up shows that promises has been kept, the case can be closed and the agreement is archived by the mediation advisor. If mediation does not produce agreement to the case or if in follow-up it is found that promises are not kept, the case returns to a mediation advisor who evaluates the new or adequate method to be used for the case. In case the mediation methods used at a school are not seen adequate or have not solved the case, the conflict can be referred to be mediated by the local victim offender mediation offices or the parties are guided to work with other professionals, such as social workers, in a school (Gellin 2010; Chapman et al. 2015a).

3.2   Outcomes of Mediation Activities in Finnish Schools

As mentioned before, the trainings for restorative approach and mediation for Finnish schools have been developed by the VERSO programme in the framework of the Finnish Forum for Mediation and the Ministry of Social Affairs and Health, which grants and evaluates the programme every year. An evaluation has been a requirement from the Ministry's side. Moreover, surveys and inquiries have been done regularly to develop the practice and trainings in the field. Every second year the wider report and data analysis of effectivity must be collected and summarised with a template established by the Ministry. The report of the data from 2016 collected and analysed by VERSO programme for this evaluation was let to the Ministry in March 2017. To provide valuable insight into mediation activities and outcomes in Finnish schools, selected findings are presented here, and the whole report will be published in Finnish on the home page of the VERSO progamme after having feedback from the Ministry. The main issues that are required in the report concerns activity of target group and volunteers in schools, quantitative data of indicators like number of cases mediated and also short opinions asked about the action from the field. Every year also a financial budget report needs to be included. During 2016 and in the spring period 2017, the workers of the VERSO programme collected the data asked about the activity in 2016 with statistic forms and surveys developed to complete the report for the Ministry.

Mediation activity is implemented to a school by trainings organised in co-operation with the VERSO programme and a school. The VERSO programme offers trainings for pupils, school staff members and head teachers and other adults in a school. Figure 2 describes the numbers and characteristics of these trainings in 2016.

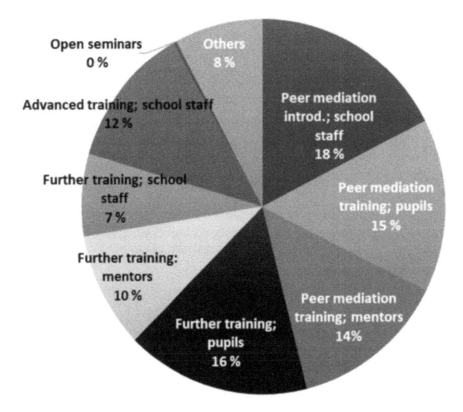

Fig. 2 The numbers and characteristics of trainings produced for schools by VERSO programme in 2016

In 2016, the VERSO programme offered a total of 269 trainings for schools in different part of the country. When starting peer mediation in a school, three phases of training are included: training for staff members to share the basic information of restorative practices and practical issues on how to implement peer mediation as one method for conflict management, peer mediation training for selected group of pupils and practical training for voluntary staff members to act as advisors for peer mediators in a school. Almost one-half (47%) of trainings were for starting peer mediation. Further trainings are offered for schools that have followed the programme of peer mediation 1 year or more, when there is usually a need to train more peer mediators. Also further training is divided in three phases, such as the starting training. In 2016, 33% of trainings were for further training. Advanced training for school staff members is a longer process where there are practice periods between the lecture days, so that learned skills can be implemented and reflected during the course. In 2016, there were 33 training modules for advanced courses, which was 12% of all trainings. According the statistics, until the end of the year 2016 there has been 704 educators who participated in advanced trainings since 2010. From the total 704 participants 348 person worked in basic education in 67 different comprehensive schools and 270 person worked in vocational institute departments in 22 different municipalities and 86 were kindergarten staff members from 8 municipalities. The participants are teachers, headmasters, special needs teachers, social councellors, student/study counsellors, youth workers and staff members from kindergartens.

In peer mediation, starting trainings there were 2142 people participating. In further trainings, there were 1300 participants in 2016. Feedback of trainings was asked in two sampling periods (March and November) after the trainings, and all persons that participated in trainings during sampling periods (=total 537 persons) gave back fulfilled questionnaire forms. Seventy-seven per cent of the answers were from pupils and 23% from staff members. The majority found trainings valuable, as 60% noticed that training was very beneficial and 38% said that trainings were quite beneficial. Only 2% had an opinion that the training was only a little beneficial. Almost all of the answerers had an opinion that they have learned to mediate, as 54% informed that they got very good skills for mediation and 46% impressed to have gotten quite good skills. Only 2% said that they got only few skills for mediation during the training. Also, the majority (93%) of trained peer mediators said that they are ready to mediate, and as well as the majority (93%) of staff members noticed that they are ready to refer cases to mediation when recognized after training.

The questionnaire about mediation cases and numbers of active mediators and their mentors was sent to 56 schools that have had their trainings for mediation in year 2014 or 2015. A total of 30 schools returned their answers in time (response rate = 53.6%).

In Figure 3 the amount of persons involved to mediation work in 30 schools are described. There were total 803 persons in duty of mediation service as voluntary actors in these 30 schools. Of the total, 79% of volunteers were pupils who act as peer mediators, 15% were working as mentors for the daily practice and 6% were trained adult mediators, who are staff member that have participated to advanced trainings.

Figure 4 details the characters of the mediated cases. In these 30 schools, there were total 997 cases mediated during 2016. The majority of the cases have been characterised as verbal or physical conflicts. From this sampling can be seen that 38% of mediated cases were about physical cases. Typically these cases are pushes, hits or fights. Also, 47% of cases were verbal such as nick naming, using bad

Fig. 3 Distribution of peer mediators, their mentors and adult mediators (n = 30)

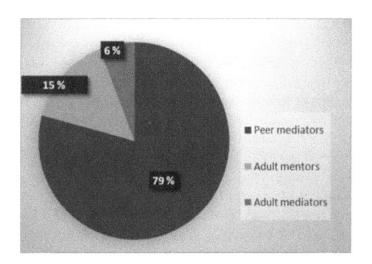

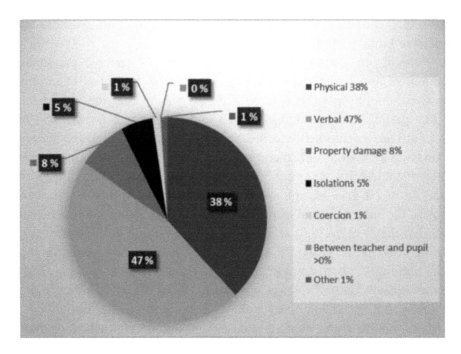

Fig. 4 The characters of mediated cases 2016

language or words, gossiping or giving negative comments about other's appearance or clothing. Additionally, 8% of cases were about property damage, typically using someone's property without permission or hiding someone's property just to cause harm. Five per cent were isolations, which usually are situations were participation in group work in lessons or participation in plays during breaks were denied by other pupils. Also, one case between a teacher and a pupil was reported and some other not detailed cases were mediated in these 30 schools during 2016.

To evaluate the effects of the mediation work done, the data was collected after further trainings in 2016. The aim of the further trainings was to teach with the experticy of experienced peer mediators and their adult mentors new voluntary pupils and staff members to work as peer mediators and mentors in their school. The questionnaire was given in 10 different further trainings to 67 participants that had worked as voluntary actors in the programme in their school during recent years. Fulfilled answer forms were received from all of them (response rate = 100%). The questions are formulated as simple as possible so that also younger pupil can answer to them. Of this, 73% of answers were from pupils and 27% from staff members. In next three figures some opinions from the informants are opened.

In Fig. 5 describes opinions about mediation. The majority of the cases had been solved in mediation, as 82% of informants had an opinion that disputes have always been solved in mediation and 18% noticed that cases were often solved. No one claimed that cases are solved seldom or never. Figure 6 gives details on the opinions concerning disputes. The majority had an opinion that there was less disputes in their school than earlier, as 18% argued that disputes were decreased a lot and 55% said that disputes were decreased quite a lot, although 27% had an opinion that disputes were decreased a little in their schools. Figure 7 describes the opinions about changes in atmosphere. The majority of the answerers said that mediation activity

Fig. 5 Have disputes been solved in school mediation?

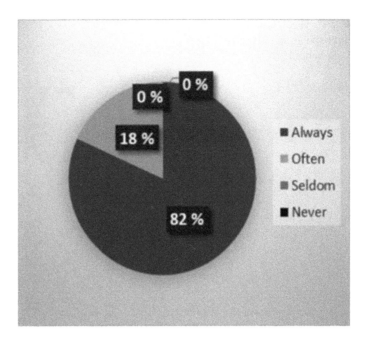

Fig. 6 Have disputes decreased in your school? (N = 67)

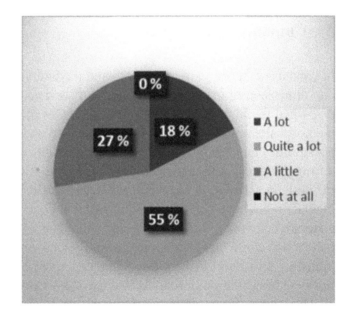

had improved the atmosphere in their schools. 6% argued that the atmosphere in a school has improve a lot and 65% of informed that the atmosphere has improved quite a lot in their schools. Additionally, 29% had an opinion that there was a little improvement for atmosphere in their school when following the mediation programme.

Fig. 7 Has the school atmosphere improved in your school? (N = 67)

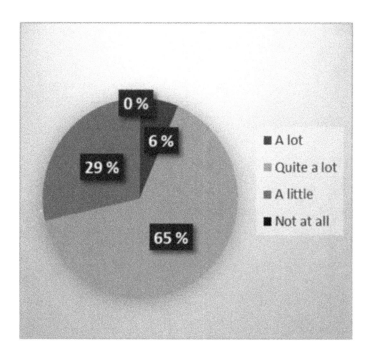

4 Concluding Remarks

In conclusion, a restorative approach and mediation in schools can be considered as one dimension to mediation activities and services in Finnish society. It is obvious that when reaching experiences and information of restorative conflict management methods already in a school, pupils can become more aware of the rights and possibilities they can use when there are conflicts during their school years or later during lifetime. Although restorative practices may not totally replace punitive methods in schools, in those schools where VERSO programme is actively used, mediation has been considered as a first practice to use in conflict situation. Thus, a restorative approach has strengthened understanding of the importance of a participatory and child friendly approach and social learning in conflict management. Statistics also indicate with no doubt that most conflicts have been successfully resolved in mediation in schools that use the VERSO programme.

The results discussed in this paper about mediation activity in Finnish schools give a picture that mediation is a working method when managing different kind of conflicts in schools. Learning of conflict resolution and improving social capacity are the main benefits that mediation practice can give to participants, as well as to those involved in mediation in their schools. However, not all members of school societies are ready the move on to restorative values when discussing bullying and misbehaviour in schools. Mediation should be offered as an alternative method when managing conflicts, and one way to decrease the resistance of using mediation is to collect and share proper and clear information of the mediation practice and principles of a restorative approach. This is an ongoing task for those offering the trainings for mediation, schools that are implementing a mediation practice, decision makers in the field of education and for academics in universities.

In Finland, in those schools that are following VERSO programme, restorative practices are used both in proactive tools in a classroom and as a reactive method when managing conflict situations during daily work in a school. As an exception to situation in many other countries, the VERSO programme has had an opportunity to work as a nationwide programme due to the co-operation and economic support from the Ministry of Social Affairs and Health. This situation gives also the basic ground and advantage for systematic evaluation and development of the approach and practices offered by the VERSO programme. Quantitative data discussed in this paper gives some understanding of the progress of action. When having both pupils and staff members trained to mediate, mediation can be used flexibly as a method for early intervention to conflicts before social tension escalates to more traumatic misbehaviour. This co-operation between pupils and staff members is valuable not only from the point of view of social learning and creating atmosphere of trust to each other, but also because challenges a hectic rhythm to school days often cause to daily work and social life in schools. However, this paper does not discuss the quality of the practices or deeper experiences reached in practice. Neither does this paper describe how restorative principles in practice in schools has been fulfilled. Peer mediation has been implemented in Finnish schools since 2001, and the trainings for whole school restorative approach have been offered since 2010. The activity of trainings and ongoing need for the trainings, as well as the feedback of the practice, give an understanding that a restorative approach and mediation are valued more and more in the field of Finnish education.

It is obvious that academic research is still needed to study the effectiveness and results of restorative approach in schools. It is important to evaluate such issues that are producing the benefits that are connected to restorative practices in order to find and understand the elements that creates quality in practices so that the schools can fully benefit from a restorative approach. Both pedagogical and youth cultural aspects should be included in these observations. Currently, the report of the doctorate research on restorative approach in Finnish schools is under completing work by the writer of this article. In that research, it has been asked if and how restorative values has been implemented and how restorative practices and mediation have affected the daily profession of educators that have actively used a restorative approach and mediation in their work. The research is based on qualitative data, and the analysis has followed the Grounded Theory process. As first findings of the results, it seems that to produce a whole school restorative approach there are three needs for educators to be fulfilled: adopting a *restorative mindset*, practicing actively *restorative participation* and considering conflicts as learning possibilities to be managed with *restorative mediation*. What are these concepts, how they can be produced and what challenges there are in implementing will be discussed in the coming dissertation, hopefully before the end of 2018.

References

Bonafé-Schmitt J-P (2012) Social mediation and school mediation. In: Barraldi C, Iervese V (eds) Participation, facilitation and mediation. Children and young people in their social contexts. Routledge, New York, pp 49–65

Chapman T, Gellin M, Aertsen I, Anderson M (2015a) Protecting rights, restoring respect and strengthening relationships. A European model for restorative justice with children and young people. European Research on Restorative Juvenile Justice, vol II. OIJJ/ECJJ, Brussels. http://www.ejjc.org/eumodel. Accessed 7 June 2017

Chapman T, Gellin M, Anderson M (2015b) Toolkit for professionals. Implementing European model for restorative justice with children and young people, vol III. OIJJ/ECJJ, Brussels. http://www.ejjc.org/eumodel Accessed 7 June 2017

Christie N (1977) Conflicts as property. Br J Criminol 17(1):1–15

Christie N (1983) Piinan rajat. Oikeussosiologian julkaisuja no 4. Helsingin yliopiston monistus-palvelut, Helsinki

Elonheimo H (2010) Nuorisorikollisuuden esiintyvyys, taustatekijät ja sovittelu. Scripta Lingua Fennica Edita, C, 299. Dissertation, University of Turku, Turku

Ervasti K, Nylund A (2014) Konfliktinratkaisu ja sovittelu. Helsinki, Edita

Fronius T, Persson H, Guckenburg S, Hurley N, Petrosino A (2016) Restorative justice in U.S. Schools. A research review. The WestEnd Justice & Prevention Research Center, San Francisco. http://jprc.wested.org/wp-content/uploads/2016/02/RJ_Literature-Review_20160217.pdf. Accessed 12 Dec 2016

Gellin M (2007) Sovittelulla riidoista ratkaisuihin. Oppilaiden osallisuus voimavarana työrauhaa turvattaessa. In: Gretschel A, Kiilakoski T (eds) Lasten ja nuorten kunta. Nuorisotutkimusseura, Helsinki, pp 56–70

Gellin M (2010) Koulussa sopu sijaa antaa – vertaissovittelun tuloksia. In: Poikela E (ed) Sovittelu. Ristiriitojen kohtaamisesta konfliktien hallintaan. PS-kustannus, Jyväskylä, pp 69–89

Gellin M (2011) Sovittelu koulussa. Opetus 2000 sarja. PS-kustannus, Jyväskylä

Gellin M, Gretschel A, Matthies A-L, Nivala E, Oranen M, Sutinen R, Tasanko P (2012) Lasten ja nuorten asema hyvinvointipalveluissa. In: Gretschel A, Kiilakoski T (eds) Demokratiaoppitunti. Lasten ja nuorten kunta 2010-luvun alussa. Nuorisotutkimusseura, Helsinki, pp 149–179

Guidelines of the Ministers of the Council of Europe on Child-friendly Justice (2011) https://rm.coe.int/16804b2cf3 Accessed 25 Apr 2017

Hopkins B (2006) Implementing a restorative approach to behaviour and relationship management in schools – the narrated experiences of educationalists. Dissertation, University of Reading, Reading

Hopkins B, Gellin M (2016) Restorative Approach in Educational Settings. Minori guistizia. Revista interdisciplinary di studi guiridici, psicologici, pedagogici e sociali sulla relazione fra minorenni e guistizia. Franco Angeli, Milano

Kiilakoski T (2009) "Parempihan se on sovitella ku ei sovitella". Vertaissovittelu, konfliktit ja koulukulttuuri. Vertaissovittelun ulkopuolinen arviointiraportti. Nuorisotutkimusseuran verk-kojulkaisuja, vol 30. Nuorisotutkimusseura, Helsinki

Kinnunen A (2012) Restoratiivisen oikeuden kehitys Euroopassa. Haaste 2012(3):23–25

McCold P (2006) The recent history of restorative justice. Mediation, circles and conferencing. In: Sullivan D, Tifft L (eds) Handbook of restorative justice. Routledge, New York, pp 23–51

Marklund L (2007) Skolmedling i teori och praktik. Licentiate's Dissertation, University of Uppsala, Uppsala

Morrison B, Vaandering D (2012) Restorative justice. Pedagogy, praxis, and discipline. J Sch Violence 11:138–155

Peachey DE (1989) The kitchener experiment. In: Wright M, Galaway B (eds) Mediation and criminal justice. Victims, offenders and community. Sage Publications, London

Pehrman T (2011) Paremmin puhumalla. Restoratiivinen sovittelu työyhteisössä. Acta Universitatis Lapponiensis 212. Dissertation, University of Lapland, Rovaniemi

Poikela E (2009) Oppimisen design. In: Ruohonen S, Mäkelä-Marttinen L (eds) Kohti oppimisen ekosysteemiä. Kymenlaakson ammattikorkeakoulujen julkaisuja, serie A (24). Kopijyvä, Jyväskylä, pp 10–17

Poikela E (2010) Oppiminen sovittelun ytimenä – restoratiivisen ohjauksen lähtökohtia. In: Poikela E (ed) Sovittelu. Ristiriitojen kohtaamisesta konfliktien hallintaan. PS-kustannus, Jyväskylä, pp 223–300

Promoting Restorative Justice for Children (2013) http://srsg.violenceagainstchildren.org/sites/default/files/publications_final/srsgvac_restorative_justice_for_children_report.pdf. Accessed 7 June 2017

The Finnish National Core Curriculum for Basic Education (2014) Perusopetuksen opetus-suunnitelman perusteet 2014. Opetushallitus, Määräykset ja ohjeet 2014:96. http://www.oph.fi/download/163777_perusopetuksen_opetussuunnitelman_perusteet_2014.pdf. Accessed 18 Mar 2017

Thorsborne M (2016) Affect and script psychology. Restorative practice, biology and a theory of human motivation. In: Hopkins B (ed) Restorative theory in practice. Insights into what works and why. Jessica Kingsley Publications, London, pp 25–45

UN Convention on the Rights of the Child (1989) http://www.ohchr.org/EN/ProfessionalInterest/Pages/CRC.aspx. Accessed 12 Dec 2016

Van Wormer K, Kaplan L, Juby C (2012) Confronting oppression, restoring justice. From policy analysis to social action. Council on Social Work Education, Alexandria

Zehr H (2002) The little book of restorative justice. Good books, Intercourse

Index

CPSIA information can be obtained
at www.ICGtesting.com
Printed in the USA
LVHW061337251020
669765LV00034B/1528